THE
MODERN FREUDIANS

THE LIBRARY OF CLINICAL PSYCHOANALYSIS

A Series of Books Edited By

Steven J. Ellman

THE
MODERN FREUDIANS

Contemporary
Psychoanalytic Technique

Edited by

Carolyn S. Ellman
Stanley Grand
Mark Silvan
Steven J. Ellman

JASON ARONSON INC.
Northvale, New Jersey
London

Production Editor: Elaine Lindenblatt

This book was set in 10 pt. New Baskerville by Alabama Book Composition of Deatsville, AL

Library of Congress Cataloging-in-Publication Data

The modern Freudians : contemporary psychoanalytic technique / Carolyn
    Ellman, editors . . . [et al.].
      p. cm.
      "The NYU Freudians."
      Includes bibliographical references and index.
      ISBN 0-7657-0158-8 (alk. paper)
      1. Psychoanalysis. 2. Freud, Sigmund, 1856–1939.
      3. Psychoanalytic counseling. I. Ellman, Carolyn S.
    BF175.M574   1998
    150.19'5—dc21
                                                   98-12097

    ISBN 0-7657-0229-0 (softcover)

Printed in the United States of America on acid-free paper. For information and catalog write to Jason Aronson Inc., 230 Livingston Street, Northvale, NJ 07647-1726, or visit our website: www.aronson.com

Contents

PART II: THE ENDURING LEGACIES

PART III: CHANGING PERSPECTIVES
ON THE THERAPEUTIC RELATIONSHIP

Acknowledgments

This book grew out of a conference that was presented at New York University on November 9–10, 1996. The impetus for this conference, which was arranged by the Freudian faculty of the NYU Postdoctoral Program in Psychotherapy and Psychoanalysis, was the realization that psychoanalysis had changed so much in the last fifty years that members of the faculty had not really defined for themselves or others why they still considered themselves "Freudian." While many faculty members felt that they had been strongly influenced by Kleinian, relational, and self-psychological points of view, others on the faculty felt that they were not so influenced; therefore, the group decided to examine the theories informing their work with patients in an attempt to decipher what was truly Freudian about it. We are grateful to the members of the Freudian faculty for their input and support in putting on the conference.

We are also indebted to the late Dr. Bernie Kalinkowitz, who was Director of the New York University Postdoctoral Program in Psychoanalysis from its inception in 1961 until his death in 1992. Because of his vision of a home for psychologists of all different theoretical persuasions and his extraordinary capacity to embrace intellectual diversity, he was able to conceive of a program where Freudians, interpersonalists, relational analysts, and independents could and do co-exist. If he was still alive, he would surely propose a track for the Kleinians. As a result of his ideas and under his leadership, we have grown, and we are grateful to him for encouraging this openness to different points of view.

We were fortunate to have Drs. Arnold Richards and Arthur Lynch join us by contributing to the book a chapter on contemporary conflict theory, even though they are not part of the NYU Faculty and were not part of the original conference. Due to Dr. Richards' training at the New York Psychoanalytic Institute and his attention as editor of the *Journal of the American Psychoanalytic Association* to divergent views and multi-perspectives on contemporary issues, we felt he would give a particularly scholarly view of the role of ego psychology in American psychoanalysis.

Special thanks to Dr. Jo Lang for her excellent leadership as Chair of the Freudian faculty, to all the students and graduates that helped run the conference, and especially to Margarita Aguilar, who was secretary of the Postdoctoral Program: her help with the conference went far beyond the call of duty.

In conceptualizing the conference we would like to thank Drs. Andrew Druck and Mark Grunes, who served on the committee with the four editors of this book. The committee tried to sort out the important areas that needed to be covered in order to give a representative view of contemporary Freudian thought.

Our thanks to Dr. Michael Moskowitz and Peter Ellman and the staff at Jason Aronson, who were there from the beginning to the end with support, excellent comments, and endless patience: notably David Kaplan, our excellent copyeditor, and Elaine Lindenblatt, who is truly a wonderful production editor.

And last but not least we would like to express our gratitude to all of our deceased colleagues who contributed to the growth and development of the Freudian track of the New York University Postdoctoral Program. We are especially grateful to Dr. Fred Wolkenfeld, who served so devotedly as Chairman of our faculty for so many years until his untimely death in 1995. We miss him and know how much he would have enjoyed the challenge of understanding what contemporary Freudian psychoanalysis is today.

Carolyn S. Ellman
Stanley Grand
Mark Silvan
Steven J. Ellman

Editors and Contributors

Abby Adams-Silvan, Ph.D., is Adjunct Clinical Professor of Psychology and Supervising Analyst, New York University Postdoctoral Program in Psychotherapy and Psychoanalysis; and Past President, Training and Supervising Analyst, and faculty member of the New York Freudian Society. Included among her writings are papers on the dying patient, on post-traumatic stress disorder, and on a specific dynamic of the seduction trauma.

Sheldon Bach, Ph.D., is Adjunct Clinical Professor of Psychology and Supervising Analyst, NYU Postdoctoral Program in Psychotherapy and Psychoanalysis; Training and Supervising Analyst (Fellow), IPTAR; and faculty member and Training and Supervising Analyst, New York Freudian Society. He is author of *Narcissistic States and the Therapeutic Process* and *The Language of Perversion and the Language of Love.*

Martin S. Bergmann is Adjunct Clinical Professor of Psychology, NYU Postdoctoral Program in Psychotherapy and Psychoanalysis; Training and Supervising Analyst, New York Freudian Society; and author of *Anatomy of Loving* and *In the Shadow of Moloch.* He is co-recipient of the 1997 Mary Sigourney Award.

Andrew B. Druck, Ph.D., is Adjunct Clinical Associate Professor of Psychology and Supervising Analyst, NYU Postdoctoral Program in Psychotherapy and Psychoanalysis; and President and Past Dean, faculty member, and Training and Supervising Analyst (Fellow), IPTAR. He is author of *Four Therapeutic Approaches to the Borderline Patient: Principles and Techniques of the Basic Dynamic Stances.*

Carolyn S. Ellman, Ph.D. (editor), is Adjunct Supervising Analyst, NYU Postdoctoral Program in Psychotherapy and Psychoanalysis; Training and Supervising Analyst, New York Freudian Society; and faculty member and Supervisor, Metropolitan Institute. Clinical Associate (Supervisor) in City University Department of Clinical Psychology, she is co-editor of *Omnipotent Fantasies and the Vulnerable Self.* She chaired the NYU Conference and is senior editor of this book.

Steven J. Ellman, Ph.D. (editor), is Adjunct Visiting Clinical Professor of Psychology and Supervising Analyst, NYU Postdoctoral Program in Psychotherapy and Psychoanalysis; Past President, faculty member, and Training and Supervising Analyst (Fellow), IPTAR; and Professor of Psychology, Clinical Psychology Program, City University of New York. Author of *Freud's Technique Papers: A Contemporary Perspective* and *The Mind in Sleep,* he is co-editor of *Enactment: Toward a New Approach to the Therapeutic Relationship* and *The Neurobiological and Developmental Basis for Psychotherapeutic Intervention.*

Elsa First, M.A., is Adjunct Clinical Associate Professor of Psychology, NYU Postdoctoral Program in Psychotherapy and Psychoanalysis; and faculty member and Training and Supervising Analyst (Adult and Child), New York Freudian Society. She has published papers on Winnicott and the interpersonal origins of play and is a frequent contributor on issues of psychoanalytic technique.

Norbert Freedman, Ph.D., is Adjunct Clinical Professor of Psychology and Supervising Analyst, NYU Postdoctoral Program in Psychotherapy and Psychoanalysis; Past President, faculty member, and Training and Supervising Analyst (Fellow), IPTAR; and Professor and Director of the Research Unit for the Study of Communication in Psychotherapy and Psychoanalysis, Health Sciences Center, SUNY, Brooklyn, NY. He has written widely on the evaluation of the communicative process in analytic treatment.

Helen K. Gediman, Ph.D., is Adjunct Clinical Professor of Psychology and Supervising Analyst, NYU Postdoctoral Program in Psychotherapy and Psychoanalysis; faculty member and Training and Supervising Analyst, New York Freudian Society; and Diplomate in Psychoanalysis, ABPP. She is author of *Fantasies of Love and Death in Life and Art* and co-author of *The Many Faces of Deceit.*

Stanley Grand, Ph.D. (editor), is Adjunct Clinical Professor of Psychology and Supervising Analyst, NYU Postdoctoral Program in Psychotherapy and Psychoanalysis; Past President, faculty member, and Training and Supervising Analyst (Fellow), IPTAR; and Training and Supervising Analyst, New York Freudian Society. Associate Professor Emeritus at the Health Sciences Center, SUNY, Brooklyn, NY, he is co-author of the books *Communicative Structures and Psychic Structures* and *Transference in Brief Psychotherapy.*

Mark Grunes, Ph.D., is Adjunct Clinical Professor of Psychology and Supervising Analyst, NYU Postdoctoral Program in Psychotherapy and Psychoanalysis; faculty member and Training and Supervising Analyst, New York Freudian Society; and faculty member, IPTAR. Author of articles on the therapeutic object relationship, he is a frequent discussant on the therapeutic relationship.

Marvin Hurvich, Ph.D., is Adjunct Visiting Clinical Professor of Psychology and Supervising Analyst, NYU Postdoctoral Program in Psychotherapy and Psychoanalysis; Professor of Psychology, Long Island University, Brooklyn Center; faculty member and Training and Supervising Analyst (Fellow), IPTAR; and faculty member and Training and Supervising Analyst, New York Freudian Society. He is co-author of *Ego Functions in Schizophrenics, Neurotics and Normals* and author of numerous articles on annihilation anxiety.

Richard Lasky, Ph.D., is Adjunct Clinical Associate Professor of Psychology and Supervising Analyst, NYU Postdoctoral Program in Psychotherapy and Psychoanalysis; faculty member and Training and Supervising

Analyst (Fellow), IPTAR; and Diplomate in Psychoanalysis, ABPP. He is author of *Evaluating Criminal Responsibility in Multiple Personality and the Related Dissociative Disorders: A Psychoanalytic Perspective* and *The Dynamics of Development and the Therapeutic Process*.

Arthur A. Lynch, D.S.W., is Adjunct Associate Professor at Columbia University School of Social Work. He co-authored the articles "Merton Gill: A View of His Place in the Freudian Firmament" and "Interactions in the Transference–Countertransference Continuum."

Martin L. Nass, Ph.D., is Adjunct Clinical Professor of Psychology and Supervising Analyst, NYU Postdoctoral Program in Psychotherapy and Psychoanalysis; faculty member and Training and Supervising Analyst, New York Freudian Society; and Professor Emeritus, Brooklyn College and City University of New York. He is the author of numerous articles on music and the creative process in composers.

Arnold D. Richards, M.D., is Training and Supervising Analyst at New York Psychoanalytic Institute, Clinical Assistant Professor of Psychiatry at New York University School of Medicine, and Editor of the *Journal of the American Psychoanalytic Association*. He has co-edited several books including *Psychoanalysis: The Science of Mental Conflict, Essays in Honor of Charles Brenner*, and *The Perverse Transference and Other Matters: Essays in Honor of R. Horacio Etchegoyen*.

Mark Silvan, Ph.D. (editor), is Adjunct Supervising Analyst, NYU Postdoctoral Program in Psychotherapy and Psychoanalysis, and faculty member and Training and Supervising Analyst, New York Freudian Society. He has co-authored several articles on topics such as hysteria, psychosexuality and the effective use of power by a woman ruler, and the incapacity to experience empathy.

Irving Steingart, Ph.D., is Adjunct Clinical Professor of Psychology and Supervising Analyst, NYU Postdoctoral Program in Psychotherapy and Psychoanalysis; faculty member and Training and Supervising Analyst (Fellow), IPTAR; and faculty member and Training and Supervising Analyst, New York Freudian Society. He is author of *Pathological Play in*

Borderline and Narcissistic Personalities and *A Thing Apart: Love and Reality in the Therapeutic Relationship.*

Jane Tucker, Ph.D., is Adjunct Clinical Assistant Professor of Psychology and Supervising Analyst, NYU Postdoctoral Program in Psychotherapy and Psychoanalysis; Clinical Associate (Supervisor), Clinical Psychology Program, City University of New York; and Associate Editor, *Psychoanalytic Psychology.*

Introduction

Carolyn S. Ellman

In our field scientific spirit and care for the object certainly are not opposites: they flow from the same source. It is impossible to love the truth of psychic reality, to be moved by this love as Freud was in his lifework, and not to love and care for the object whose truth we want to discover. All great scientists, I believe, are moved by this passion. Our object, being what it is, is the other in ourselves and ourself in the other. To discover truth about the patient is always discovering it with him and for him as well as for ourselves and about ourselves. And it is discovering truth between each other, as the truth of human beings is revealed in their interrelatedness. While this may sound unfamiliar and perhaps too fanciful, it is only an elaboration, in nontechnical terms, of Freud's deepest thoughts about the transference neurosis and its significance in analysis. [Loewald 1970, pp. 297–298]

In what follows I shall endeavor to collect together for the use of practicing analysts some of the rules for the beginning of the treatment. Among them there are some which acquire their impor- tance from their relation to the general plan of the game. I think I am well-advised, however, to call these rules "recommendations" and not to claim any unconditional acceptance of them. The extraordinary diversity of the psychical constellations concerned, the plasticity of all mental processes and the wealth of determining factors oppose any mechanization of the technique; and they bring it about that a course of action that is as a rule justified may at times prove ineffective, whilst one that is usually mistaken may once in a while lead to the desired end. These circumstances, however, do not prevent us from laying down a procedure for the physician which is effective on the average. [Freud 1913, p. 123]

Even among staunch Freudians the debates about what remains of classical psychoanalysis as described by Freud are very intense. In 1923 Freud said, "The assumptions that there are unconscious mental processes, the recognition of the theory of resistance and repression, the appreciation of the importance of sexuality and the Oedipus complex, these constitute the principal subject matter of psychoanalysis and the foundations of its theory," and he added, "No one who cannot accept them all should count himself a psychoanalyst" (1923, p. 247). In a recent article Leo Rangell (1996) says what is more "specifically analytic is the direction towards the unconscious, the intrapsychic and the scanning for conflictual states. These are the essential and pathognomonic concerns of analysis" (p. 143).

When the Freudian faculty at the New York University Postdoctoral Program in Psychotherapy and Psychoanalysis set out to do a conference on contemporary Freudian theory and technique, it was because we wanted to define for ourselves (as well as for others) what criteria we used when we said we were "Freudians." Had we modified and changed our positions so much that we ourselves, when put to the test, might actually be unclear as to our "true selves"? Many leading analysts such as Wallerstein (1990) have questioned how different the different schools of thought really are. He says that we should call ourselves analysts if we have a common ground centered on the technical ideas of transference and resistance, and that we should look for the common ground between us and not focus on our differences. Rangell (1996) disagrees strongly with this position and feels that we must spell out exactly what is Freudian and try to encompass the changes that have occurred into a larger theory in order to try and preserve some scientific integrity.

All of us in this book identify ourselves as Freudians. Are we clinging to some outdated notion of ourselves? Have we refused to look at the changes that have occurred in our ways of dealing with patients in the last twenty-five to thirty years or to acknowledge the profound nature of these changes in our identity? The answer to why we are Freudians and what distinguishes contemporary Freudian technique at New York University is the essence of this book.

It is a little over a hundred years ago that the word *psychoanalysis* came into being in a paper called "Heredity and the Aetiology of the Neurosis" prepared by Freud for a French neurological review. He said, "I owe my results to a new method of psycho-analysis" (Freud 1896, p. 151). And within five or six years "he was beginning to collect around him a group of men of like interests, attracted by his ideas and prepared to work within this general method [of free-association]" (Wollman, 1971, p. 137). Within ten years Adler, Federn, and Rank had joined Freud, and by 1908 Ferenczi had come. Jung, Binswanger, Abraham, Brill, and Jones were already interested in this method and visited Freud from abroad. They were interested in how to treat hysterical patients. Freud had published his famous *Studies on Hysteria* in 1895, and he had also written *The Interpretation of Dreams* in 1900, in which there was clearly a new theory of the mind.

And as the movement developed, it seemed most natural to its members that they should call themselves after the method that they practiced. They were psychoanalysts. In April 1908, the informal Wednesday evening meetings, at which they came together to discuss their ideas and the progress of cases, became known as the Vienna Psychoanalytical Society. In the same year the first International Psychoanalytical Congress was held at Saltzburg. [Wollman 1971, pp. 137–138]

The concept of the unconscious was long known to philosophers and poets, but no one had tried to systematically examine the manifestations of the unconscious in a scientific fashion. How shall we live our lives in a moral fashion was for Socrates the fundamental question of human existence, but Plato, Shakespeare, Proust, Nietzsche, and Freud complicated the issue by insisting that there are deep, dark, and uncontrollable currents of meaning in the unconscious. Wollman concludes that Freud "led people to think about their appetites and their intellectual powers, about self-knowledge and self-deceit, about the ends of life and about man's profoundest passions and about his most intimate or trivial failings, in ways that would have seemed to earlier generations at once scandalous

and silly" (p. ix). And, one of his greatest contributions was that he created
a truly unique therapeutic technique by inventing the "analytic situation."
As Steingart (1995) states, "Freud created not only a new theory of human
nature but, interrelated with that theory, a new type of human relationship,
whatever might be the theoretical orientation of the analyst" (pp. 108–
109).

In trying to understand the psychoanalytic situation it is interesting to
note how few papers on technique Freud actually wrote.

During a half century of clinical work and in some 300 scientific
publications, Freud wrote relatively little on the subject of technique.
Between 1895 and 1937, he dedicated some 20 papers—not counting
the case studies whose primary purpose was to prove the validity of
scientific hypotheses, not to demonstrate his therapeutic method—to
the question of what principles should guide the analyst in conducting
a psychoanalytic treatment. Of these, only a handful are . . . explicit
in technical instruction. . . . Most importantly, however, it was Freud's
skepticism about the usefulness of establishing strict rules in the
training of future analysts that restrained him. He believed that only
general guidelines could be laid down and that their application had
to be left to tact and experience, particularly in the form of a training
analysis. [Lohser and Newtown 1996, pp. 11, 13]

Freud wanted to leave many things open to the future. He said in
1923,

Psychoanalysis is not, like philosophies, a system starting out from a
few sharply defined basic concepts, seeking to grasp the whole
universe with the help of these and, once it is completed, having no
room for fresh discoveries or better understanding. On the contrary,
it keeps close to the acts in its field of study, seeks to solve the
immediate problems of observation, gropes its way forward by the
help of experience, is always incomplete and always is ready to correct
or modify its theories. [p. 253]

In reality, contrary to the popular belief that Freud was rigidly holding on
to certain beliefs, his theory was always changing. As Strachey points out in
1943 in *The Freud–Klein Controversies,*

[If] Freud's own discoveries and theories had been made, not by a single man in the course of one lifetime, but by a succession of men over a longer period of years [such as the changes from the seduction theory to his views on infantile sexuality, the change from the topographic model to the structural model, the changing views on narcissism and the ego-ideal and superego, and the development of the dual instinct theory] . . . it is not very fantastic to suppose that every one of such modifications . . . would have provoked crises exactly comparable to our present one and to the many others which may be ahead. Nevertheless, as things in fact turned out, there were no such disruptions; the innovations and corrections succeeded one another with the utmost smoothness. [King and Steiner 1991, pp. 606–607]

Strachey was right. The transitions aren't smooth today and the debates are so intense and complicated that people are turning further and further away from theory. As far back as 1976, George Klein was urging that we do away with metapsychology and just focus on the clinical theory. And in the introduction to a recent book, Glen Gabbard, a leading psychoanalyst, says that early in his career it became apparent to him that no one theory had all the answers to the challenges he confronted in clinical practice. "Empirical validation of one theory as superior to another is so complicated in our field that we must use clinical usefulness as the major test" (Gabbard 1996, p. xi). But while it is possible to feel threatened by these changes and it may prove difficult to really integrate them all, it is also challenging and productive. As Riccardo Steiner says in the conclusion of *The Freud–Klein Controversies,*

In spite of the difficulties [caused by the bitter debates that almost destroyed the British Psychoanalytic Society] . . . the scientific life of the Society was characterized by an explosion of creativity in all sorts of directions. One has only to remember the work of Melanie Klein and her post-war pupils W. R. Bion, H. A. Rosenfeld, and H. Segal, on psychosis; and the contributions of M. Balint, J. Bowlby, and, above all, D. W. Winnicott, especially during the fifties and the sixties. . . . Especially when the narcissism of the small differences does not interfere too much, the existence of different groups can lead to a

very lively comparison of ideas and viewpoints *even today* (my emphasis). [King and Steiner 1991, pp. 916–917].

We particularly like to turn to *The Freud–Klein Controversies* not only
because of the fascinating debates that occurred then but because the New
York University Postdoctoral Program is also an institute where many
different points of view are represented (Freudian, relational, interpersonal, and independent). We are proud that this respect for different
points of view was upheld here, thanks to the program's founder, Bernie
Kalinkowitz. We don't think there is anyone on the Freudian faculty who
has not been affected in some way or other by object relations theory, by
Kohut, by infant research, by the new findings in brain research, and
particularly by the continually expanding thoughts about the nature of the
therapeutic process. From our own faculty, we have already conceived of
such new concepts as "analytic trust" (Ellman 1991, 1992), "pathological
play" (Steingart 1995), the "therapeutic object relationship" (Grunes
1984), the "four psychologies" (Pine 1990), "narcissistic states of consciousness" (Bach 1985, 1994), the importance of the "self-reflective function"
(Grand 1995), and the role of "transformation" during treatment (Freedman 1994). Many other ideas keep emerging as we take on the challenge
of understanding new phenomena (especially in nonsymbolizing and
action-oriented patients).

But what are the major controversies today and what is the real
challenge to Freudian technique? Just as the major controversies in 1943
centered on whether the mental development of infantile object relationships as defined by Melanie Klein was compatible with the theory of
instinctual development as put forth by Freud, today the major theoretical
struggle seems to be over what has been called the one- or two-person
systems. Some people think about it as the "classical" position versus the
"intersubjective" position (Dunn 1995). The last ten years have focused us
more in some ways on what goes on in us rather than on what goes on in
the patient. Is there any real analytic space or is everything part of this
two-person system? What is the nature of the transference? What is the real
relationship? Are we a projection of the patient or is the patient a
projection of us? Is there any reality outside of the situation we are
creating? How much is a repetition from the past, which will inevitably lead
to reconstructive work, and how much is a new relationship that is being

formed in the present, which can lend itself to a treatment based only on the here and now? Do interpretations cure, or does the relationship cure, or is it a combination of both? In the debate over the classical model versus the intersubjective point of view (as put forth by Hoffman 1993, Jacobs 1991, Ogden 1986, 1994, Renik 1993) each theory is being forced, as Jonathan Dunn (1995) says, to rethink and spell out "(1) What are the bedrock concepts employed by each model to ground its theory of human nature and (2) how does each model (and others) conceptualize the primary force driving the mode and determining the direction of the psychoanalytic treatment process?" (p. 734).

The importance of the relationship to the analyst has been stressed by Freudians for many years (Greenson 1965, 1967, Loewald 1960, Stone 1961). What is new is how much it is being stressed, how much (or how little) one concentrates on surface versus unconscious material, and how important are intrapsychic conflicts versus the emerging transference-countertransference dialogue (with a particular focus on the analyst's inner life).

> The object of investigation, the analysand, as well as the investigator, the analyst, although each has a considerable degree of internal psychic organization and relative autonomy in respect to the other, can enter a psychoanalytic investigation only by virtue of their being relatively open systems, and open to each other. And each in his own ways must renounce a degree of autonomy for the sake of the investigation. Neither the object of investigation nor the investigator can be dealt with theoretically as though a simple subject–object confrontation obtained. We even have to qualify our speaking of investigator and object, insofar as the object, by the very nature of the psychoanalytic process, becomes an investigator of himself, and the investigator-analyst becomes an object of study to himself. [Loewald 1970, p. 278]

In the 1960s, criticism by Stone (1961) and Greenson (1965) was directed against the rigid, overly rational, detached attitude thought to be classical. No one was more outspoken about how the distortions of the classical position led to a confused image of the role of the analyst and the real relationship in the treatment situation than Leo Stone (1961):

We must, to be sure, concern ourselves with the absurd misinterpre-
tations, exaggerations or other misuses of the "mirror" concept
indulged in by severely compulsive or self-indulgent personalities, or
as a rationalization for passive anxiety, or through uncritical enthusiasm for what is thought to be the letter of the law. . . . The true
analyst can be relied on to be warmly tolerant and understanding in
the ultimate test, as the expression of his genuine emotional and
intellectual commitment to his task and of his mature view of human
suffering and inner conflict, regardless of how his feelings may
fluctuate in certain immediate situations. [pp. 33–34]

It is particularly with the difficult patient that the issue of the
relationship comes up, not only because these patients often induce such
severe countertransference, but also because they often need more from
the therapist. Since these were not specifically the patients Freud was
writing about (even though many of them would fall in these categories)
and since so many of the people writing in this area developed their
theories around the early mother–child relationship, it has been particularly important to see how contemporary Freudians have thought about
these issues. Just as Kohut's (1971, 1973) and Bach's (1985) ideas led to a
modification of the treatment of the narcissistic patient, Klein (1946) made
us think of projective and introjective mechanisms, and the ideas of Bion
(1967), Winnicott (1960), and Modell (1976) greatly influenced many
clinicians to think about the "holding environment" and the "containing"
function of the analyst. None of these thinkers, however, specifically
stressed the internal life of the analyst as being crucial to the nature of the
interaction and how the treatment progressed; instead, the emphasis now
(in contemporary debates) is on this detailed examination of the analyst's
internal states, to understand not only what the patient is communicating
(for example, by projective identification) but also the uniqueness of the
therapist–patient relationship. "The intersubjective challenge of the 90's
embodies the notion that the very formation of the therapeutic process is
derived from an inextricable intertwined mixture of the clinical participants' subjective reactions to one another" (Dunn 1995, p. 723). Not only
is this a challenge to the objective observer concept (long held as an ideal
in classical treatment), but some writers are even suggesting that the
therapeutic action only occurs through some "enactment" between the two
parties (Renik 1993).

The debate about the importance of the relationship has endured for half a century, with some analysts supporting the central role of the new relationship and yet remaining in the Freudian camp (Ellman 1997, Grunes 1984, Loewald 1960, Stone 1961), and others seeing even the so-called real relationship as something that ultimately has to be analyzed in order to complete the treatment (Arlow and Brenner 1990). The argument over the centrality of the relationship clearly led to the significant breaks in psychoanalysis into different schools and is a key issue in terms of the nature of the therapeutic process and cure (with some theorists emphasizing interpretation as the crucial element in the cure and others seeing the relationship itself as the essential curative factor). Freud mentioned the concept of countertransference only four times in his career (Ellman 1991), and he was clearly afraid to emphasize the analyst's reactions. Instead, he highlighted the dangers of the countertransference, particularly when the transference became intense and highly eroticized. Perhaps his being protective of the new science made him fearful of revealing too much of his inner life or having his colleagues do the same (for example, see Aron and Harris [1993] on Ferenczi).

Freud's self-analysis never stopped and it was the inspiration for many of his great insights (for example, the Oedipus complex), but ultimately he did feel it was the patient's drives, the patient's transferences, and the patient's intrapsychic conflict that propelled the analyst and treatment process in one direction or another and that the goal of the treatment was to understand the patient's psychic reality. "Evenly hovering attention" (Freud 1913) was essential in the treatment in order to use one's own unconscious to understand the other. As Steingart (1995) emphasizes, Freud devised a technique to really understand the structure of the analysand's psychic reality, which was now "lovingly elevated in importance" (p. 121). Freud used everything available to him at the time (especially his own dreams) to try to understand the unconscious mind, and the psychoanalytic situation was devised to facilitate that investigation (in that respect he felt we should analyze our countertransference to protect the patient and to free one from bias).

Today, however, for whatever complicated historical and philosophical reasons, some analysts feel free to say what they really do. Is this because analysts have become more aware of the complexities of human interactions, owing to all the exposure to early infant research? Is it because we now have a greater understanding of the subtle impact of one person on another because of our years of studying nonverbal communication and the language of the body? And have these years of exposure to deconstructivism led to a new view of the authority of the analyst (and authority in general), with an aim to divest the analyst of his so-called power? Whether the investigation into the patient's inner life is furthered or interfered with by the focus on the inner life of the analyst is one of the challenges to contemporary Freudians.

This book discusses theoretical, clinical, and historical issues. It is extremely important to understand the context in which the present controversies exist in order to try and sort out how much of our thinking and rethinking has been influenced by our culture and the politics of psychoanalysis itself, and three chapters are devoted to this. Chapter 1 emphasizes the influence of ego psychology on contemporary thought. Chapter 2 discusses the influence of object relations theory on contemporary Freudians. The final chapter (Chapter 13) gives an historical perspective from one of our faculty who has not only lived through many of these changes but has written extensively on the history of psychoanalysis.

Part II (Chapters 3, 4, and 5) is devoted to understanding how many of Freud's original concepts (such as the unconscious, the id, the ego, transference, resistance, free association, and the oedipal complex) are still considered crucial by the NYU contemporary Freudians. The answers are not necessarily what one would expect.

The next two parts focus more on technique. Part III addresses the crucial issues of the role of the transference, the real relationship, and intersubjectivity (Chapters 6, 7, and 8). Part IV (Chapters 9, 10, and 11) focuses on the psychoanalytic treatment of the narcissistic and borderline patient. Since it is here that one expects the greatest overlap with other schools, we particularly asked these authors to focus on what they consider crucial to their definition of being a Freudian.

Chapter 12 summarizes the book and focuses on the crucial differences between our Freudian position and other orientations (Kleinian, relational, and self psychology). We hope by exploring all these different facets of the Freudian position today we will have succeeded in showing the reader and ourselves how we have integrated over a hundred years of psychoanalytic thought, how our exposure to so many different points of view has changed (or not changed) us, and how we hope we have emerged as better analysts and observers of ourselves and others. We are indebted to

Sigmund Freud for inventing such an infinitely fascinating thing called "psychoanalysis."

REFERENCES

Arlow, J. A., and Brenner, C. (1990). The psychoanalytic process. *Psychoanalytic Quarterly* 59:678–692.

Aron, L., and Harris, A., eds. (1993). *The Legacy of Sandor Ferenczi.* Hillsdale, NJ: Analytic Press.

Bach, S. (1985). *Narcissistic States and the Therapeutic Process.* New York: Jason Aronson.

——— (1994). *The Language of Love and the Language of Perversion.* Northvale, NJ: Jason Aronson.

Bion, W. R. (1967). *Second Thoughts: Selected Papers on Psychoanalysis.* New York: Jason Aronson.

Dunn, J. (1995). Intersubjectivity in psychoanalysis: a critical review. *International Journal of Psycho-Analysis* 76:723–738.

Ellman, S. (1991). *Freud's Technique Papers: A Contemporary Perspective.* Northvale, NJ: Jason Aronson.

——— (1992). Psychoanalytic theory, dream formation and REM sleep. In *Interface of Psychoanalysis and Psychology,* ed. J. Barron, M. Eagle, and D. Wolitsky, pp. 357–374. Washington, DC: American Psychological Association.

——— (1997). An analyst at work. In *More Analysts at Work,* ed. J. Reppen, pp. 91–115. Northvale, NJ: Jason Aronson.

Freedman, N. (1994). More on transformation enactments in psychoanalytic space. In *The Spectrum of Psychoanalysis: Essays in Honor of Martin S. Bergmann,* ed. A. K. Richards and A. D. Richards, pp. 93–110. Madison, CT: International Universities Press.

Freud, S. (1896). Heredity and the aetiology of the neurosis. *Standard Edition* 3:143–156.

——— (1913). On beginning the treatment. *Standard Edition* 12:121–144.

——— (1923). Two encyclopaedia articles. *Standard Edition* 18:235–259.

Gabbard, G. (1996). *Love and Hate in the Analytic Setting.* Northvale, NJ: Jason Aronson.

Grand, S. (1995). A classic revisited: clinical and theoretical reflections on Stone's widening scope of indications for psychoanalysis. *Journal of the American Psychoanalytic Association* 43:741–764.

Greenson, R. R. (1965). The working alliance and the transference neurosis. *Psychoanalytic Quarterly* 34:155–181.

——— (1967). *Technique and Practice of Psychoanalysis.* New York: International Universities Press.

Grunes, M. (1984). The therapeutic object relationship. *Psychoanalytic Review* 71:123–143.

Hoffman, I. Z. (1983). The patient as interpreter of the analyst's experience. *Contemporary Psychoanalysis* 19:389–422.

Jacobs, T. J. (1991). *The Use of the Self: Countertransference and Communication in the Analytic Situation.* New York: International Universities Press.

King, P., and Steiner, R. (1991). *The Freud–Klein Controversies 1941–45.* London: Routledge.

Klein, G. S. (1976). *Psychoanalytic Theory: An Exploration of Essentials.* New York: International Universities Press.

Klein, M. (1946). Notes on some schizoid mechanisms. In *The Writings of Melanie Klein,* vol. 3, pp. 1–24. London: Hogarth, 1975.

Kohut, H. (1971). *The Analysis of the Self.* New York: International Universities Press.

——— (1973). Thoughts on narcissism and narcissistic rage. *Psychoanalytic Study of the Child* 27:360–400. New Haven, CT: Yale University Press.

Loewald, H. W. (1960). On the therapeutic action of psychoanalysis. In *Papers on Psychoanalysis,* pp. 221–256. New Haven, CT: Yale University Press, 1980.

——— (1970). Psychoanalytic theory and the psychoanalytic process. In *Papers on Psychoanalysis,* pp. 277–301. New Haven, CT: Yale University Press, 1980.

Lohser, B., and Newtown, P. M. (1996). *Unorthodox Freud.* New York: Guilford.

Modell, A. H. (1976). The "holding" environment and the therapeutic action of psychoanalysis. *Journal of the American Psychoanalytic Association* 24:285–308.

Ogden, T. H. (1986). *The Matrix of the Mind.* Northvale, NJ: Jason Aronson.

——— (1994). The analytic third: working with intersubjective clinical facts. *International Journal of Psycho-Analysis* 75:3–19.

Pine, F. (1990). *Drive, Ego, Object and Self: A Synthesis for Clinical Work.* New York: Basic Books.

Rangell, L. (1996). The "analytic" in psychoanalytic treatment. How analysis works. *Psychoanalytic Inquiry* 16(2):140–166.

Renik, O. (1993). Countertransference enactment and the psychoanalytic process. In *Psychic Structure and Psychic Change: Essays in Honor of Robert S. Wallerstein, M.D.,* ed. M. J. Horowitz, O. F. Kernberg, and E. M. Weinshel, pp. 135–158. Madison, CT: International Universities Press.

Steingart, I. (1995). *A Thing Apart.* Hillsdale, NJ: Jason Aronson.

Stone, L. (1961). *The Psychoanalytic Situation.* New York: International Universities Press.

Wallerstein, R. S. (1990). Psychoanalysis: the common ground. *International Journal of Psycho-Analysis* 71:3–20.

Winnicott, D. W. (1960). The theory of the parent–infant relationship. In *The Maturational Processes and the Facilitating Environment,* pp. 37–55. New York: International Universities Press, 1965.

Wollman, R. (1971). *Sigmund Freud.* Cambridge, London: Cambridge University Press.

PART I

THE EVOLUTION
OF FREUDIAN THOUGHT

1

From Ego Psychology to Contemporary Conflict Theory: An Historical Overview

Arnold D. Richards
Arthur A. Lynch

Ego psychology is rooted in the third and final phase of Freud's theorizing (Rapaport's [1959] classification), and takes "The Ego and the Id" (1923) and "Inhibitions, Symptoms and Anxiety" (1926) as its foundational works. More specifically, it grows out of Freud's final model of the mind, the structural hypothesis of id, ego, and superego. Levy and Inderbitzen (1996) aptly define ego psychology in terms of the underlying assumptions of Freud's structural hypothesis: "Ego psychology is: a systematic and coordinated conceptualization of various mental activities grouped together by virtue of their similar aims and behavioral manifestations especially associated with delay or control of instinctual discharge, on the one hand, and adaptation to reality opportunities and danger on the other" (p. 412).

In "The Ego and the Id," Freud explained why the structural hypothesis was preferable to the earlier topographic point of view, which used the property of consciousness to characterize mental activity. This model with its three structural agencies constituted a balanced approach to psychic functioning that allows for both environmental and biological determinants, for both purpose and drive and for both the reality principle and the pleasure principle. In "Inhibitions, Symptoms, and Anxiety," Freud considered the clinical implications of his earlier partitioning of the human mind. He began by identifying an error in the prestructural theory: the formulation that repression causes anxiety. He then shifted from an energetic model to a meaning model, the central idea being that childhood wishes are associated with childhood dangers related to loss. These dangers are loss of the object (a significant person), loss of the object's love, loss of or injury to the genitals (castration), and fear of punishment (guilt). On this model a threatening wish seeking expression in consciousness signals danger to the ego, which occasions anxiety. In Freud's monograph, the ego is at the center of exploration but the primary importance of relationships, internal and external, real and fantastic, is also brought into focus. This emphasis on the relational or interpersonal was anticipated in "Group Psychology and the Analysis of the Ego" (1921), where Freud wrote, "In the individual's mental life, someone else is invariably involved, as a model, as an object, as a helper, as an opponent; and so from the very first individual psychology, in this extended but entirely justifiable sense of the words, is at the same time social psychology as well" (p. 69).

Arlow noted in a personal communication that the clinical material informing the structural hypothesis is to be found in a number of cases Freud published around the same time. These include "Some Character Types Met With in Psychoanalytic Work" (1916), "Mourning and Melancholia" (1917), "A Child is Being Beaten" (1919), "Associations of a Four-Year-Old Child" (1920a), "The Psychogenesis of a Case of Homosexuality in a Woman" (1920b), and "Some Neurotic Mechanisms in Jealousy, Paranoia, and Homosexuality" (1922).

Modern ego psychology begins with the contributions of Richard Sterba, James Strachey, and Anna Freud. It took shape in the 1930s, as analytic theorists probed further the clinical, and especially the technical, implications of the structural hypothesis. Many contributions were made during this era by such theorists as Wilhelm Reich, Hermann Nunberg, Karl Abraham, and Paul Federn, and many more were made in ensuing years by theorists like Edward Glover, René Spitz, Erik Erikson, and Annie Reich. The most important contributors, however, were Anna Freud, Heinz Hartmann, Rudolf Loewenstein, Ernst Kris, Phyllis Greenacre, Otto Fenichel, and Edith Jacobson, all of whom extended or modified Freud's theory in varying degree.

Two crucial papers of 1934, Sterba's "The Fate of the Ego in Analytic Therapy" and Strachey's "The Nature of the Therapeutic Action of Psychoanalysis," laid the groundwork for the technical modifications that arose in the aftermath of the structural hypothesis by offering two contrasting visions of the theory of therapeutic action. On the one hand, Sterba described a therapeutic split in the patient resulting in an experiencing ego and an observing ego. The analyst was to side with the latter, helping patients to incorporate the analyst's observing function in order to strengthen their own. Strachey stressed incorporation from the side of the superego rather than the ego. The analyst was to help the patients diminish the harsh, judgmental character of their conscience by offering for identification and incorporation his greater tolerance for drive expression.

These contrasting viewpoints came to the fore in two pivotal events of 1936. In the Marienbad symposium of that year, Strachey's emphasis on the patient's introjection of the analyst's superego and on the importance of the resulting superego alliance seemed to carry the day, though not without dissent (Friedman 1988). Nevertheless, Anna Freud's *The Ego and the Mechanisms of Defense*, published that same year, echoed Sterba's concern with the technical importance of strengthening the patient's observing ego in order to achieve mastery over the experiencing ego. Anna Freud's clinical contribution to this task was to single out the ego's unconscious defensive operations as perhaps the most important set of ego activities entering the treatment.

Many later contributions to the theory of pathology, technique, and development owed a debt to Anna Freud's *Ego and the Mechanisms of Defense*. Following its publication, the history of psychoanalytic technique, from an ego psychology standpoint, can be seen to revolve around a single issue: the clinical role of the analysis of conflict and defense opposed to the analysis of unconscious mental content. The position taken on this key issue provides a basis for differentiating among the major contributors to the theory of technique. The issue is central to the differences between Anna Freud and Melanie Klein, and also serves to distinguish the technical recommendations of Sterba, Strachey, Nunberg, Fenichel, and Hartmann, Kris, and Loewenstein.

Levy and Inderbitzen (1996) note how Anna Freud's reframing of the technical issue of the analyst's attitude complemented an attentiveness to the patient's observing ego. This latter emphasis is the ego-psychological tributary flowing from Sterba's influential paper of 1934. As Levy and Inderbitzen remark,

> Her recommendation that the analyst listen from a point equidistant from id, ego and superego emphasized the importance of neutrally observing the influence of all three psychic institutions. However, the analyst's activity (interventions) always begins with and is directed toward the ego and in this sense the analyst is actually nearer to the ego than to the id or superego. The ego wards off not only derivatives of instinctual drives but also affects that are intimately connected with the drives. She advocated that priority be given to the interpretation of defenses against affects as well as defenses against instinctual drives. [p. 414]

Anna Freud's ego-psychological rationale for Freud's technical requirement of analyst neutrality, an issue that has generated controversy to the present day, was influential during this period. Greenacre's (1954) advocacy of the blank screen with no disclosure or social contact stood at one extreme, while a middle position was taken by Leo Stone (1961), who recommended benign neutrality and physicianliness. Others staked out a position in the middle by advocating the role of the real relationship as a therapeutic and curative factor. Ralph Greenson (1965) wrote of the working alliance, Elizabeth Zetzel (1956) of the therapeutic alliance, and Hans Loewald (1960, 1971) of the role of the relationship. At the other extreme stood Sandor Ferenczi's (1920) active therapy, Franz Alexander's (1956) corrective emotional experience, and Harry Stack Sullivan's outright disregard of the transference. Theorists at this more active end of the spectrum believed that the analyst's direct involvement in the patient's treatment was necessary for a lasting therapeutic effect.

Within psychoanalytic ego psychology, Sterba's concern with the fate of the ego has been more influential than Strachey's attentiveness to a therapeutic partnership between analyst and analysand superegos. Strachey's position is continued in the Kleinian, object relations, and self psychological schools, whereas the Sterba–Anna Freud line extends to the development of American ego psychology in the 1940s and 1950s. This was also the period when analysts who had lived and worked in Central Europe in the 1930s, and immigrated to the United States later that decade and in the 1940s, continued Freud's 1920s exploration of the structure and functioning of the ego. Its members were Anna Freud (who immigrated to England), David Rapaport, Hermann Nunberg, Robert Waelder, Ernst Simmel, Siegfried Bernfeld, Erik Erikson, Otto Fenichel, Edith Jacobson, Margaret Mahler, and the triumvirate of Heinz Hartmann, Ernst Kris, and Rudolf Loewenstein.

THE HARTMANN ERA

What was the ego-psychological paradigm that grew out of the collective efforts of these emigré theorists? Whereas the ego of Freud's topographical theory was conceptualized mainly in opposition to the id, the pioneer ego psychologists took a much larger purview. For them, the ego was a complex structure, emerging, as Freud had noted, out of the perceptual apparatus, and functioning as an executive forging compromises among id, superego, and external reality.

Hartmann, Kris, and Loewenstein (1946), proposed revisions to the Freudian models of mind, development, pathogenesis, and technique. They understood survival as a primary motivating force, and adaptation to the environment as essential to this end. The reality and pleasure principles were reconceptualized in line with this insight. One result of this effort was the transmuting of psychoanalysis into a general psychology of the human condition, ranging from the pathogenic to the normal.

Hartmann's 1939 monograph *The Ego and the Problem of Adaptation* is in the spirit of Freud's lifelong project of creating a bio/psycho/social model. Hartmann emphasized that the individual is born with innate psychic structures (the primary autonomous ego functions of perception, memory, thought, and motility) into an average expectable environment, and that the individual's personality is molded by this social surround. The child growing up in a familial and societal world learns to fit in or adapt to the environment. The alternatives are to change the environment (alloplastic adaptation), to change oneself (autoplastic adaptation), or to leave the environment. Hartmann and Kris (1945), like Freud, stressed that "psychoanalysis does not claim to explain human behavior only as a result of drives and fantasies; human behavior is directed toward a world of men and things" (p. 23). They believed that the child in interaction with the environment acquires secondary autonomous ego functions, and develops a sense of self and other, while mental equilibrium is promoted by an ego that mediates inner and outer imperatives (fitting them together). The adaptive viewpoint emphasized the role of the environment in the shaping of conflicts and added the interpersonal dimension to the psychoanalytic intrapsychic emphasis. It should be recognized that during the forties and fifties both ego psychologists and the interpersonal school were exploring the influence of relationships and the role of the environment on the individual.

A second thrust of Hartmann's theoretical project was to widen the categories of motivation from the more confined aims of libidinal pleasure and destruction, or love and hate, proposed by Freud. Hartmann retained Freud's energic model and language but offered the concept of neutralization as a way out of Freud's narrow and experience-distant drive/energy/instinct box. Neutralized libido came to include a range of experiences from lust, sensuousness, and intimacy to friendliness, warmth, and affection. Neutralized aggression likewise subsumed a spectrum of experience, from self-assertion and competitive strivings to hate and destructiveness. Each had its place in the individual's panoply of affects.

Hartmann, Kris, and Loewenstein's work (1946, 1949) provided the rationale and impetus for observational research on infants and children. The thrust was to study how mother–child interactions affected the developing ego and the sense of self and other. Hartmann (1950) wrote that "the development of object relations is co-determined by the ego; object relations are also one of the main factors that determine the development of the ego" (p. 105). Contemporaries of Hartmann joined this object relations conversation: Anna Freud (1965) elaborated the concept of developmental line, Edith Jacobson (1964) investigated the self and object worlds, and Margaret Mahler (1963; Mahler et al. 1975) provided the classic formulations of separation and individuation. Attention was directed to the impact of the preoedipal period of childhood on later development as well as to the ways in which external controls, deriving in part from the child's transactions with the parents, are internalized. These various strands were woven into an ego-psychological/object relations fabric.

Edith Jacobson's contributions deserve special mention. She postulated an undifferentiated instinctual energy at birth which, *"under the influence of external stimulations"* (1964, p. 13, emphasis added), develop into libidinal and aggressive drives. Frustration and gratification, laid down as memory traces of the ambivalent conflicts of childhood, organize affective experience. Jacobson's work figured in debates over the concept of identity in the 1950s and 1960s. Erikson took one position and Greenacre, Mahler, and Jacobson another. For Erikson (1956) identity was like a beach; it remains the same yet changes with the tide: "The term identity . . . connotes both a persistent sameness within oneself . . . and a persistent sharing of some kind of essential character with others" (p. 57). Erikson acknowledged the importance of childhood development, but maintained that a lasting and stable identity is not formed until the close of adolescence. He placed considerable emphasis on social role, values, and ideals. Jacobson took exception to Erikson's formulations. She felt that his theory overemphasized social-descriptive aspects and lacked a clear metapsychological presentation of identity formation. Further, his focus on processes of late adolescence and early adulthood gave short shrift to the immense influence of early childhood. For Jacobson (1964), identity was equated with self-feeling or self-awareness, qualities that emerged in the process of self and object differentiation: "I would prefer to understand by identity formation a process that builds up the ability to preserve the whole psychic organization—despite its growing structuralization, differentiation and complexity—as a continuity at any stage of human development" (p. 27).

In regard to psychopathology, ego psychologists did not limit their purview to neurosis. In a paper on schizophrenia, Hartmann (1953) described the failure of the capacity to neutralize aggressive energy and thereby to build adequate defensive structures as the most significant etiological factor in the development of this psychosis. Arlow and Brenner (1964) presented in essence the same thesis but without the economic/energic language. The ego psychological purview extended also to the investigation of character and personality disorders, including the oral character (Glover 1925), the anal character (Abraham 1921), the phallic-narcissistic character (W. Reich 1933), the hysterical character (Marmor 1953), the masochistic character (Stein 1956), the as-if personality (Deutsch 1942), the impostor (Abraham 1925), and the perverse character (Arlow 1971). Jacobson (1964), in her work on identity, noted that from the clinical standpoint "serious identity problems appear to be limited to neurotics with specific narcissistic conflicts, and to borderline and psychotic patients" (p. 29). This expansion in diagnostic categories eventuated in both a clinical recognition of the widening scope of psychoanalysis (Stone 1954), and of the need for careful empirical studies, for example

the Menninger research project (a long-term follow-up of forty-two patients) and the Hampstead index (an in-depth study of the psychoanalytic
case material of a two-year-old child).

Clinical Implications of Ego Psychology

Many of the contributions to the theory of ego psychology had general
implications for psychoanalytic technique. Anna Freud (1936) shifted the
technical emphasis of observation to the ego. She noted that it was only
through the patient's ego that the analyst could observe the presentations
of the id, ego, and superego with equal attention. Hence, she concluded
that the ego is the agency through which analysis occurs. Hartmann's work
broadened the scope of understanding beyond the individual's psychopathology to include the total personality, where both nonconflictual functioning and ego autonomy play important roles. Hartmann described how
autonomous functions can facilitate (e.g., through self-observation and
verbalization) or inhibit (e.g., through purposive thinking) free association. Loewenstein (1982) noted, "if the main though not exclusive interest
of psychoanalysis is the study of conflict in man, the *tools* of this study are
the autonomous functions" (pp. 213–214). Nevertheless, these functions
may at times serve resistance and become objects of the analysis. Hartmann
(1939) called this unexpected occurrence a "change of function." Loewenstein (1963) moved the understanding of resistance beyond the basic rule
by calling attention to the distinction between resistances mobilized to
address core conflicts and those mobilized against the emergence of a
particular feeling or thought.

Neutralized energy was regarded as a reservoir by which the ego could
support its aims and functions independently of drive pressure. Likewise,
neutralized energy fueled the ego's defenses against drive demands.
Clinically, Hartmann's theoretical concepts provided the impetus for ego
psychology to explore such concepts as reality testing, sublimation, altru-
ism, modes of internalization, ideal formation, and self-esteem regulation.
These contributions provided a "shift in emphasis . . . [that led to]
significant consequences" (Loewenstein 1954, p. 189), without changing
the basic psychoanalytic technique. These ranged from considering the
effects on interpretations of speech, timing, and direction to redefining
the main therapeutic goals from recovering repressed material to modify-

ing the ego's mode of functioning. Nunberg (1955) concisely captured the clinical outcome and goals of ego psychology in noting that "the changes which are achieved through treatment in the ideal case involve the entire personality and are as follows: the energies of the id become more mobile, the superego becomes more tolerant, the ego is freer from anxiety and the synthetic function is restored" (p. 360).

Interpretation and Clinical Process

Ego psychology shifted the emphasis in technique from the recovery of the repressed to the modification of the patient's ego, including the alteration of automatic defensive functions. Interpretation, although not the only mode of intervention, is the major intervention that results in insight (Kris 1956a), the critical element in lasting personality and behavioral change. Loewenstein (1951, 1957, 1958) saw interpretation as a continuous effort aimed at broadening the patient's understanding of how the past remains dynamically integral to current experiences. Loewenstein (1958) argued for a view of interpretation as a process that respects the unique personalities of analysand and analyst both as individuals and in the therapeutic interaction. Kris (1951) also noted the analyst's role as "participant-observer," a dynamic presence in the analytic situation. Loewenstein provided a framework to guide the analyst in the work of discovering the unconscious meanings that underlie the patient's communications. The analyst gathers evidence for his conjectures from the patient's verbal and nonverbal communication. This careful approach placed a new emphasis on the role of speech (Hartmann 1951, Loewenstein 1956, 1961) that increased the personalized sense of the treatment process. Loewenstein (1951) wrote: "Interpretations deal with the individual experiences of a human being. They aim at widening the conscious knowledge of the individual about himself and should therefore deal with the psychological realities of the individual" (p. 5). This aspect of ego psychology is often missed by critics who view it as impersonal and mechanistic.

Kris (1956b), in his paper "The Personal Myth," elaborated how a person's unique history infuses the self-image with the important early fantasy. The personal myth is preserved as a "treasured possession" and the person reenacts the repressed fantasy in various aspects of life. The personal myth serves multiple functions, acting as a defense and as a pattern of life. Its interpretation fosters the analysand's reintegration. A major achievement of the contemporary successors of ego psychology has been to elaborate the place of unconscious fantasy and the behavior of the individual. "The unacceptable wishes of childhood are part of the persistent unconscious fantasies that seek resolution in the present through compromise formation. As we develop, these fantasies mature and shape our special interests and character traits, determine our behavior, and produce our neurotic symptoms. The essential plot or narrative of unconscious wishes and fears endures even as their manifestations are transformed" (Bachant et al. 1995a, p. 75).

Transference and Countertransference

We have also noted (Lynch et al. 1997) that Freud's definition of transference in 1905 laid the groundwork for the recognition of the therapeutic value of the interactive aspects of the transference. He characterized transference phenomena as "new editions or facsimiles of the impulses and phantasies which are aroused and made conscious during the progress of the analysis; . . . they replace some earlier person by the person of the physician. To put it in another way: a whole series of psychological experiences are revived, not as belonging to the past, but as *applying to the person of the physician at the present moment*" (p. 116, emphasis added).

Freud (1912, 1915) went on to note that transference is found in every adult relationship, a point emphasized by Loewenstein (1969), Brenner (1982), and Bird (1972). Brenner, for example, notes that what distinguishes the therapeutic relationship from the ordinary adult relationship is not the presence of transference but its use by the analyst to analyze psychic conflict (Bachant et al. 1995b).

The concept of countertransference did not become a subject for close investigation until the 1950s, when discussions of the concept burgeoned in the literature. The most systematic papers of this time were written by Annie Reich (1951, 1960, 1966), who followed in the ego psychological tradition. Like other contemporary contributors, Reich chose a broader definition of countertransference than Freud's, but one that stopped short of embracing the analyst's total response to the analysand.

Countertransference . . . comprises the effects of the analyst's own unconscious needs and conflicts on his understanding or technique. In such instances the patient represents for the analyst an object of the past onto whom past feelings and wishes are projected, just as it happens in the patient's transference situation with the analyst. The provoking factor for such an occurrence may be something in the patient's personality or material or something in the analytic situation as such. [1951, pp. 138–139]

Loewenstein (1957) highlighted the difference between, on the one hand, reactions in the analyst that are induced by the analysand, and, on the other, true countertransferential feelings and responses. The former were to be understood as an expression of activity in the analytic relationship. Regarding the distinction between countertransference and the analyst's total response to the analysand, A. Reich (1966) noted that the analysand is responded to not only as an object for unconscious strivings but as an object in reality as well. To achieve empathy, she maintained, the analyst must have some object libidinal investment in the analysand. Countertransference occurs only when unconscious infantile strivings are expressed in intense and inappropriate feelings, responses, or actions. Thus, she wrote, "If, for private reasons, the analyst . . . is too charged with his private problems, too many conflicts will be mobilized, too many inner resistances stirred up, or some instinctual impulses too near to breakthrough will threaten" (p. 352). It is the intensity of these conflicts that blocks understanding, interferes with technique, and leads to a breakdown of the analytic task. Within contemporary conflict theory, Arlow (1971, 1985), Boesky (1982), Brenner (1976, 1982, 1985), Jacobs (1983, 1986), McLaughlin (1981, 1988), and Silverman (1985) are among those who have contributed to the expansion and modification of the current clinical status of countertransference.

Initiating a different line of thought, Paula Heimann (1950) and Margaret Little (1951) advocated broadening countertransference to include the total response of the analyst. Maxwell Gitelson (1952) and M. B. Cohen (1952) identified the place of interactions between analyst and analysand; Heimann (1950) stressed that the analyst's emotional response is important for empathy and that countertransference is a creation of the analysand as well as of the analyst. This body of work by ego psychologists and object relations theorists provided the grounding for contemporary debates about transference actualization and enactment. Contributors to these debates include Abend (1989), Boesky (1982), Chused (1991), Jacobs (1993), McLaughlin (1991), Ogden (1982, 1983), Sandler (1976a,b) Sandler and Sandler (1978), and Schwaber (1983). Various subtexts of these debates, which have galvanized discussion (Lynch et al. 1997), include the place of philosophical relativism and social constructivism, the clinical valorization of the here and now, the status of the real relationship, the impact of the analysand on the analyst, and the role of the analyst's self-revelation and self-disclosure.

CONTEMPORARY CONFLICT THEORY

The ego-psychological tradition has also come to fruition in the theoretical viewpoint commonly referred to as modern structural theory, although contemporary conflict theory is perhaps a more apt designation and is one that we prefer. This viewpoint was developed primarily by a group of American analysts who trained in the late 1940s and early 1950s and were analyzed and supervised, for the most part, by emigrés from Central Europe. Jacob Arlow, David Beres, Charles Brenner, Martin Wangh, and Leo Rangell were members of this original group; all but Rangell attended the New York Psychoanalytic Institute. After completing their training, Arlow, Beres, Brenner, and Wangh met together and subsequently with their teachers and supervisors (Hartmann, Kris, Lewin, Loewenstein, et al.) to examine critically the received psychoanalytic wisdom of their time. Out of this examination, which focused on the concepts of anxiety, repression, defense, and symptom formation, the modern structural viewpoint emerged.

What precisely is the relationship between ego psychology and contemporary conflict theory? The latter is an outgrowth of the former, inasmuch as it devotes "considerable attention to the role, function, and characteristics of the ego" (Arlow 1963, p. 576). Yet, as Boesky (1988) has observed, the two are not synonymous, as contemporary conflict theory focuses on the essential interrelatedness of id, ego, and superego. Indeed, Rangell (1988) has suggested "id/ego/superego/external reality psychology" as a more appropriate designation for the theory that embraces the central presupposition of Freud's structural hypothesis—that psychoanalysis is primarily a psychology of conflict. Contemporary conflict theory approaches mental life and all psychic phenomena as the expression of intrapsychic forces in conflict and the resulting compromises. The thrust of contemporary conflict theory has been to refine and amend Freud's hypothesis in order to achieve a fuller appreciation of the range and scope of conflicts and compromise formations in mental life and to develop a more powerful psychoanalytic treatment approach.

Initially, this approach led to the espousal of structural concepts as more useful, clinically, than concepts associated with Freud's topographic model. Even within the structural model, moreover, the dynamic and genetic viewpoints were given precedence over the economic/energic. Arlow and Brenner's *Psychoanalytic Concepts and the Structural Theory* (1964) is an important articulation of this viewpoint. Its verdict has been underscored by Boesky (1988), who observes that Freud's concepts of psychic energy are no longer accepted by those espousing contemporary conflict theory.

Along with this selective use of structural concepts comes a trend toward loosening the dependence of conflict theory on Freud's model of the three psychic agencies. Beres gave voice to this trend in "Structure and Function in Psycho-Analysis" (1965), as did Hartmann (1964) in "Concept Formation in Psychoanalysis." Beres argued that Freud always understood the psychic structures as "functional groups" and that his emphasis was always on issues of organization and process. Sharing Arlow and Brenner's belief that theoretical concepts are ways of organizing clinical phenomena, Beres urged analysts to follow the functional direction of Freud's theorizing, an approach that viewed the structural entities of id, ego, and superego as metaphorical rather than concrete.

Beres's cautionary advice has generated a range of theoretical responses. One set of responses, associated with the work of Arlow and Brenner, has been to dissociate contemporary conflict theory from the metapsychological propositions that Freud imported into his structural theory. Arlow, Brenner, Beres, and Boesky all argue for the jettisoning of economic concepts, such as cathexis and decathexis, that are far removed from clinical observation. The modern structural emphasis on unconscious fantasy as an ego function, an emphasis growing out of an influential body of work by Arlow (1969a) and Beres (1962), is consistent with this trend.

The progressive loosening of contemporary conflict theory from Freud's formulations of id, ego, and superego has resulted in a more clinically based focus on the components of psychic conflict, a development accompanied by a widening of the experiential and dynamic realm of conflict. The shift in emphasis is from id, ego, and superego as components of conflict to the dynamic constellations closest to the data of observation.

The common frame of reference of modern conflict theorists has not precluded their espousal of different clinical emphases. Two major variations, both legacies of ego psychology, focus on the interpretation of conflict and compromise formation in the context of unconscious fantasy (Arlow, Blum, Brenner, Abend, Boesky, Rangell, Rothstein) and on the patient's resistance to awareness of the operation of defenses (Busch 1995, Gray 1994). The latter perspective is cautious about interpreting unconscious content, emphasizing instead an analytic partnership that facilitates the patient's self-discovery and emerging capacity for self-analysis. Busch links therapeutic success to the extent to which, during analysis, the patient's unbypassed ego functions have been involved in a consciously and increasingly voluntary partnership with the analyst.

An important controversy among proponents of contemporary conflict theory concerns the technical role of the patient–analyst relationship. At issue is the active use of the relationship as opposed to a greater emphasis on interpretation. This attachment/interpretation dialectic has been a major theme of ego-psychological discourse since the 1930s. It was a subject of dispute at the Marienbad symposium of 1936, where Sterba held that attachment was preliminary to understanding, whereas Strachey contended that it was the vehicle of structural change. The debate was continued at the Edinburgh symposium of 1962, where Gitelson, arguing in the spirit of Strachey, held that attachment was "a restructuring experience in itself, operating on the entire psychic apparatus and not just the ego or the superego" (Friedman 1988, p. 51).

The next installment of this debate, occurring in the 1960s and 1970s, revolved around the concept of the therapeutic alliance. The proponents of this concept, Elizabeth Zetzel and Ralph Greenson, saw it as redressing the inadequate attention to the real relationship that typified the reigning ego-psychological approach. Their position was opposed by Brenner (1979), who considered the concept superfluous and even countertherapeutic, and by Martin Stein, whose paper "The Unobjectionable Part of the Transference" (1981) offers the clearest statement of the way in which positive transference can be enlisted by patient and analyst together in the service of resistance. It is fair to say that the ego-psychological tradition, from Sterba through Fenichel and Kris to Arlow and Brenner, has been cautious about using the analytic relationship as a lever of treatment. Yet contemporary analysts trained in the ego-psychological tradition (e.g., James McLaughlin, Owen Renik, Theodore Jacobs, and Judith Chused) are among those who have alerted us to the importance of the analyst's subjective experience as a guide to understanding the patient. These analysts propound a range of positions regarding the nature and extent of the analyst's participation in the therapeutic process, but they share an appreciation of the analyst's subjectivity and find value in the enactments that occur inevitably in analytic treatment.

Contemporary conflict theory, building on the foundations of ego psychology and a spectrum of psychoanalytic theories, is an evolutionary, as opposed to revolutionary, viewpoint, since it takes Freud's conflict psychology as a conceptually and clinically adequate perspective. To be sure, it is a perspective subject to ongoing emendation (as in the work of Arlow, Brenner, and Rangell) and expansion (as in the work of Renik, Jacobs, McLaughlin, and Chused). It is noteworthy that Brenner, in his most recent writings (1993, 1994), has dispensed entirely with Freud's model of id, ego, and superego in expounding conflict and compromise formation. And Arlow, for his part, has long argued against the clinical-explanatory importance of a structural model with reified psychic agencies: "Id, ego, and superego," he has remarked, "exist not in the patient but in psychoanalytic textbooks" (personal communication). Still, other prominent contemporary structuralists continue to believe that the tripartite model remains the most illuminating and clinically useful way to understand conflict and compromise. Clearly there is no "last word" in contemporary conflict theory, and future decades will witness continuing advances in our understanding of, and clinical approaches to, "the mind in conflict" (Brenner 1982).

Having attempted to elucidate the influences and controversies along specific lines of inquiry in the history of psychoanalytic development, we end with a disclaimer: it is not possible to neatly divide psychoanalysis into independent schools with disparate theories and techniques. Rather, psychoanalytic history bears witness to an ongoing process of accommodation and mutual influence. There is a central core of theory from Freud to the present with many diverse elaborations. Often, seemingly radical differences among theories diminish in their clinical presentation. Like any science, psychoanalysis will continue to generate diverse and conflicting positions; it will continue also to be influenced by contributions from the social and natural sciences. Amid these currents of change, a firm grasp of our collective history and scientific influences will help us to avoid the partisan squabbles and irrational battles that too often have plagued our field.

REFERENCES

Abend, S. (1979). Unconscious fantasy and theories of cure. *Journal of the American Psychoanalytic Association* 27:579–596.

———— (1989). Countertransference and psychoanalytic technique. *Psychoanalytic Quarterly* 58:374–395.

Abraham, K. (1921). Contributions to the theory of the anal character. *International Journal of Psycho-Analysis* 4:400–418.

———— (1925). The history of an impostor in the light of psychoanalytic knowledge. *Psychoanalytic Quarterly* 4:570–587.

Alexander, F. (1956). *Psychoanalysis and Psychotherapy*. New York: Norton.

Arlow, J. A. (1963). The supervisory situation. *Journal of the American Psychoanalytic Association* 11:576–594.

———— (1969a). Fantasy, memory, and reality testing. *Psychoanalytic Quarterly* 38:28–51.

———— (1969b). Unconscious fantasy and disturbances of conscious experience. *Psychoanalytic Quarterly* 38(1):1–27.

———— (1971). Character perversion. In *Currents in Psychoanalysis*, ed. I. M. Marcus, pp. 317–336. New York: International Universities Press.

———— (1985). Some technical problems of countertransference. *Psychoanalytic Quarterly* 54:164–174.

Arlow, J. A., and Brenner, C. (1964). *Psychoanalytic Concepts and the Structural Theory*. New York: International Universities Press.

Bachant, J. L., Lynch, A. A., and Richards, A. D. (1995a). The evolution of drive theory: a response to Merton Gill. *Psychoanalytic Psychology* 12:565–573.

———— (1995b). Relational models in psychoanalytic theory. *Psychoanalytic Psychology* 12:71–87.

Beres, D. (1962). The unconscious fantasy. *Psychoanalytic Quarterly* 31:309–328.

———— (1965). Structure and function in psycho-analysis. *International Journal of Psycho-Analysis* 46:53–63.

Bird, B. (1957). A specific peculiarity of acting out. *Journal of the American Psychoanalytic Association* 5:630–647.

———— (1972). Notes on transference: universal phenomenon and hardest part of the analysis. *Journal of the American Psychoanalytic Association* 20:267–301.

Boesky, D. (1982). Acting out: a reconsideration of the concept. *International Journal of Psycho-Analysis* 63:39–55.

———— (1988). Comments on the structural theory of technique. *International Journal of Psycho-Analysis* 69:303–316.

Brenner, C. (1976). *Psychoanalytic Technique and Psychic Conflict.* New York: International Universities Press.

———— (1979). Working alliance, therapeutic alliance and transference. *Journal of the American Psychoanalytic Association* 27:137–158.

———— (1982). *The Mind in Conflict.* New York: International Universities Press.

———— (1985). Countertransference as compromise formation. *Psychoanalytic Quarterly* 54:155–163.

———— (1994). Mind as conflict and compromise formation. *Journal of Clinical Psychoanalysis* 3(4):473–488.

———— (1995). Some remarks on psychoanalytic technique. *Journal of Clinical Psychoanalysis* 4(4):413–428.

Busch, F. (1995). *The Ego at the Center of Clinical Technique.* Northvale, NJ: Jason Aronson.

Chused, J. F. (1991). The evocative power of enactments. *Journal of the American Psychoanalytic Association* 39(3):615–640.

Cohen, M. B. (1952). Countertransference and anxiety. *Psychiatry* 15:231–243.

Deutsch, H. (1942). Some forms of emotional disturbance and their relationship to schizophrenia. *Psychoanalytic Quarterly* 11:301–321.

Erikson, E. H. (1956). The problem of ego identity. *Journal of the American Psychoanalytic Association* 4:56–121.

Ferenczi, S. (1920). The further development of an active therapy in psychoanalysis. In *Further Contributions to the Theory and Technique of Psychoanalysis.* New York: Brunner/Mazel.

Freud, A. (1936). *The Ego and the Mechanisms of Defense.* New York: International Universities Press, 1946.

———— (1965). *Normality and Pathology in Childhood: Assessment of Development.* New York: International Universities Press.

Freud, S. (1905). Fragment of an analysis of a case of hysteria. *Standard Edition* 7:112–122.

———— (1912). The dynamics of transference. *Standard Edition* 12:97–108.

———— (1915). Observations on transference-love. *Standard Edition* 12:157–171.

———— (1916). Some character types met with in psychoanalytic work. *Standard Edition* 14:309–336.

———— (1917). Mourning and melancholia. *Standard Edition* 14:237–258.

———— (1919). A child is being beaten. *Standard Edition* 17:175–204.

———— (1920a). Associations of a four-year-old child. *Standard Edition* 18:266.

———— (1920b). The psychogenesis of a case of homosexuality in a woman. *Standard Edition* 18:146–172.

———— (1921). Group psychology and the analysis of the ego. *Standard Edition* 18:65–144.

———— (1922). Some neurotic mechanisms in jealousy, paranoia, and homosexuality. *Standard Edition* 18:221.

———— (1923). The ego and the id. *Standard Edition* 19:1–66.

———— (1926). Inhibitions, symptoms and anxieties. *Standard Edition* 20:87–176.

———— (1937). Analysis terminable and interminable. *Standard Edition* 23:209–254.

Friedman, L. (1988). *The Anatomy of Psychotherapy.* Hillsdale, NJ: Analytic Press.

Gitelson, M. (1952). The emotional position of the analyst in the psychoanalytic situation. *International Journal of Psycho-Analysis* 33:1–10.

Glover, E. (1925). Notes on oral character formation. *International Journal of Psycho-Analysis* 6:131.

Gray, P. (1994). *The Ego and Analysis of Defense.* Northvale, NJ: Jason Aronson.

Greenacre, P. (1954). The role of transference—practical considerations in relation to psychoanalytic therapy. *Journal of the American Psychoanalytic Association* 2:671–684.

Greenson, R. R. (1965). The working alliance and the transference neurosis. *Psychoanalytic Quarterly* 34:155–181.

Hartmann, H. (1939). *Ego Psychology and the Problem of Adaptation.* New York: International Universities Press.

———— (1950). Psychoanalysis and developmental psychology. In *Essays on Ego Psychology: Selected Problems in Psychoanalytic Theory*, pp. 108–109. New York: International Universities Press, 1964.

———— (1951). Technical implications of ego psychology. In *Essays on Ego Psychology: Selected Problems in Psychoanalytic Theory*, pp.142–154. New York: International Universities Press, 1964.

———— (1953). Contribution to the metapsychology of schizophrenia. In *Essays on Ego Psychology: Selected Problems in Psychoanalytic Theory*, pp. 182–206. New York: International Universities Press, 1964.

———— (1964). Concept formation in psychoanalysis. *Psychoanalytic Study of the Child* 19:11–47. New York: International Universities Press.

Hartmann, H., and Kris, E. (1945). The genetic approach in psychoanalysis. *Psychoanalytic Study of the Child* 1:11–30. New York: International Universities Press.

Hartmann, H., Kris, E., and Loewenstein, R. M. (1946). Comments on the formation of psychic structure. *The Psychoanalytic Study of the Child* 2:11–38. New York: International Universities Press.

———— (1949). Notes on the theory of aggression. *Psychoanalytic Study of the Child* 3/4:9–36. New York: International Universities Press.

Heimann, P. (1950). On countertransference. *International Journal of Pyscho-Analysis* 31:81–84.

Jacobs, T. (1983). The analyst and the patient's object world: notes on an aspect of countertransference. *Journal of Clinical Psychoanalysis* 31:619–642.

———— (1986). On countertransference enactments. *Journal of the American Psychoanalytic Association* 34:289–307.

———— (1993). *The Use of the Self.* Madison, CT: International Universities Press.

Jacobson, E. (1964). *Self and the Object World.* New York: International Universities Press.

Kris, E. (1951). Ego psychology and interpretation in psychoanalytic therapy. *Psychoanalytic Quarterly* 20:15–30.

———— (1956a). On some vicissitudes of insight in psychoanalysis. *International Journal of Psycho-Analysis* 37:445–455.

———— (1956b). The personal myth. *Journal of the American Psychoanalytic Association* 4:653–681.

Levy, S., and Inderbitzen, L. (1996). Ego psychology and modern structural theory: consolidation of ego psychology. In *Psychiatry*, vol. 1, ed. A. Tasman, J. Kay, and J. Lieberman, pp. 412–413. Philadelphia, PA: Saunders.

Little, M. (1951). Countertransference and the patient's response to it. *International Journal of Psycho-Analysis* 32:32–40.

Loewald, H. W. (1960). On the therapeutic action of psycho-analysis. *International Journal of Psycho-Analysis* 43:16–33.

———— (1971). Some considerations on repetition and repetition compulsion. *International Journal of Psycho-Analysis* 52:59–66.

Loewenstein, R. M. (1951). The problem of interpretation. *Psychoanalytic Quarterly* 20:1–14.

———— (1954). Some remarks on defenses, autonomous ego, and psychoanalytic technique. *International Journal of Psycho-Analysis* 35:188–193.

———— (1956). Some remarks on the role of speech in psychoanalytic technique. *International Journal of Psycho-Analysis* 37:460–468.

———— (1957). Some thoughts on interpretation in the theory and practice of psychoanalysis. *Psychoanalytic Study of the Child* 12:127–150. New York: International Universities Press.

———— (1958). Remarks on some variations in psychoanalytic technique. *International Journal of Psycho-Analysis* 39:202–210.

———— (1961). Introduction to panel: the silent patient. *Journal of the American Psychoanalytic Association* 9:2–6.

———— (1963). Some considerations on free association. *Journal of the American Psychoanalytic Association* 11:451–473.

———— (1969). Developments in the theory of transference in the last fifty years. *International Journal of Psycho-Analysis* 50:583–588.

———— (1982). Ego autonomy and psychoanalytic technique. In *Practice and Precept in Psychoanalytic Technique: Selected Papers of Rudolph M. Loewenstein*, pp. 211–228. New Haven: Yale University Press.

Lynch, A. A., Richards, A. D., and Bachant, J. L. (1997). *Interaction in the transference/countertransference continuum.* Paper presented at the 40th International Psychoanalytic Association Conference, Barcelona, Spain.

Mahler, M. S. (1963). Thoughts about development and individuation. *Psychoanalytic Study of the Child* 18:307–324. New York: International Universities Press.

Mahler, M. S., Pine, F., and Bergman, A. (1975). *The Psychological Birth of the Human Infant: Symbiosis and Individuation.* New York: Basic Books.

Marmor, J. (1953). Orality in the hysterical personality. *Journal of the American Psychoanalytic Association* 1:656–671.

McLaughlin, J. T. (1981). Transference, psychic reality and countertransference. *Psychoanalytic Quarterly* 50:639–664.

—— (1988). The analyst's insights. *Psychoanalytic Quarterly* 57:370–388.

—— (1991). Clinical and theoretical aspects of enactment. *Journal of the American Psychoanalytic Association* 39(3):595–614.

McLaughlin, J. T., and Johan, M. (1992). Enactments in psychoanalysis. *Journal of the American Psychoanalytic Association* 40:827–841.

Nunberg, H. (1931). The synthetic function of the ego. *International Journal of Psycho-Analysis* 12:123–140.

—— (1955). *Principles of Psychoanalysis.* New York: International Universities Press.

Ogden, T. H. (1982). *Projective Identification and Psychotherapeutic Technique.* New York: Jason Aronson.

—— (1983). The concept of internal object relations. *International Journal of Psycho-Analysis* 64:227–241.

Rangell, L. (1988). The future of psychoanalysis: the scientific crossroads. *Psychoanalytic Quarterly* 57:313–340.

Rapaport, D. (1959). A historical survey of psychoanalytic ego psychology. In *Psychological Issues*, vol. 1, ed. G. F. Klein, pp. 5–17. New York: International Universities Press.

Reich, A. (1951). On countertransference. In *Annie Reich: Psychoanalytic Contributions*, pp. 136–154. New York: International Universities Press.

—— (1960). Further remarks on countertransference. In *Annie Reich: Psychoanalytic Contributions*, pp. 271–287. New York: International Universities Press.

—— (1966). Empathy and countertransference. In *Annie Reich: Psychoanalytic Contributions*, pp. 344–360. New York: International Universities Press.

Reich, W. (1933). *Character Analysis.* New York: Orgone Institute Press.

Renik, O. (1993). Analytic interaction: conceptualizing technique in light of the analyst's irreducible subjectivity. *Psychoanalytic Quarterly* 57:523–552.

Sandler, J. (1976a). Actualization and object relationships. *Journal of the Philadelphia Association for Psychoanalysis* 3:59–70.

—— (1976b). Countertransference and role-responsiveness. *International Review of Psycho-Analysis* 3:43–47.

Sandler, J., and Sandler, A. (1978). On the development of object relationships and affects. *International Journal of Psycho-Analysis* 59:285–296.

Schwaber, E. (1983). Psychoanalytic listening and psychic reality. *International Review of Psycho-Analysis* 10:379–392.

Silverman, M. (1985). Countertransference and the myth of the perfectly analyzed analyst. *Psychoanalytic Quarterly* 54:175–199.

Stein, M. H. (1956). The problem of masochism in the theory and technique of psychoanalysis. *Journal of the American Psychoanalytic Association* 4:526–538.

———— (1981). The unobjectionable part of the transference. *Journal of the American Psychoanalytic Association* 29:869–892.

Sterba, R. (1934). The fate of the ego in analytic therapy. *International Journal of Psycho-Analysis* 15:117–126.

Stone, L. (1954). The widening scope of indications for psychoanalysis. *Journal of the American Psychoanalytic Association* 2:567–594.

———— (1961). *The Psychoanalytic Situation.* New York: International Universities Press.

Strachey, J. (1934). The nature of the therapeutic action of psychoanalysis. *International Journal of Psycho-Analysis* 15:127–159.

Zetzel, E. (1956). Current concepts of transference. *International Journal of Psycho-Analysis* 37:369–376.

2

The Influence of Object Relations Theory on Contemporary Freudian Technique

Marvin Hurvich

The term *object relations* includes so many meanings that an entire symposium could be devoted to their delineation, comparison, and contrast. Regarding the concept of object, we may be referring to a mental representation as an organization of meanings, to a fantasy, to a developmental capacity, or to a basic personality structure, with levels of developmental capacities (Perlow 1995), including dynamic properties that go beyond just being a representation. In addition, there are disagreements of various kinds such as the extent of internal versus external sources of mental objects, their relative status as experiential or nonexperiential, their relation to motivation, and the relative maturity of the mental representation in terms of its differentiation and integration and its developmental level.

The popularity of an object relations approach today is demonstrated by the fact that the number of books and articles from this perspective is approaching the output on borderline and narcissistic pathology of a few years ago. The issue of object relations is also a central focus in current ideological warfare among various schools and positions on the contemporary psychoanalytic scene. Object relations theories are being contrasted with classical theory, the latter being portrayed as a drive/defense theory (Greenberg and Mitchell 1983) or a drive/structural theory (Summers 1994).

Object relations theories centrally refer to events occurring within the psychic sphere, conceptions that are based importantly on internalization processes. In the scholarly and comprehensive accounts of Greenberg, Mitchell, Summers, and others, the crucial place in classical theory of identification in particular, and of internalization more generally, has been insufficiently acknowledged. Relevant here is the work of Helene Deutsch (1942) on the failure of identification in as-if personalities, Greenson (1954) on the struggle against identification, Sandler and Rosenblatt (1962) on the representational world, and Schafer (1968) and Meissner (1981) on internalization. Jacobson (1954, 1964), Spitz (1965), Mahler (1972), Loewald (1978), and Kernberg (1980) have all made major contributions to object relations theory, and have integrated drive, ego, and object relations into their formulations. Fred Pine's (1990) delineation of the four psychologies of drive, ego, object, and self is another noteworthy example.

Many contemporary Freudian analysts are interested in the potential value of contributions by object relations theorists to a broadening and deepening of a contemporary Freudian perspective. These contributions have come from analysts identified with a classical Freudian position, and also from some not so identified, especially from Melanie Klein and theorists from the British object relations group.

Because of the view that the concern of classical theory with drive and defense reflects an alternative to a concern with object relations, this chapter begins with a condensed overview of how object relations issues were important in Freud's writings. The major contributions of object relations theorists are discussed.

A key to Freud's entire approach was that the etiology of neuroses lay in the psychological and social realms, as well as in biological spheres, the latter being the predominant psychiatric view at the time. In the libido theory, each instinctual drive has an object, and Freud differentiated the kind of object relationship consistent with each stage of libidinal development. In a footnote added in 1910 to "Three Essays" (1905) he wrote:

The most striking distinction between the erotic life of antiquity and our own no doubt lies in the fact that the ancients laid the stress upon the instinct itself, whereas we emphasize its object. The ancients glorified the instinct and were prepared on its account to honor even an inferior object; while we despise the instinctual activity itself, and find excuses for it only in the merits of the object. [p. 149]

Also in "Three Essays," Freud wrote that the child at the breast becomes the "prototype of every relation of love" (p. 222), and that the finding or choosing of an object was actually a refinding, that it is based on a previous internalization.

Freud's 1911 theory of psychosis (1911a) was object relations centered, focusing on a withdrawal of the libidinal cathexis from a significant person and from the mental representation of that person as the event that ushered in the psychotic process.

Freud (1914) defined anaclitic (dependent) and narcissistic bases for finding an object, that is, object choice or interpersonal relations. His distinction between narcissistic libido and object libido is the first described foundation for self and object representations.

In 1917, Freud underscored object loss as the key basis for melancholia, and further that identification or internalization of the lost object was an effort to retain the object, that identification is a preliminary stage of object choice, and that an identification replaces the object cathexis of the lost object. Thus, Freud explicitly formulated the representation of objects, in addition to drive derivatives, as an aspect of psychic reality and unconscious content. Also, his concept of the superego as the internalized voice of the parents was reflected in his famous metaphor that the shadow of the object falls on the ego. The superego as the internalization of the critical voice of the parents underscores this construct as both a major mental structure, and as an internal representation and continuation of a relationship with the parents.

Additionally, Freud (1921) distinguished *identification* from *object love*, the wish to *be* the object in contrast with the wish to *have* the object. This distinction makes a place for a difference between the pleasure of sexual satisfaction, on the one hand, and feelings of contentment and security involved in an identification-merger with the object, on the other (Hensler 1991, Joffe and Sandler 1967).

Freud (1921) clarified falling in love as involving the object being put in the place of the ego ideal. In 1923, he described the ego in terms of a group of functions, but also as a precipitate of abandoned object cathexes. He stated that the makeup of the ego is importantly influenced by the history of those object choices.

Abraham (1924) presented a set of stages in the development of object love to parallel the stages of libidinal development.

In 1926, Freud asserted that anxiety is a reaction to the felt loss of the object, and two of the four basic dangers formulated by him relate to loss of the object and loss of the object's love. Here, the object is initially external, but eventually also internal.

Freud (1938/1940) described internalization in terms of an inner object relation:

> This new psychical agency [i.e., the superego] continues to carry on the functions which have hitherto been performed by people [the abandoned objects] in the external world: it observes the ego, gives it orders, judges it, and threatens it with punishments, exactly like the parents whose place it has taken. [p. 205]

Here, Freud is describing the ego being divided into two formations that are in an active dynamic interrelationship, that is, an internalized object relationship. It is worth noting that Freud did not formulate the mechanisms clarifying how such an interaction is possible.

In his later work, Freud showed a growing appreciation of the importance of the mother–infant bond, both for the development of ego structure, and for the relation with the mother as "established unalterably for a whole lifetime as the first and strongest love-object and as the prototype of all love relations—for both sexes" (1938/1940, p. 188).

As Laplanche and Pontalis wrote in their authoritative *The Language of Psychoanalysis* (1973), "In Freud's work, the concept of identification comes little by little to have the central importance which makes it, not simply one psychical mechanism among others, but the operation itself whereby the human subject is constituted" (1973, p. 206).

Within contemporary Freudian thought is the premise that psychoanalysis has always tied drive, defense, and object relational concepts together (Spruiell 1988), and that since Freud's description of the basic dangers in 1926, psychoanalytic structural theory has been an object relations theory (Boesky 1991). The centrality of internalization processes and of object relations in psychoanalytic developmental psychology is axiomatic (Blanck and Blanck 1979, 1986, Jacobson 1964, Kernberg 1976, Mahler et al. 1975, Spitz 1965).

Of the various developmental lines she delineated, Anna Freud (1963) described the one from emotional dependence to emotional self reliance and adult object relationships as the most basic one, and that these issues have been important from the beginning. She was able to integrate psychosexual level, object relations stage, and ego development factors to provide an important way of describing preoedipal pathology that goes beyond psychosexual stages but also includes them.

Erikson (1950) described internalization of relationships, and integrated psychosexual and psychosocial perspectives. Hartmann (1952), Fraiberg (1969), and McDevitt (1975) delineated object constancy. Jacobson (1964) was able to encompass, within the Freudian structural model, an integration of drive derivatives, affects, defensive functioning, object relations, and psychic structure formation in a developmental model that centers on object relations.

Loewald (1951) emphasized the embeddedness of the individual in a medium of object relations. Nevertheless, he underscored the importance of separateness and individuation, and the need for personal responsibility for one's own life. Loewald was addressing the importance of a *one-person psychology*, without downplaying the two-person psychology. Indeed, as Modell (1984) has pointed out, a two-person psychology is necessary for Freudian theory, and is not a replacement of it. The juxtaposition of one-person and two-person formulations is found in ideological debates, but a theoretical frame that encompasses both and attends to their interrelationships is a better alternative than either one alone. Even defensive activity is not limited to a one-person model (Modell 1984).

Modell (1984) attemps to integrate object relations within the structural model. One of his major points is that it is the identification with a "good object" (p. 212) that enables the person to achieve mastery over id impulses. A survey of the classical literature on analyzability led Bachrach and Leaff (1978) to conclude that ego strength and object relations have been seen as the most important issues.

Mahler's (1972) delineation of the separation-individuation phases can be understood as a description of preoedipal development, with emphasis on the interrelated unfolding of drive factors, ego processes, and object relations.

Other key contributions to object relations theory came from Klein, Fairbairn, Winnicott, and Balint. Only some of the most central issues will be considered here.

Melanie Klein took the object relations aspect of Freud's libido theory and made it more central, stressing that the internalized good object forms the ego core, and the importance of the object for ego growth. She expanded Freud's conception of the inner world, and described a view of the mind as a stage on which an inner drama is played out, with the players being fantasied objects and part objects. She postulated an interrelationship among *internal* objects, unconscious phantasies, and drives that has a good deal of clinical utility. Internal objects are seen as the content of unconscious phantasies, and unconscious phantasies are the psychic representations of libidinal and aggressive instinctual drives. She took Freud's concept of the death instinct seriously, and emphasized the importance of envy as one of its earliest and most important manifestations. Klein formulated that, early on, the object is split into good and bad based on gratifying and frustrating experiences, and she saw the relative preponderance of positive over negative drives and affects as a crucial variable influencing psychic health.

She delineated three possible sources for internal objects: an innate basis, concrete bodily interactions, and as a result of the introjection of experiences with external objects. She assumed that internal objects undergo a developmental progression. Initially, they are apprehended as concrete and physically present, then as representations of an object in the psyche and in the person's memory system, and finally, as a symbolic representation in words or in other symbolic forms (Hinshelwood 1989, Money-Kyrle 1968, Segal 1958). A major contribution of Klein and her group to psychoanalysis, beyond making the object notion more central in intrapsychic life, was the focus on the intersubjective processes in transference and countertransference.

Klein's concept of projective identification as modified and expanded by Heimann (1950), Bion (1952, 1967), Racker (1953), and Grinberg (1962) includes interpersonal and intersubjective, as well as intrapsychic aspects, and provides much of the theoretical underpinning for the currently popular concept of enactments (Chused 1991).

David Rapaport (1959) once opined that Melanie Klein had substituted an *id mythology* for an *ego psychology*. Schafer (1997), more recently, has maintained that the work of some contemporary Kleinians is essentially

Freudian and includes its own version of an ego psychology. This latter aspect is reflected in an ongoing interest by these workers in delineating specific clinical descriptions of ego weaknesses and cognitive impairments that are based on intrapsychic conflicts that seriously interfere with the analytic work.

Another contribution of Klein is the delineation of cetain concepts and the demonstration of their clinical utility: greed, envy, gratitude, omnipotence, projective identification, part objects, splitting, and the paranoid-schizoid and depressive positions. Primitive and pathological envy is especially important in more disturbed patients. My clinical impression is that pathological envy is one of the central sequelae of childhood psychic trauma. That is, the patient's anger and disappointment over the negative events in his early object relations are activated and potentiated when the patient compares him/herself to the therapist or to a friend regarding some attribute, possession, or perceived accomplishment of the other. This becomes a key resistance in the therapy, and a basis for hatred of the therapist or other who is perceived as having been more fortunate and blessed by fate. Also clinically very valuable, I think, are the notions of successful and blocked mourning and reparations, which have been developed in Kleinian theory.

The paranoid-schizoid and depressive positions were formulated in terms of changes in relation to the object, and on internal or fantasied object relations. They are seen to involve characteristic anxieties, defensive operations, and qualities of object relationships. From the analyst's perspective they are *mental models* with certain attributes. From the patient's experience, they are *states or attitudes of mind*, a creation of related fantasies of and relationships to objects with typical anxieties and defenses. An ongoing dynamic relationship between the two positions is seen; neither one is always in control. It is a Kleinian truism that the more the depressive features predominate over paranoid and schizoid, and love prevails over hate, the better the prognosis for change. Tracking the interplay between the two positions, from fragmentation to integration and back, is a major task of Kleinian analysts, and can be useful to Freudian analysts as well.

Fairbairn (1944), more explicitly than Klein, attempted to develop a comprehensive object relations theory, which he saw as an evolutionary step following the focus on impulse and then on the ego. He held that impulses are object seeking; that repression is primarily directed against bad objects rather than against memories or impulses per se; that when repression fails, other defenses come into play, namely, phobic, obsessional, hysterical, or paranoid "techniques," or taking onto the self the "badness" experienced toward the object (moral defense). And he asserted that the clinging to painful experiences, so common in psychopathology, is better understood as relevant to relationships with bad internal objects, than in terms of a repetition compulsion. He gave more importance to the environmental object in addition to a more delineated theory of internalized objects. He emphasized that it is *object relations* that are internalized, not just self and object representations. He further conceptualized internal objects as dynamic structures, with the capacity for psychological activity, such as perceiving, thinking, and feeling, and with degrees of capacity for independent functioning.

Fairbairn thus conceived of the personality as housing semiautonomous divisions, with inner conflict, not among id, ego, and superego components, but among agencies or endopsychic structures, all based on internalized object relations: the central ego and the ideal object, the libidinal object and the exciting object, and the antilibidinal object and the rejecting object. The return of the repressed is now the return of the bad object. The bases for psychopathology are not conflictual impulses or intolerable memories, but rather, intolerably bad internalized objects, claimed Fairbairn (1943).

Fairbairn emphasized the unfolding and development of dependency, and underscored the nurturant aspect of libido rather than the sexual features. He saw object seeking, safety, and connection as more central than pleasure and pain as regulating principles.

In this regard, he also emphasized that the infant is entitled to be treated and loved as a person in his own right. This now completed the triad: Freud stressed the oedipal father, Klein the preoedipal mother, and Fairbairn, along with Winnicott, the rights of the infant.

Fairbairn formulated the schizoid position as the key psychopathological paradigm rather than the depressive or the hysterical, and he accented the process of splitting of the object in repression and in the process of internalization, which he limited to a pathological process.

He posited that when infantile neediness is overly frustrated, the youngster comes to fear the destructiveness of his own need-saturated love. Rather than experiencing everything bad coming from the outside, the pleasure ego (Freud 1911b), Fairbairn (1944) underscored the "moral defense" as taking the parents' "badness" onto the self, the youngster preferring to be a sinner in a livable world, rather than a saint in a world of intolerably bad objects. To Freud's five sources of resistance (1926), Fairbairn added the resistance to change based on the fear of loss of the connection with the internalized object. This is a valid one, and quite useful, in my experience, though it overlaps with Freud's superego resistance.

Ogden (1990) has clarified the theoretical basis for the dynamic properties of the internal object, implied in Freud's, Klein's, and Fairbairn's formulations. Ogden points out that an internal object in Fairbairn's system both has the capability for perception, thought, and feeling, just as the whole ego does, while also being a split-off part of the ego (self) as a result of being internalized, that is, substantially identified with an object representation. As Ogden formulated it:

> Because the ego suborganization is itself capable of generating meanings, its identification with an object representation results in a shift in the way that person thinks of itself. That which was originally an object representation becomes experientially equivalent to a self representation of one of the split-off facets of the ego. . . . Such a dual split would result in the formation of two new suborganizations of the ego, one identified with the self in the external object relationship and the other thoroughly identified with the object. [pp. 149–150]

This formulation is helpful in understanding the experiences of patients with dissociative reactions, where inner personified persecutors utilize current issues in dominating and reprimanding the patient.

Winnicott (1958, 1965) has provided concepts and ways of understanding that have deepened our work with more disturbed patients. He gave us the holding environment, the good-enough mother, the use of an object, true and false self, ego relatedness, the stage of concern, the capacity to be alone, and impingement into the infant's going on being. His valuable recommendations are to allow the insight to come within the patient's own omnipotence, and to understand the importance of not being destroyed by the patient's anger so the patient can develop a clearer distinction between fantasy and reality. His concept of the transitional object as the first "not-me" possession and the beginning of symbolization and of play has become widely utilized by many Freudian analysts. Modell (1968) has extended transitional objects to the transitional object relationship, a way of relating to others characteristic of those patients who do not recognize the separateness of the other, and where the other is experienced mainly as a need satisfier. Grunes (1984) has described the therapeutic object relationship as an important ingredient in the work with such patients.

Michael Balint (1968), along with Winnicott, provided concepts and techniques for dealing with patients not suitable for standard analysis. Both authors made a clear distinction among patients based on structural considerations. Balint differentiated between malignant and benign regression, and gave us the idea of regression as an aspect of the therapeutic action with some patients, regression in the service of progression. He described ways to respond to the patient at the *basic fault,* a metaphor for deficient and defective ego development, where treatment may be facilitated by creating a special, empathic atmosphere. Here, the experience of the patient is regressed, so that the words of adult language are not understood to have their ordinary meaning, a regressive position that is based on a time prior to the development of words. Balint's recommendation of a special atmosphere with these patients is based on the idea that the malignant form of regression is more likely to occur when the analyst's behavior, demeanor, and way of intervening and interacting implies to the patient either his omnipotence or omniscience. This recognition that the regressed patient often profits from changes in the frame and interactive style has been helpful for many Freudian analysts working with more disturbed patients.

The most comprehensive effort thus far to integrate Fairbairn and Klein's object relations views within a contemporary Freudian framework is Kernberg's (1976) model, importantly influenced by the work of Mahler and Jacobson. Affect and cognition are integrated by initial intrapsychic experiences, and in turn link the libidinal and aggressive drive systems with internalized object relations, which are internalized in self-object dyadic units, characterized by a particular affect tone. These object relations units are major building blocks of intrapsychic structure, and the drive aspects of intrapsychic conflict are seen to be expressed through the object relations units. Character defenses reveal the triggering of one self and object dyadic grouping, which defends against a repressed and opposed self and object unit (Kernberg 1980).

The view put forth here is not only that object relations theories are an integral part of contemporary classical frameworks, but that concepts from the object relations schools have additionally enriched contemporary Freudian theory. Further, a classical framework can usefully and adequately encompass many of these conceptualizations and insights. This is not meant to ignore or gloss over the difficulties of integrating concepts from the various psychoanalytic positions, nor to underplay the controversies regarding specific issues, considerations not delineated in this chapter.

Object relations issues, such as object relations and interpersonal relations, one- and two-person psychologies, intrapsychic and interpersonal, real relationship and transference relationship, here-and-now versus past influences on the transference, the relations between transference and enactment, and the conceptions of transference-resistance versus transference–countertransference, are conceptualized by current Freudian writers.

These considerations can be found in various combinations. Gill's (1982) emphasis on the value and importance of interpreting resistances to recognizing transference manifestations, the employment of transference interpretations early in the analytic work, and on a more dominant place for transference interventions in analysis altogether, preceded and laid the foundation for his later interactional two-person focus. He pointed out that in the analytic situation, intrapsychic conflicts may be reflected in the interpersonal relation between patient and analyst. He also stated that defense is an intrapsychic concept, while resistance is an interpersonal one. Even here, a case has later been made for interactional aspects of defense (Dorpat and Miller 1992). Gill (1991) subsequently stated that in psychoanalysis and psychotherapy alike, interaction is inevitable, but that in analysis, the goal is to analyze it. Oremland (1991) has depicted both psychoanalysis and psychoanalytically oriented psychotherapy as involving interpretation of the transference, while interactive psychotherapy employs the transference-as-interaction to mitigate symptoms and suffering.

There are positions where the analyst considers him/herself both an interactionist and an adherent of a one-person psychology. An illustration of some of the layered complexities of these issues is Boesky's (1990) view that he is able to account for the important dyadic aspects of the interaction between analyst and patient within an intrapsychic point of view, while still maintaining that resistance is a mutual creation of patient and analyst. He holds to the premise that psychoanalysis is limited to the intrapsychic sphere, and that this is true for all observations about the interaction between the analyst and the patient.

Classical analysts have different positions on the extent to which the analyst serves as a participant observer (Renik 1993), and even what the term *participant observer* means (Boesky 1990). In Renik's (1993) view, it is the interaction between the patient's and the analyst's interpretations that can lead to analytic progress.

Acknowledging the interactional quality of the analytic dyad, however, can lead to opposite foci. For example, Sandler (1976) emphasizes the patient's attempt to induce the analyst to play a role in his own reenacted transference drama. Schwaber (1992), on the other hand, sees counter-transference as the analyst's retreat from the patient's point of view.

An issue that has interactional implications is enactments. For some (Jacobs 1986), both transference and countertransference enact-ments are seen to provide information useful for analytic work. Others (Brenner 1982) understand transference and countertransference as in-distinguishable, genetically and dynamically. But the patient's transference is analyzed in conjunction with the analyst, while countertransference should not be.

Another major controversy involves the therapeutic and working alliances versus the transference. Both Zetzel (1956) and Greenson (1967) defined the therapeutic alliance as a working relationship between thera-pist and patient, following Freud's concept of the positive transference (1915a), and his characterization of the analytic situation as involving the analyst allying himself with the patient's ego (1937) so that the uncon-trolled parts of the id can be integrated with the ego. For Zetzel, the alliance is part of the real object relationship between patient and analyst, which promotes the utilization of the patient's autonomous ego functions, so necessary for him/her to fulfill the functions of an analytic patient. The transference, on the other hand, is seen as the vehicle for the patient using the analyst as the object of displaced and unsettled infantile fantasy. For Greenson (1967), the two most important kinds of object relations in analysis are transference manifestations and the working alliance. Green-son claimed that a working alliance, which includes associating to and efforts to comprehend the analyst's interpretations, is necessary for a process of working through to take place.

Brenner (1979), on the other hand, holds that the transference concept is sufficient to cover all instances where the notion of a therapeutic alliance has been invoked.

A comment by Boesky (1990) provides a most relevant ending for this brief sampling of some ways object relations theories have influenced contemporary Freudian thought: the way the analyst contributes to the psychoanalytic process merits additional intensive elucidation.

REFERENCES

Abraham, K. (1924). A short study of the development of the libido, viewed in the light of mental disorders. In *Selected Papers of Karl Abraham*, pp. 418–501. New York: Basic Books.

Bachrach, H., and Leaff, L. (1978). "Analyzability": review of the clinical and quantitative literature. *Journal of the American Psychoanalytic Association* 26:881–902.

Balint, M. (1968). *The Basic Fault.* London: Tavistock.

Bion, W. (1952). Group dynamics: a review. In *Experiences in Groups*, pp. 141–192. New York: Basic Books.

——— (1967). *Second Thoughts.* New York: Jason Aronson.

Blanck, G., and Blanck, R. (1979). *Ego Psychology*, vol. 2. New York: Columbia University Press.

Boesky, D. (1990). The psychoanalytic process and its components. *Psychoanalytic Quarterly*, 54:550–584.

——— (1991). Conflict, compromise formation, and structural theory. In *Conflict and Compromise: Therapeutic Implications*, ed. S. Dowling. Madison, CT: International Universities Press.

Brenner, C. (1979). Working alliance, therapeutic alliance, and transference. *Journal of the American Psychoanalytic Association* 27:137–158.

——— (1982). *The Mind in Conflict.* New York: International Universities Press.

Chused, J. (1991). The evocative power of enactments. *Journal of the American Psychoanalytic Association* 39:614–639.

Deutsch, H. (1942). Some forms of emotional disturbance and their relationship to schizophrenia. *Psychoanalytic Quarterly* 11:301–321.

Dorpat, T. L., and Miller, M. L. (1992). *Clinical Interaction and the Analysis of Meaning: A New Psychoanalytic Theory.* Hillsdale, NJ: Analytic Press.

Erikson, E. (1950). *Childhood & Society.* New York: Norton.

Fairbairn, W. R. D. (1944). The repression and the return of bad objects (with special reference to the "war neuroses"). In *Psychoanalytic Studies of the Personality*, pp. 59–81. London: Routledge & Kegan Paul, 1952.

——— (1944). Endopsychic structure considered in terms of object-relationships. In *Psychoanalytic Studies of the Personality*, pp. 82–136. London: Routledge & Kegan Paul, 1952.

Fraiberg, S. (1969). Libidinal object constancy and mental representation. *Psychoanalytic Study of the Child* 24:9–47. New York: International Universities Press.

Freud, A. (1963). The concept of developmental lines. *Psychoanalytic Study of the Child* 18:245–265. New York: International Universities Press.

Freud, S. (1905). Three essays on the theory of sexuality. *Standard Edition* 7:135–243.

———— (1911a). Psychoanalytic notes on an autobiographical account of a case of paranoia (dementia paranoides). *Standard Edition* 12:3–80.

———— (1911b). Formulations on the two principles of mental functioning. *Standard Edition* 12:218–226.

———— (1914). On narcissism: an introduction. *Standard Edition* 14:73–102.

———— (1915a). Observations on transference love. *Standard Edition* 12:157–171.

———— (1915b). Instincts and their vicissitudes. *Standard Edition* 14:117–140.

———— (1917). Mourning and melancholia. *Standard Edition* 14:237–258.

———— (1921). Group psychology and the analysis of the ego. *Standard Edition* 18:67–143.

———— (1923). The ego and the id. *Standard Edition* 19:3–66.

———— (1926). Inhibitions, symptoms and anxiety. *Standard Edition* 20:77–175.

———— (1937). Analysis terminable and interminable. *Standard Edition* 23:216–253.

———— (1938/1940). An outline of psychoanalysis. *Standard Edition* 23:144–207.

Gill, M. (1982). *Analysis of Transference. Vol. 1: Theory and Technique.* New York: International Universities Press.

———— (1991). Indirect suggestion: a response to Oremland's *Interpretation and Interaction.* In *Interpretation and Interaction: Psychoanalysis or Psychotherapy,* by J. D. Oremland, pp. 137–163. Hillsdale, NJ: Analytic Press.

Greenberg, J., and Mitchell, S. (1983). *Object Relations in Psychoanalytic Theory.* Cambridge, MA: Harvard University Press.

Greenson, R. (1954). The struggle against identification. *Journal of the American Psychoanalytic Association* 21:200–217.

———— (1967). *The Technique and Practice of Psychoanalysis.* New York: International Universities Press.

Grinberg, L. (1962). On a specific aspect of countertransference due to the patient's projective identification. *International Journal of Psycho-Analysis* 31:81–84.

Grunes, M. (1984). The therapeutic object relation. *Psychoanalytic Review* 71:123–143.

Hartmann, H. (1952). The mutual influences in the development of ego and id. *Psychoanalytic Study of the Child* 7:9–30. New York: International Universities Press.

Heimann, P. (1950). On counter-transference. *International Journal of Psycho-Analysis* 31:81–84.

Hensler, H. (1991). *Freud's "On Narcissism": An Introduction,* ed. J. Sandler, E. Person, and P. Fonagy, pp. 195–215. New Haven, CT: Yale University Press.

Hinshelwood, R. (1989). *A Dictionary of Kleinian Thought*. London: Free Association Books.

Jacobs, T. (1986). On countertransference enactments. *Journal of the American Psychoanalytic Association* 34:289–307.

Jacobson, E. (1954). The self and the object world: vicissitudes of their infantile cathexes and their influence on ideational and affective development. *Psychoanalytic Study of the Child* 9:75–127. New York: International Universities Press.

———— (1964). *The Self and the Object World*. New York: International Universities Press.

Joffe, W., and Sandler, J. (1967). Some conceptual problems involved in the consideration of disorders of narcissism. *Journal of Child Psychotherapy* 2:56–66.

Kernberg, O. (1976). *Object Relations Theory and Clinical Psychoanalysis*. New York: Jason Aronson.

———— (1980). *Internal World and External Reality*. New York: Jason Aronson.

Laplanche, J., and Pontalis, J-B. (1973). *The Language of Psychoanalysis*. New York: Norton.

Loewald, H. W. (1951). Ego and reality. *International Journal of Psycho-Analysis* 32:10–18.

———— (1978). Instinct theory, object relations, and psychic structure formation. In *Papers on Psychoanalysis*, pp. 207–218. New Haven, CT: Yale University Press.

Mahler, M. (1972). On the first three subphases of the separation-individuation process. *International Journal of Psycho-Analysis* 53:333–338.

Mahler, M., Pine, F., and Bergman, A. (1975). *The Psychological Birth of the Human Infant*. New York: Basic Books.

———— (1979). *Selected Papers of Margaret Mahler*, vols. 1 & 2. New York: Jason Aronson.

McDevitt, J. B. (1975). Separation-individuation and object constancy. *Journal of the American Psychoanalytic Association* 23:713–742.

Meissner, W. (1981). Internalization in Psychoanalysis. *Psychological Issues*, Monograph 50. New York: International Universities Press.

Modell, A. (1968). *Object Love and Reality: An Introduction to a Psychoanalytic Theory of Object Relations*. New York: International Universities Press.

———— (1984). *Psychoanalysis in a New Key*. Madison, CT: International Universities Press.

Money-Kyrle, R. (1968). Cognitive development. *International Journal of Psycho-Analysis* 49:691–698.

Ogden, T. H. (1990). *The Matrix of the Mind*. Northvale, NJ: Jason Aronson.

Oremland, J. D. (1991). *Interpretation and Interaction: Psychoanalysis or Psychotherapy*. Hillsdale, NJ: Analytic Press.

Perlow, M. (1995). *Understanding Mental Objects*. London: Routledge.

Pine, F. (1990). *Drive, Ego, Object and Self: A Synthesis For Clinical Work*. New York: Basic Books.

Racker, H. (1953). A contribution to the problem of countertransference. *Psychoanalytic Quarterly* 26:313–324.

Rapaport, D. (1958/1959). A historical survey of psychoanalytic ego psychology. *Psychological Issues* 1:5–17.

Renik, O. (1993). Analytic interaction: conceptualizing technique in the light of the analyst's irreducible subjectivity. *Psychoanalytic Quarterly* 62:553–571.

Sandler, J. (1976). Countertransference and role responsiveness. *International Review of Psycho-Analysis* 3:43–47.

Sandler, J., and Rosenblatt, B. (1962). The concept of the representational world. *Psychoanalytic Study of the Child* 17:128–145. New York: International Universities Press.

Schafer, R. (1968). *Aspects of Internalization.* New York: International Universities Press.

——— (1997). *The Contemporary Kleinians of London.* Madison, CT: International Universities Press.

Schwaber, E. A. (1992). Countertransference: the analyst's retreat from the patient's vantage point. *International Journal of Psycho-Analysis* 73:349–361.

Segal, H. (1957). Notes on symbol formation. *International Journal of Psycho-Analysis* 38:39–45.

Spitz, R. (1965). *The First Year of Life.* New York: International Universities Press.

Spruiell, V. (1988). The indivisibility of Freudian object relations and drive theories. *Psychoanalytic Quarterly* 57:597–625.

Summers, F. (1994). *Object Relations Theories and Psychopathology.* Hillsdale, NJ: Analytic Press.

Winnicott, D. W. (1958). *Collected Papers.* New York: Basic Books.

——— (1965). *The Maturational Processes and the Facilitating Environment.* New York: International Universities Press.

Zetzel, E. (1956). Current concepts of transference. *International Journal of Psycho-Analysis* 37:369–376.

——— (1958). Therapeutic alliance in the analysis of hysteria. In *The Capacity for Emotional Growth,* pp. 182–196. New York: International Universities Press, 1970.

PART II

THE ENDURING LEGACIES

Overview of Controversies

Martin L. Nass

Two of the chapters in Part II address technical issues in psychoanalysis, while the third goes to the basic underpinnings of forms of communication—the symbol. There are some common threads among the chapters that highlight current issues in psychoanalysis.

The history of psychoanalysis and psychoanalytic technique can best be understood through its chronological development. To be unaware of history is to repeat the same mistakes made in the course of the development of psychoanalytic thought, albeit unwittingly. From its beginnings, psychoanalysis has always had its roots in an empirical methodology through which theoretical constructs always followed clinical observations. Freud's approach continuously moved from clinical observations to theory, and then refining or modifying theory through further observations. The fact that he left his prior work in print and never directly refuted it has resulted in criticisms of psychoanalysis that were based on concepts and ideas that are no longer held to be valid. For example, much of the current trend in some quarters toward self-disclosure in analysis can be traced to

Ferenczi's attempts at "mutual analysis" (Dupont 1988). Countertransference feelings are not used as data for the understanding of the analytic dialogue, but are revealed to the patient as helpful information. This "wild analysis" does not stem from a solid theoretical understanding of the transference but is used as a means of discharging the analyst's own feelings. Similarly, cathartic methods of treatment popular a decade or two ago in primal scream therapy and in encounter groups can be traced to the tried and discarded cathartic method of Breuer and Freud in the 1890s (Breuer and Freud 1893). Stanley Grand (Chapter 5) highlights this area in his discussion of the self-reflective function of the analytic process, particularly where it applies to issues in the transference. Affective discharge and self-revelations do not in themselves build character structure.

The formulation of psychoanalytic perspectives on understanding the empirical findings that were obtained often turned on which aspects of these findings were given greater focus when theoretical formulations were developed. This has been true throughout the history of psychoanalysis, where dissenting schools often took one aspect of basic psychoanalytic tenet and expanded it into an encompassing theory, viz. Alfred Adler. From Abraham's (1911, 1924) shift in emphasis to projective mechanisms in depression away from Freud's (1917) emphasis on internalization, the Kleinian perspective and the focus on projective mechanisms grew. Freud's emphasis on internalization provided for the development of the structural theory and eventually of ego psychology (Coltrera 1994). The work of Hartmann (1939) and Hartmann, Kris, and Loewenstein (1946) made room for the study in psychoanalysis of nonconflictual aspects of behavior and for the expansion of a developmental perspective in psychoanalysis, first presented by Freud in 1926. This latter has resulted in expansion of technique, making analysis possible in situations where analysands would previously have been considered unanalyzable. Techniques for addressing early nonverbal aspects of the psychoanalytic encounter have been developed (Coltrera 1979), partly made possible through the understanding of nonverbal interactions in the form of "enactments" (McLaughlin 1991) and by greater awareness of the psychoanalytic encounter as repeating the circumstances of early maternal reciprocal dialogue. Analytic understanding has moved from the "blank screen" stereotype of the analyst to the analyst as actively involved (with the kind of patient reported in these three chapters) in helping to reestablish early failed dialogue.

The three chapters in Part II each address some aspect of these issues.

The authors are addressing the enduring legacies of psychoanalysis and what has been particularly meaningful to them in psychoanalytic thought. Psychoanalytic truths are hard won, always following from clinical findings. Freud also stated that psychoanalysis was an art of interpretation in which the appearance and working through of transference phenomena through regressive recall is its most powerful therapeutic instrument. Its cornerstones were for him the assumption that there are unconscious mental processes, the recognition of the theory of resistance and repression, and the appreciation of the importance of sexuality and of the Oedipus complex. "These constitute the principal subject-matter of psycho-analysis and the foundation of its theory. No one who cannot accept them all should count himself a psycho-analyst" (Freud 1923, p. 247).

For me the vitality of psychoanalysis is its ability to grow with new knowledge and incorporate the current thinking of many fields into its approach. The evolving nature of psychoanalysis is such that it is an organically growing, open-ended theory in which there is built-in room for expansion for more current concepts. For, example, in the 1890s when the current thinking in physics was based on a hydraulic model, that's where psychoanalytic theory had its position; in the 1990s, as much of the thinking in the so-called hard sciences is based on chaos theory, there is room in a psychoanalytic point of view to account for this theory. Chaos theory is now being applied to psychoanalysis and to the therapeutic process with some exciting observations that have focused on nonlinear, complex autonomic nervous system activity. By observing sequences of states and monitoring the rapid changes that take place dramatically following inter- or intrapersonal distress, researchers have shown that confronting painful feelings and thoughts decreases measured autonomic arousal.

The recent findings in neurobiology have also been confirming what we have known developmentally for a very long time—that early dialogue and interaction stimulate a neurological feedback system and stimulate development, resulting in greater brain activity and in structural changes in the brain, that there are open, growing systems whose paths are more in keeping with chaos theory than simple linear development, and that behavior is far more complex than we ever imagined. Our work in some ways attempts to reestablish these failed dialogues and to reestablish a sense of trust in our patients. This developmental point of view is most active and vital in psychoanalytic thought and connects to some of Freud's early work in neurobiology. We are moving toward the future in many ways, but we also have a strong tie to our roots, so that we can profit and learn from the insights and the errors of our predecessors and use them to move ahead. This is why a developmental perspective is so critical in our understanding of psychoanalytic process (Shore 1994).

These three chapters address some issues in psychoanalytic thought from very different approaches. The common link among them is the continuity of Freud's thinking, although modified, into the present time.

Grand (Chapter 5) addresses the place of self-reflection in the psychoanalytic process and takes us through some of the current controversies in the field regarding which theory of pathogenesis is best. He rightfully criticizes the technical fashions in the field and demonstrates the lack of commonality among them that would preclude the designs of a comparison research. He also provides us with a great deal of information on the history of technique.

Adams-Silvan and Silvan (Chapter 3) demonstrate through a clinical anecdotal process that Freud's basic principles involving the use of transference run through all psychoanalytic and psychotherapeutic approaches, and even the most radical technical modifications continue this line of understanding. They highlight the empirical nature of Freud's work and correctly point out that theory was developed to organize and codify observations. They show that the basic psychoanalytic approaches were set down over a hundred years ago.

In their writings, Grand and Adams-Silvan and Silvan address questions of technical modifications in so-called classical psychoanalysis. However, since psychoanalysis as I see it has been evolving over the past hundred years, aren't the evolutionary technical changes from the basic model the inevitable growth in terms of expansion of knowledge as well as in the differences in the kinds of people who are now amenable to psychoanalytic treatment? There are many patients treated by psychoanalysis today who would not have been considered analyzable twenty-five or thirty years ago, and this has been made possible by increased knowledge of dealing with character issues, working with nonverbal and preverbal issues and bringing them into the analytic dialogue. However, Freud's basic principles that I mentioned earlier are still operating. Consequently, Grand's question of whether it is useful to still call the technical shifts "modified analysis" in my opinion should be answered in the negative since they still meet the basic criteria for what constitutes a psychoanalytic process by Freud in 1923. The greater attention paid to preverbal and nonverbal aspects of behavior are developmental aspects of the growth of psychoanalytic methodology and need to be understood from the perspective of the historical growth of psychoanalysis. The history of an idea in its development includes and presupposes all of what has contributed to its present state; for example, an ego psychology presupposes the inclusion of an id psychology as well. Consequently, the evolutionary changes in psychoanalytic technique that are a the result of empirical findings should not be regarded as "modified" but as current developmental changes in methodology.

Freedman's discussion of symbolism (Chapter 4) goes to the heart of one of the analyst's main functions—that of interpretation and supplying meaning to the analysand's narrative. Freedman discusses symbolization as a process of shaping meaning and gives us an historical perspective on some of the seminal thinkers in this field. He discusses symbolization from a developmental perspective in which the analyst helps the patient to raise symbolization to a higher level through the analytic process. Raising the developmental level of the patient's capacity to symbolize helps create greater space and thus greater reflective capacity and room for increased psychic growth.

Thus, the analyst helps the patient make sense out of his or her life, and helps through interpretation to reconstruct experience and to show how the past operates in the present in an automatic manner. As ego psychology with its emphasis on form and style developed, technical issues of timing and manner of communication to the patient became as important as or more important than the content of what is transmitted. Loewenstein's (1956) paper on the role of speech in psychoanalysis highlights the importance of the act and style of speaking as well as what the patient is saying. He also emphasizes the role of speech as an objectification involved in bringing outside that which is inside. Freud's dictum (and this was stated before ego psychology) that the interpretation should be addressed to the psychic surface where the resistance and the affect state of the patient are clearly identifiable is a truism in present-day technique. This was systematically elaborated by Edward Bibring in 1954 in his paper on psychoanalysis and psychotherapy. He clearly sketches out what constitutes an interpretation and the varieties of technical interventions used in psychoanalysis, ranging from suggestion and abreaction to confrontation and clarification.

Interpretation is the only technical intervention that addresses unconscious material and connects the past with the present. Technical maneuvers involving preinterpretive strategies are vital in the preparation for an interpretation. The role of self-reflection and introspective curiosity is vital for the conduct of an analysis. How does one help to achieve this in a nonreflective patient? Grand's patient Mrs. J. had difficulty with transference space, which resulted in her only being able to tolerate his empathic attunement to her distress and an inability to reflect on her experience. His interpretations were experienced as unempathic and her style was to experience her difficulties as stemming from external sources. Such patients present immeasurable challenges to the psychoanalyst. While empathic attunement is a vital factor in working with such individuals, an active approach on the part of the psychoanalyst to help promote reflective awareness and introspection is crucial. While Grand speaks of the identification with the analyst as a means of enabling the patient to work more readily in the analytic modality, it seems to me that this is but one aspect of promoting self-reflection. In addition, something more active on the part of the analyst to help the patient become more reflective is crucial. The patient needs to be helped to see what he or she is doing and this cannot be accomplished strictly by an identification with the methodology when there is no introspective curiosity. This technical problem is addressed by both Bibring (1954) and Coltrera (1981), who indicate that the analyst needs to help the patients observe their behavior. Bibring suggests that helping the patient to reflect involves preinterpretive strategies of confrontation and clarification. By showing the patient his or her actions from the external vantage point, one can show the individual what he or she is doing. This also addresses the importance of character style in that the person defends against an internal experience by externalizing and seeing the source of feelings and actions to originate in the outside world. Such technical interventions are not new but are vital in the treatment of individuals with poor self-reflective capacities and are active strategies to help them to look at themselves.

These technical advances in the treatment of patients with early developmental disturbances have made it possible to address early nonverbal and preverbal issues as they manifest themselves in the treatment situation (Coltrera 1979). By tuning in and confronting and clarifying behavior that is outside of the patient's awareness but is shown through actions or through enactments with the analyst, this material that often presents in nonverbal and in nondiscursive form can be examined and discussed in the analysis. This has made it possible to open up an entire area of psychoanalytic work to a group of patients who previously had been considered unanalyzable. Calling attention to nonverbal behavior (and often the manifestation of preverbal behavior) has moved psychoanalytic technique into a whole new area of possibilities. This to me is evolutionary and not strictly a radical departure from the basic model. A developmental position of psychoanalysis, first addressed by Freud in 1926, is now possible through our understanding of the recent work in child development, developmental neurobiology, and through the courageous work of pioneering psychoanalysts.

An early step in this direction was made by Edward Bibring (1937), who made what to me was a monumental contribution to the Marienbad Symposium of 1936. It was clearly ahead of its time and anticipated a good deal of the work of Hans Loewald, who some 25 years later (Loewald 1960) fleshed out what happens between analyst and patient during the psychoanalytic process from a developmental perspective. Loewald has been rediscovered recently by many people and perhaps Bibring's work will also receive more of the recognition it deserves. For example in 1936, he had a distinct developmental perspective on the role of the analyst, which Loewald wrote about in 1960. Bibring (1937) said,

> Psychoanalysis achieves a loosening of fixation, removal of repression, weakening of repetition compulsions and a *restoration of development.* . . . I believe that the patient's relationship to the analyst from which a sense of security emanates is not only a precondition of the procedure but also effects an immediate consolidation of his sense of security which he has not successfully acquired in childhood. [pp. 176–177]

Forty years later, Harry Guntrip (1975) made a similar statement from the *patient's* point of view in comparing his own analytic experiences with Fairbairn and with Winnicott: "To find a good parent at the start is the basis of psychic health. In its lack, to find a genuine 'good object' in one's analyst is both a transference experience and a real life experience" (p. 156).

Clearly, good clinicians have always been practicing in manners that reflected a deep understanding of what they were doing and were available to their patients despite many stereotyped views of analysis and the role of the analyst as strictly a projection of the patient's internal world who functioned as a blank screen.

Adams-Silvan and Silvan raise some interesting questions in their chapter concerning what is psychoanalytic versus what is psychotherapeutic. It would be interesting to know under what conditions, other things being equal, they would recommend psychotherapy versus psychoanalysis and under what conditions they would interrupt the patient's associative flow. Interpretation on the part of the analyst is vital to the psychoanalytic process and still meets all of Freud's criteria as to what constitutes psychoanalysis (Freud 1923). They also raise some interesting issues regarding analysts' choice of when, how, and at what level of depth to intervene with the patient. These have been addressed by Freud in his technical papers (Freud 1912, 1913, 1914) in which the depth of an interpretation should be a function of the psychic surface marked by the resistances (Coltrera 1981). Clear technical guidelines that have evolved with the development of the empirical idea have made our work more orderly, still imaginative and creative, but not impossible.

These three chapters serve to highlight the wide scope of what can be subsumed under the heading of "contemporary Freudian psychoanalysis." It encompasses a variety of positions, and one needs to keep an historical perspective concerning the evolution and development of psychoanalysis in order to understand what happened over the years, why it happened, what technical changes evolved, and why they did. To do so is to follow in the tradition of Freud in which empirical observations are the basic building blocks of theoretical formulations and are used to continuously revise them. Such a perspective will enable us to avoid the errors made over the history of psychoanalysis and avoid the pitfalls of "wild analysis" discussed by Freud as early as 1910.

REFERENCES

Abraham, K. (1911). Notes on the psychoanalytic investigation of depressive insanity and allied conditions. In *Selected Papers on Psychoanalysis*, pp. 137–156. New York: Basic Books, 1960.

———— (1924). The influence of oral erotism on character development. In *On Character and Libido Development*, ed. B. Lewin, pp. 151–164. New York: Basic Books, 1966.

Bibring, E. (1937). On the theory of the therapeutic results of psychoanalysis. *International Journal of Psycho-Analysis* 18:170–189.

———— (1954). Psychoanalysis and the dynamic psychotherapies. *Journal of the American Psychoanalytic Association* 2:745–770.

Breuer, J., and Freud, S. (1893). On the psychical mechanism of hysterical phenomena: preliminary communication. *Standard Edition* 2:1–17.

Coltrera, J. T. (1979). Truth from genetic illusion: the transference and the fate of the infantile neurosis. *Journal of the American Psychoanalytic Association* 27 (suppl):289–313.

———— (1981). On the nature of interpretation: epistemology as practice. In *Clinical Psychoanalysis*, ed. S. Orgel and B. D. Fine, pp. 83–129. New York: Jason Aronson.

———— (1994). *Here and now and then: some technical issues in narcissism.* Paper presented to the Psychoanalytic Association of New York, January.

Dupont, J. (1988). *The Clinical Diaries of Sándor Ferenczi.* Cambridge, MA: Harvard University Press.

Freud, S. (1910). "Wild" psycho-analysis. *Standard Edition* 11:221–227.

———— (1912). Recommendations to physicians practising psycho-analysis. *Standard Edition* 12:111–120.

———— (1913). On beginning the treatment. *Standard Edition* 12:123–144.

———— (1914). Remembering, repeating and working-through. *Standard Edition* 12:147–156.

———— (1917). Mourning and melancholia. *Standard Edition* 14:243–258.

———— (1923). Two encyclopaedia articles. *Standard Edition* 18:235–259.

———— (1926). Inhibitions, symptoms and anxiety. *Standard Edition* 20:87–172.

Guntrip, H. (1975). My experience of analysis with Fairbairn and Winnicott. *International Review of Psycho-Analysis* 2:145–156.

Hartmann, H. (1939). *Ego Psychology and the Problem of Adaptation.* New York: International Universities Press, 1958.

Hartmann, H., Kris, E., and Loewenstein, R. (1946). Comments on the formation of psychic structure. *Psychoanalytic Study of the Child* 2:11–38. New York: International Universities Press.

Loewald, H. (1960). On the therapeutic action of psychoanalysis. *International Journal of Psycho-Analysis* 41:16–33.

Loewenstein, R. M. (1956). Some remarks on the role of speech in psychoanalysis. *International Journal of Psycho-Analysis* 37:460–468.

McLaughlin, J. T. (1991). Clinical and theoretical aspects of enactment. *Journal of the American Psychoanalytic Association* 39:595–614.

Shore, A. (1994). *Affect Regulation and the Origin of the Self.* Hillsdale, NJ: Lawrence Erlbaum.

3

Freud After All

Abby Adams-Silvan
Mark Silvan

We feel in one world; we think, we give names to things in another; between the two, we can establish a certain correspondence, but we do not bridge the interval.
—M. Proust

The tall, bespectacled, 50-year-old man sits hunched over in the patient's chair, his arms extended between his spread knees, hands clasped. For the first time in one-and-a-half years of once- and twice-weekly treatment, the analyst sees him wearing slacks and a sport shirt instead of his otherwise invariable pinstripe suit, Hermes tie, custom-made pastel shirt with immaculate white collar and cuffs, and gold cufflinks. His 12-year-old daughter sits in the waiting room—also a first. The patient is miserable; he speaks of his lover, his wish to marry her, and his distress at his daughter's declaration that if he does so she will never again visit him. He cannot, he says, hurt her that way.

Mr. Smith has not been able to resolve the issue. Twice he has set, and twice he has canceled wedding dates, but now, he says, it is definite. He will *not* marry. He is not angry but simply cannot allow himself that happiness, and certainly not at his daughter's expense.

He's quiet and, after a long pause, he says, "I don't understand anything, and I can't do anything. You have any ideas?"

And the analyst says, "Look, the only thing we really know is that the feelings of helplessness have something to do with being left and leaving. We know about the seduction by your cousin (male) and your mother being right there in the next room, and how you felt so betrayed and alone that you left home—*not* feeling angry—and barely spoke to anyone in your family for years."

There is a long silence. Mr. Smith responds: "I was just thinking, you know. I was born in December, so I started school very young. I was 5—5!—and my mother took me for my first day of school. I was born in December so I was the youngest in my class. I was so scared. I cried and cried. She left me in the school yard and drove off with my father. I think that I have never felt so alone in my life. I could never, *never* do that to my child."

Mr. Smith is crying. There is a pause. "Dwelling on the past won't help. Even though I know it's what I'm supposed to do here. I need answers—you really leave me too much on my own."

Then he says, "By the way, did I tell you that my daughter is starting in a new junior high school? I wish she didn't live so far away. . . ." His associations proceed.

What have you heard and seen? What do you know? Not much in ordinary manifest content terms. But an analytic thinker starts, from the first descriptive words, to speculate, to listen for confirmation or negation, to wonder what was done or said, to think how it might be done differently—or the same, and to ask why an intelligent, wealthy businessman, capable of self-appraisal and object relationships, is not in a more intensive treatment. And what kind of treatment is he in anyhow?

He is seen once weekly, sometimes twice; his conscious wish not to come more often and to remain seated rather than to lie down is being gratified and for now not addressed. Nevertheless, even in this very brief vignette we see that the technical mode is free associative and dynamic interpretive, that the characterological, defensive, and symptomatic importance of an adolescent incestuous seduction has clearly been addressed, that transference is deep enough so that fantasies based on it are utilized for defensive control.

And what of Mrs. Jones? Another patient, different questions.

It is her *fifth* session of the week. She is a most attractive, well-spoken, 35-year-old woman who looks more like 25. She has been in treatment for only a few months. Always rather seductively dressed, today she wears very, very tight shorts, a scoop-necked, closely contoured silk tee shirt, white-dyed alligator loafers, and carries a giant, buttery-soft leather pouch handbag that has been left open and into which her hand dives from time to time to extract various items: a watch, a linen handkerchief, a note pad, a mirror. She is the picture of a glowingly healthy, well-educated, well-bred, cosmopolitan socialite.

Mrs. Jones speaks dramatically and readily, and given what you an analytic thinker might have already wondered, her verbal associations are not surprising. She talks first about a liposuction she had had in the past, and that she now was thinking of repeating the procedure. She then speaks of her husband's ill health and her concerns for him, and her own childhood experience with a life-threatening illness from which, for six months, she, herself, her parents, and the physicians expected her to die. She certainly is glad she didn't, mostly because her own children would never have been born. She speaks for quite a while, the material associatively connected to her early brush with death. She weeps a little, but when she starts to describe the abdominal surgery necessitated by her childhood illness, she begins to cry even more, and the verbal associations cease. The therapist decides to help, repeats her last articulated words and connects them to the silence. Then, based on an attempt to understand and integrate *all* the material, verbal and nonverbal (the liposuction, the handbag, the bringing out of specific items, the illness, the reference to children, life vs. death, and surgery, followed by the emergent dominance of resistance), the analyst wonders aloud if perhaps some feelings about the patient's abortion in early adolescence, about which she had spoken in her previous session, have somewhere aroused a feeling of which Mrs. Jones has never been aware before—or at least has not let herself speak about.

The patient's weeping abates and she says she has decided to tell the truth—even though she knows it will disgust and alienate the therapist. In fact, she has had seven—maybe eight—abortions. She weeps again. The therapist listens attentively and is concerned not to support one or another side of an obviously active conflict manifested in a repetition compulsion. She does not recoil or condemn, of course; neither does she assume the patient really needs to be consoled. Now she waits.

Is this a classical model treatment based on ego-psychological techniques? Should it not be? This is an exhibitionistic, delightful, bright, and articulate young woman; a conflicted patient suffering from early external traumata, the oedipal fantasies thereof, and trapped in a self-destructive repetition compulsion.

Well, all that is true, but three things have been omitted: (1) the patient began the session by abruptly and impulsively hugging the analyst; (2) the patient is sitting facing the analyst, not lying on the couch; and (3) from the time the patient began to weep, she was addressing not the analyst but the analyst's small dog, which was curled up in the patient's lap.

The fact is, the patient apparently can speak about painful and conflict-laden material only to the dog, whose acquaintance she has made because very early in her treatment she had heard quiet, low, little-dog noises, which she believed were "crying from loneliness" and which were intolerable to her. The dog was brought into the session to reassure her and at this time in treatment was regularly present.

As with Mr. Smith, what kind of treatment is Mrs. Jones in? Classical analysis? Certainly not, though her sessions marched along on identifiable associative lines. The answer we propose is that both these patients are in the tradition of Freud's psychoanalytic treatment. Not in an attenuated or modified or parametric or impure(!) Freudian treatment, but *Freud's* treatment, most profoundly because what the therapists are doing is following Freud's basic principles as to technique, behavior, assumptions, and intervention. Note that we substitute *Freud* for *Freudian*. It is our contention that the words *Freudian, orthodox, rigid,* and even *classical* have come to refer not necessarily to Freud's thought but often to a misunderstanding of it that is outdated, in need of revision, and presently subject to new, enlarged, and better understandings.

First, in both these treatments, the analyst/therapist has determined the immediate technical mode according to his best judgment of what is the need of the patient at this time, trying to understand the real, latent communication of that need, attending as well as possible to the conscious and derivative, unconsciously determined indications given by the patient.

Then, the analyst has undertaken to listen as much as possible in a unique way, in Freud's way, hovering so as to remember, nonjudgmental, evaluative, absorptive, absorbed, informed, self-aware, and himself oscillating in and out of a primary process mode. All this with the underlying assumption that everything is meaningful and worth watching and listening to. All this is clearly demonstrated in Freud's earliest clinical work, to which we will return. Finally, the therapists are making certain clinical assumptions that are historically Freud's—assumptions with which they approach every treatment and that are time-tested, replicable, demonstrable, and positively antique in longevity.

First and foremost, we know that what the analyst actually saw and heard was important, but only the beginning of understanding. It is the meaning of what was manifest, the latent content, that will in the end help the analyst help the patient to understand himself and, if he wishes to, change. Fundamental to this is Freud's theory of unconscious determination and the dominance of the descriptive unconscious in everyday life.

We know, too, that the *sequence* of thoughts and behavior manifestations is revealing, precisely because the same unconscious determination governs the associative process. So when Mr. Smith's associations move from the statement that he will not marry to the statement that he is not angry but unable to allow himself a pleasure, we know that it is somehow connected; when he responds to the analyst's intervention about abandonment with a memory of school, we know that that will be of significance way beyond the manifest content, no matter how complete of itself it seems to be. Meaning may be hidden, but potentially may be discerned in connections.

In the same way, when Mrs. Jones seductively and unexpectedly embraces her analyst, and proceeds to move from thoughts of liposuction (something has been forced out of her) to danger, to death, to children, to life-and-death surgery, all the time pulling objects from her bag, her analyst is naturally reminded—because she is listening in the analytic mode recommended by Freud—of the previous session and of abortion. Further, Freud's concept of symbolism is surely informative, especially with reference to the items recovered from the pocketbook. We are not sure of the meaning of the embrace: Was she "aborting" the treatment, and/or repeating the impregnation? Was she pleading for reassurance that she is not revolting and disgusting, and/or making the therapist complicit as a transference acting-out? We are asking, and expecting answers to, Freud's questions based on Freud's assumptions.

Similarly, Mr. Smith dresses informally when he brings his daughter. We are not sure of the meaning, but we are sure it has meaning. Is he in some way identifying with her youth, that is, a mild, not inappropriate regression? Perhaps Mr. Smith in his distress about (we later discover) abandonment by his mother to a forbidden gratification that—we can speculate—required him to flee from a regression to negative oedipal gratification, is in some way engaging in oedipal rejection as he rejects his girlfriend Jane. Is this an important transference re-creation?

And that, of course, is the crucial other "antique" concept we are using: transference, the touchstone, the sine qua non for the closest approximate understanding we can have of the formative veridical and fantasy life of the patient. As understood in Freud's psychoanalytic theory, transference—interpersonal and object—occurs in all relationships as a manifestation of the repetition compulsion. Different therapists utilize this principle in different ways, depending on patient need, but there is a difference between the knowledge of the concept and how it is used; it may be honored, for example, in avoiding its discussion, because that would, at a given point, frighten or even devastate the patient. Can we imagine a good practitioner telling Mrs. Jones that she may be in fantasy embracing her seducer so as to repeat the unconscious gratification of self-mutilation and the destruction of an inner object? Or, since we know that to make a genetic interpretation of the transference will tend to attenuate it, we may be silent so as to allow it to flourish rather than dissipate, if the time is not yet ripe.

We recognize that transference is always with us, coloring all exchanges. Even though it may seem to be real based on the real therapeutic situation that everyone faces, our understanding is that it still is transference, based on universal experiences of childhood. For example, when a patient is distressed at having to pay a fee, we recognize the childhood roots in distress over emotional "payment" in compliance, love, gratitude to the caregiver. If a patient feels humiliated by lying down, may this not have its roots in the universal humiliations experienced by the child who is indeed small and left out of the grown-ups' lives in many ways? The analyst and the analytic situation are humiliating only because of the transference, the childhood roots. Our understanding of the scenario that the patient will create and re-create in the transference is the primary data that informs the analyst of the patient's inner world, past and present.

Further, the assumption of predictable, universal childhood developmental sequences is historically the orderly psychosexual, subject/object and structural developmental sequences that can be used to help our understanding of the clinically unique in the universal context. Infant observation, one of the new disciplines, yields predictable sequences. How could any animal development possibly be random or idiosyncratic? As Freud (1925) said, "it became possible to confirm . . . (the sexuality of children) . . . by direct observation. Indeed, it is so easy to convince oneself of the regular sexual activities of children that one cannot help asking with astonishment how the human race can have succeeded in overlooking the facts . . ." (p. 39). The new disciplines expand, but hardly replace, Freud's developmental models or observational techniques.

Theory, at its best, is primarily a way of organizing observations. With expanding observations, Freud was constantly revising his own theories, and so, too, have his intellectual heirs. But these changes do not represent a diminution of understanding, only an accretion, providing only that the mobilizing observations—whether they validate or refute—be accurate.

An extraordinary number of Freud's assumptions and ideas were first articulated in "On the Psychical Mechanism of Hysterical Phenomena: The Preliminary Communication" (Freud and Breuer 1893) and "Studies on Hysteria" (Freud and Breuer 1893–1895). Over a hundred years old, they legally qualify as antique: the technique of free-association; the importance of listening; the idea of neutrality; there are no spontaneous fluctuations, only a demonstrable psychic determinism available through association; the primacy of following the patient; the importance of secrets; the importance of association of events and the sequence of manifest content, which can tell us important information about unconscious and preconscious meanings; that memories may be traumatic, and therefore are technically significant; allowing "strangulated affect" to find a way out through speech is psychotherapeutic; the principle of abstinence; understanding the resistance; that symptoms will make sense and therefore must never be ignored; using suggestion to alleviate symptoms is not truly therapeutic; the importance of multiple trauma; the importance of recollection in mourning; that conflict and defense are dynamically crucial to the form taken by hysterical symptoms, that no patient is monosymptomatic; the principle of symbolization, with multiple determination for conversion and/or other hysterical symptoms, and the role of conflict and defense. Nor should we forget Freud's emphasis on the importance of biological factors, which are today at the forefront in the study of neuropsychology.

And then in 1900 Freud became our great cartographer, carried by dreams to the shadowy regions of the mind, and mapping his journey for us. The object of our psychotherapy remains today the widening of conscious awareness, bringing what is out of awareness into the light. As we have shown, it is more than a hundred years since the technique to do so, based on pragmatic observation, began to be available. With *The Interpretation of Dreams* (1900) almost a hundred years ago, Freud demonstrated most profoundly how to move what is out of immediate consciousness into awareness, what that conscious awareness is, and why these pragmatic techniques of free association can be so psychotherapeutically successful.

Not too much later, he made clear that a patient brings into treatment expectations based on the past, re-creating his old interpersonal relationships and object relations (i.e., the transference). Equally significant, he tells us that it is the fantasy content of those object relationships and relations that are crucial in psychic development, and that they can be reconstructed and corrected in psychotherapy.

We wish to return here to the theory of conflict and defense, articulated and central since the *Studies* and *Interpretation of Dreams*. In fact, these are the concepts that most distinguish Freud's psychotherapy from other schools of thought. "Conflict" is our identifier. It is his assumption that all human beings live with inner conflict, which, depending on the balance of force-of-impulse and counterforce against enactment, will be more or less characterologically and/or symptomatically significant in their lives. Mr. Smith and Mrs. Jones surely suffer from repressed conflict. Pathogenetic or not, conflict, the active struggle against unknown and/or unacceptable wishes, is a concept that, for followers of Freud's psychoanalysis, is universal and invariably useful in understanding human behavior.

As clinicians, our most pragmatic as well as theoretical question is: What is the unacceptable wish? Then: How does this human being keep herself from becoming aware of it? When and where did she learn this? Why? Most especially we ask: Why is the struggle unresolved and the conflict still active, rather than an optimal balance being achieved?

These are questions arising from Freud's psychoanalytic assumptions, from, in his words, "the psychology which is founded on psychoanalysis" (1911b, p. 218). In his treatment we remind ourselves always to look for the forbidden wish and consider how we may, if it is considered desirable, best help raise that wish to consciousness. The assumption is that if we can do so it will be available for mature evaluation, accepted as a wish/fantasy, more benignly channeled, and an inner balance achieved.

If at all possible (and it may not be) the psychoanalyst will use the transference, which re-creates not only what the patient is aware of having felt in the past, but what the patient no longer remembers. Of course, when the transference cannot be used it is harder for the therapist to be able to "turn his own unconscious . . . towards the transmitting unconscious of the patient" (Freud 1912, p. 115). On the patient's side, it is harder to experience the regression that allows the forbidden impulse to rise close enough to the surface.

The psychoanalyst who has listened, whose personal, theoretically informed search has in some way revealed the patient's conflict, must then make a decision as to whether or not she will intervene as therapist: articulate the forbidden wish or not, based on the patient's capacity to use what is said, for example, "I think for a long time you may have been afraid that . . ." Or say nothing about it. Or make one or another intervention to facilitate the patient's capacity to discover, understand, and hold himself in esteem.

No matter what the decision, it is based on the assumption of conflict and defense, derivative transference, moral neutrality, and the need to listen. Above all, it is based on Freud's principle of conducting treatment according to the patient's needs and capacities. The forbidden wish, for example, will always be there, but bringing it into awareness may be marvelously mutative, therapeutically supportive, or devastating. Clinical decisions based on theory, in conjunction with memory and the therapeutic moment, must constantly be made.

In other words, our treatment must be, in the most profound way, empathic. Not wild, it must be carefully disciplined by study, knowledge, constant self-analysis, experience, observation, and open-mindedness. But, above all, in touch with this patient at this moment: empathic.

As an example, let us return to the therapy session with Mrs. Jones, and to the associative sequence (behavioral and verbal) that led to the therapist's intervention regarding the patient's abortion. That intervention invoked further information that had been consciously withheld, accompanied by authentic feelings of sorrow and shame. At that point, technique based on Freud's theory indicated a passive response by the therapist; she "listens attentively and is concerned not to support one side or another side of an obviously active conflict manifested in a repetition compulsion. She does not recoil or condemn, of course; neither does she assume the patient really needs to be consoled. Now she waits" (this chapter, p. 3).

The therapist intervened as she did because she assumes the ubiquity of unconscious fantasy, which will be symbolically and/or partially manifested in behavior, in treatment or otherwise. This behavioral enactment provides, at least temporarily, the gratification of the unacceptable wish as a piece of overt behavior, which may be either dystonic (a symptom of other distress) or relatively comfortable (a syntonic part of character structure).

In treatment, the process of decoding the manifest symbolic behavior and arriving at the unconscious fantasy involves, as we have said, a close attention to sequence as well as content. When accurately translated, it is possible to identify conflicted unacceptable, rejected wishes that have remained active but outside the patient's awareness. The search for the unacceptable conflicted wish is, as we have said above, one of the hallmarks of a treatment based on Freud's theory.

In that consistent scan for that unacceptable idea, thought, or impulse, the therapist notices whatever she can. Dressed seductively, in a way that called attention to breasts and flat abdomen, Mrs. Jones carried a large bag holding many objects that she displayed: a watch (time, menstrual cycles?), handkerchief (sorrow, moisture, sanitary napkin?), a note pad (the imminence of communication?), a mirror (narcissistic reassurance? creating another being by means of reflection?).

These possible symbolic equivalents may or may not be demonstrably accurate ex post facto, but they do demonstrate the principle of symbolism. The succeeding verbal associations seem to the therapist to lead clearly to the conclusion that abortion was on the patient's mind—the conscious content to which Freud (1911a) particularly enjoins us to give priority: "The analyst should always be aware of the surface of the patient's mind at any given moment" (p. 92). But further intervention would seem to be a counterindicated interruption. Why?

The therapist intervenes when some self-protective device—defense, symptom, character problem—interferes with the flow of associations, the interventions being contingent on the patient's needs and capacities and on the availability to the therapist of pertinent information from past associations or from the body of knowledge compiled from pragmatic, observational, and experimental means. There may be many interventions or few, investigative or supportive. Whatever the type of intervention, that is, dynamic interpretation, overt encouragement, simple reflection, or defense analysis, it is intended to help the patient return to associations to whatever extent the patient is capable, while the therapist notes the apparent moment of demonstrable resistance. So long as the patient is speaking or somehow expressing herself in a relatively nondefensive way (understanding that some defenses are always operative, and that sometimes speech is itself counterproductive and obstructively defensive), the therapist informed by Freud listens, watches, and waits quietly so that the patient can reach more and more deeply within herself to what has been rejected by the self. The therapist *accepts* so that, in Bach's (1985) words, "The treatment can belong to the patient" (p. 222).

That acceptance, the movement with the patient, not following a preconceived idea or agenda (Bach 1985), is, we submit, the most empathic stance that can be taken. It leads to what Ellman (1991) calls "trust in the analytic situation" (p. 94n) and encourages the flow of communication and the concomitant deepening of the transference for which the analyst/therapist waits. With that deepening comes the possibility of bringing what is unknown into awareness and, therefore, the opportunity for a reevaluation of what is really to be forbidden by the mature self and what is instead only the product of infantile unconscious fantasy: primary process productively transformed.

All this is dependent on the structural concept of id, just as ideas of integration and therapeutic value are dependent on the concept of ego. Unconscious fantasy, conflict, symbolism, and primary process are best organized utilizing the concept of id. How could there be conflict or the gratification of unconscious fantasy without repressed wishes? In principle there could be no ego without an id since our psychology posits that it is the interplay between ego, superego, and id that is responsible for the characteristics of personality and for symptom formation. The psychodynamic triumvirate is posited to be mutually interdependent, functioning optimally when functioning in easy alliance, the ego serving to provide realistic and optimal paths for id gratifications, opportunities that flourish under a benign and approving superego, which is also moderated by the reality-testing function of the ego. Schur (1966) notes that the relationship of the three structures is indispensable to the idea of conflict.

In our treatment procedure we allow for the expression of id derivatives by the use of free association, and we engage ego and superego in the verbal interaction between therapist and patient. This is true because the purpose of free association is to minimize the learned impediments to the expression of impulse derivatives such as critical thinking, conceptual goals, and selectivity based on judgement and intellect.

Verbal interaction with the therapist, on the other hand, is dependent on—and facilitative of—self-reflection, reality testing, cognition, and other functions of ego and superego. Our interventions are oriented to enhance these structures so as to provide more constructive pathways of expression (discharge) to the id. There is no inherent destructive opposition of ego and id; harmony, not aversion, is the optimal developmental thrust.

However, Freud himself (1926) offers this caveat: "It must not be supposed that these very general ideas are pre-suppositions on which the work of psycho-analysis depends. On the contrary, they are its latest conclusions, and are open to revision. Psycho-analysis is founded securely upon the observation of the facts of mental life; and for that very reason its theoretical superstructure is . . . subject to constant alteration" (p. 266). We must be attentive constantly, however, to the fact that what does not change in Freud's psychoanalysis, or the therapeutic treatment based upon it, is that very primacy of observation as the secure foundation for hypothesis, theory, and technical strategy. In that sense, all serious clinical practitioners may be said to be heirs of Freud.

Psychoanalysts have been for some time disinclined to expostulate in terms of id psychology. Rather, ego psychology has been a dominant theme in theory and praxis roughly since Freud's death in 1939 (Sandler et al. 1973). Schur (1966) details this in an historical as well as theoretical context in his extensive monograph, "The Id and the Regulatory Principles of Mental Functioning." According to Moore and Fine (1990), "The id is now a concept in relative disuse, and is generally regarded as subsidiary to the ego" (p. 91). We have been able to find only two articles with the word *id* in the title since 1984. Slap and Saykin (1984) report not a single article from 1974 to 1984.

Freud conceptualized the hypothetical construct of the id as a mental structure or agency, the contents of which "could be thought of as somatic and/or psychical. However, the lines between somatic and psychical, id and ego, were never clarified" (Stewart 1967, p. 72). Particularly useful to the clinical psychoanalyst is Freud's own descriptive functional construct of the id as representing

the dark, inaccessible part of our personality. . . . Logical laws of thought do not apply . . . above all . . . the law of contradiction. Contrary impulses exist side by side, without cancelling each other out

or diminishing each other. . . . Nothing corresponds to the idea
of time. . . . Wishful impulses are virtually immortal. . . . The id
knows no judgments of value: no good and evil, no morality. . . .
[Repressed pathogenic] wishful impulses . . . can only be recognized as belonging to the past, can only lose their importance . . .
when they have been made conscious by the work of analysis, and it is
on this that the effect of therapeutic treatment rests to no small
extent." [1933, pp. 73–74]

The relative power of ego versus id was subject to different evaluations
by Freud at different times (Schur 1966). His final conviction was, "This
oldest portion of the psychical apparatus (the id) remains the most
important throughout life" (1940, p. 145, n. 2).

In practice it seems obvious that, specifically acknowledged or not, it
is not possible to speak of ego without implying id. Further, depending on
the flow of associations as against the appearance of defenses (resistance),
it is possible to gauge the relative strength of the structural processes at any
given moment. Nor should we forget that the dominance of the ego/
superego is as potentially negative as the dominance of the id. Mr. Smith is
too controlled; Mrs. Jones is subject to loss of impulse control. If we use
Freud's (1923) analogy of horse and rider, Mr. Smith's ego has hobbled his
id-mount; Mrs. Jones pretends she has chosen freely the dangerous course
along which she is being hurtled by the uncontrolled force of her own
impulsive id-steeds.

If Mr. Smith and Mrs. Jones are descriptively so very different with
respect to their indicated dynamics, we would expect to employ different
therapeutic techniques to achieve different therapeutic goals. We hope to
help Mr. Smith to loosen the restraints on pleasurable gratifications, and
Mrs. Jones to find the strength to rein in her desires in a less self-destructive
way. What is notable, however, is that formulated in this way there is a
transcendent goal that is the same for each patient: that the capacity to
experience constructive pleasurable gratification in love and work be
optimally realized—the pleasure principle in optimal relation to the reality
principle.

As we have said, our therapeutic goals are a harmonious balance of id,
ego, and superego, and it is in that structural context that Freud outlines
the various requirements of technique. He speaks of first "an extending
(for the weakened ego) of self-knowledge" (1940, p. 177) by relatively

intellectual means. This is followed (after some time) by properly construed and timed constructions that enlarge memory and leave "the ego,
emboldened by the certainty of our help (daring) to take the offensive in
order to reconquer what has been lost" (p. 178). Insight and resistance
oscillate, each evoking the other, with the overcoming of resistance proving
to be the most time-consuming and difficult task of all.

When resistance is overcome, however, the struggle between id and
ego/superego becomes available to us and this is facilitated by

> the natural upward drive (of the unconscious) which desires nothing
> better than to press forward across its settled frontiers into the ego and
> so to consciousness. . . . The outcome (of the struggle between the
> id and ego) is a matter of indifference: whether it results in the ego
> accepting, after a fresh examination, an instinctual (i.e., id) demand
> which it has hitherto rejected, or whether it dismisses it once and for
> all. In either case . . . the compass of the ego has been extended and
> a wasteful expenditure of energy has been made unnecessary. [p. 179]

Can an analyst who follows Freud also posit transcendent, universal
techniques by means of which these universal goals may be accomplished?
We know that specific technical strategies simply cannot be referred to a
generally applicable model. No two patients are the same, any more than
any two clinicians are the same. Differences on both sides are immediately
manifest: the same patient would have a different course of treatment with
each analyst/therapist; the same analyst/therapist will evaluate and treat
each patient differently. From the first moment of contact paths of
communication diverge. Certainly Freud never meant for technique to be
a stricture on the patient or the analyst. Technical devices exist to facilitate
the capacity of the patient to lead the way, not to constrict by rule, and this
has been true since the introduction by Freud of the method of free-
associative observation—waiting and listening—in 1900 in *The Interpretation of Dreams* and the treatment of Rat Man in 1909. The analyst must
be intrapsychically and intellectually free to follow, not programmed by
theory to selective apperceptions.

Ellman (1991) points out that Freud himself was not primarily
interested in developing and writing about technique per se, once he had
discovered that method of association.

Freud oscillated in his clinical interest in psychoanalysis and . . . as he progressed he was a good deal more interested in the discoveries the method yielded than in this new method of observation itself. . . . He did not . . . develop or internalize his technique. . . . After World War I he was conducting mainly training analyses for people who were expressly interested in psychoanalysis and not necessarily (or overtly) interested in a therapeutic analysis. [pp. 286–287]

Ellman also describes the variability and inconsistencies of Freud's own treatment techniquess. It is, therefore, noteworthy that Freud was able to use the results of the observations based on his own and others' differing techniques. In other words, he honored the validity of different technical applications.

There is implicit in all this an enduring counsel by Freud that there are two superordinate, universally applicable technical devices, the first of which is the primacy of the patient's own words. In 1908, in the minutes of the Vienna Psychoanalytic Society, he is quoted, saying, "The psychoanalyst no longer seeks to elicit material in which he is interested, but permits the patient to follow his natural and spontaneous train of thought" (Nunberg and Federn [1962], quoted by Ellman [1991], p. 294). Here then is the first universal technique: following the patient.

However, this freedom for the patient is hardly enough for therapeutic gain. It must be matched by a second universal, what we have elsewhere called a prototechnique (Adams-Silvan 1993) that allows us to understand the patient's communications and that must precede and then support any communication by the therapist to the patient. This prototechnique is the second of Freud's enduring and generally applicable clinical devices: analytic listening, which "is made up of two indissoluble and mutually interactive elements: listening and remembering as psychoanalytic phenomena distinct from ordinary listening and remembering" (Adams-Silvan 1993, p. 314). Analytic listening must encompass not only the manifest content but also a sensitivity to the latent content, which is to be discerned in cadence, rhythm, timing, sequence, parapraxes, grammatical usage—a microanalysis, as it were, of all the qualities of communication.

Analytic listening is based on that familiar injunction to maintain "the same evenly supended attention . . . in the face of all one hears" (Freud 1912, pp. 111–112). What is often not added, however, is that Freud is here making that statement with reference to a special quality, not just of apprehending the material—all the material—but of the analyst remembering what has been heard and remembering in a special way.

When the analyst does not exert a conscious effort to attend, evaluate, and remember, then unconscious memory will become effective (Freud 1912). It is an analogue for the therapist of the injunction to free associate for the patient; both patient and clinician engage in listening and remembering in a regressive mode. This regressive mode oscillates for both between inner experience, evocative memories, and intellectual processes and eventually brings the order of understanding into the apparent chaos of free association.

In other words, Freud enjoins all practitioners to suspend purposive, selective, secondary process listening. Instead, he counsels the abandonment of syntactical judgment in favor of an awareness that is nonselectively receptive and dominated by the principles of primary process. In this way the therapist will be able to "turn his own unconsciousness, like a receptive organ, towards the transmitting unconscious of the patient" (Freud 1912, p. 115).

In this general technical precept we have a statement regarding the id of the psychoanalyst and its role in treatment technique, stressing the connection between evenly hovering attention, which involves a partial cognitive regression, and an optimal capacity to remember. The analyst's remembering of the patient's material is often experienced as both qualitatively and quantitatively different from how the analyst remembers in other aspects of his life: a detail from some past association pops forcefully into awareness during a present communication, unbidden, often apparently irrelevant, but actually intimately and informatively connected with what the patient is saying. It would seem that this is indeed, on the descriptive face of it, an id arousal in the analyst.

It seems clear that this is a function of how the analyst has listened, as though by becoming that analyzing instrument, by listening in a free-floating regressed mode, the analyst has come to share in some manner of identification, whatever of the patient's inner world and organizing fantasies have been communicated. The analyst's controlled regression— his temporary intentional abandonment of secondary process thinking— leads via shared memory to empathic attunement. This is different from the dynamics of countertransference phenomena that are distinguished as, at least in part, the products of the analyst's conflicts, albeit stimulated by the patient's productions. In countertransference the analyst experiences derivatives of his own memory, while here we have reference to the patient's memories, as shared by the analyst. Arlow (1993) also addressed this phenomenon.

We do not really understand the functions of memory that explain this phenomenon of shared memory, but every analyst can describe it. The patient is speaking, or, in fact, may even be silent, is moving or still, and there comes apparently abruptly into the analyst's mind a memory or image of something that has been said or done earlier in the treatment, sometimes even years before; a phrase, anecdote, something remembered from the treatment past. Sometimes it seems almost irrelevant to the manifest matter on hand, sometimes more pertinent, but the chances are that the analyst can most profitably subject that memory to a joint scrutiny. It will most likely be connected in some crucial and eventually demonstrable way to the matters on hand. How often, indeed, do we hear the patient say exactly what we have been thinking. It is a dazzling experience!

The very irrationality of the experience can be unsettling as well as exciting, however—that irrational, thoughtless quality that connects it with the regressive quality of the analyst's listening. We have not been thinking; but we have been hearing, and we experience our analytic surprise. Perhaps we have been "taken in" in an infantile way (as Freud [1912] says, unconscious to unconscious), so that those memories of what we have heard from our patients have not been subjected to so much secondary process and editing. We listen as an ignorant small child does, and remember in the same way, as though we are creating new associative connections as well as fitting material into already established mnenic groups. This would mimic the experience of the patient in the acquisition of his original experience, and may be a function of the identificatory process that leads to empathy.

Lewin (1955) and Stein (1965) persuasively liken the analytic situation to a dream experience for the patient. In fact, when Stein says "something analogous to the dream work takes place in the apparently wide-awake patient," he adds "*or in the apparently wide-awake analyst*" (p. 81) (emphasis ours). He does not expand on this point, but using the same analogue for analytic listening, we might say that to the extent that the analyst abandons judgments of valence (hovers attentively), she or he is in part engaging with the patient in a dreamlike state, wherein what is perceived and experienced is characterized by primary process id modes; such as condensation and displacement. Then, however, the dreamers, analyst and patient, would both eventually have the need for secondary revision, to eliminate incoherence and lacunae, and to make sense of the material— the engagement of ego and superego.

This brings us inevitably to the point where the universal goal of increased harmony among psychic structures, and the universal technical means of analytic listening by therapist and free-association by patient, must be understood as the obligato background to specific technical strategies.

Depending on what the therapist has understood, or not understood, he will have to decide at any given moment whether or not to intervene, and if so, how. With particular attention given to derivatives of id, ego, and superego processes, there will be constant unique variations and fluctuations of balance, which is reflected in manifest content and behavioral demonstration. The clinician must decide how to use what the patient has communicated, taking into consideration his symptoms, character, and the overall nature and severity of his pathology. The patient's communications can potentially always be understood within the rubric of Freud's general psychology, while the technical response is always determined by the patient's unique need.

The therapist also must be constantly judging (now using ego skills) how to approach and have an impact on the patient's psychic reality, while remaining in touch with the immediate surface of the mind, as we have said. "It is not our job to dazzle," Freud says. It is our job to share understanding and to try to realize the possibility of healing by fostering the patient's capacity for insight, reevaluating of fantasies, widening of consciousness and shifts in the intrapsychic balance of internal processes that bring changes in the optimal love of self.

The judgment of how best to have such an impact is often dependent on gauging whether there should be any intervention at all and, if so, should it be oriented to id or ego/superego?

Mr. Brown, an analysand who was able to tolerate long periods of uninterrupted free association and who had, in fact, developed a transference neurosis, called the evening before his fifth session of the week and requested an earlier time for business reasons. He might, he said, have to cancel the session if it could not be rescheduled since he was unexpectedly called out of town. An earlier appointment would enable him to have his session before leaving town. The therapist told him there was no earlier time available, and the patient subsequently called to say he would keep his appointment anyhow. As fate would have it, the session preceding Mr. Brown's was canceled at the last minute, so when he arrived it was clear that indeed an earlier time had been unused. Mr. Brown was furious; he had been lied to, and this at a time when he was furious at his mother yet again. He virtually roared his rage, high pitched and voluble. He had struggled to understand that his mother had often lied, now he knew it, and his analyst lied too!

The therapist had several choices: should she say and do nothing, allowing the rage to continue as long as it would, that is, an id-oriented response? Should she make a transference/defense interpretation based on Mr. Brown's conscious experience, that is, an invitation to self-observation and evaluation, an ego/super-ego oriented response? "I think you are reacting to me just as you were reacting to your mother when you believed she was lying. Perhaps it happens with others as well. We both hear how intense and distraught you are, how hard it is to contain yourself so that you can think about it all. Perhaps in some way you are often reacting to your mother, even though the feelings seem to have been triggered by someone else."

Should she try to calm the patient so that he can reasonably work out the possibilities, that is, an ego-oriented response? "Stop a moment if you can. Perhaps we can really use this to understand when you become so terribly angry. I know how deeply upset you are—there must be many reasons why you feel so intensely—which keeps you from being able to imagine other reasons, and then you lose your sense of trust. What do you think?"

Should she wait until the affect changes and then seek to widen awareness by an interpretation formulated to arrive at repressed transference affect, that is, an id/ego response? "It seems to me that perhaps your feelings were so intense because you were not only angry, but there were other emotions under that. If I lie, if your mother lies, how can you trust? If you can't trust, that, I think, would be lonely and frightening. Under such a scary rage might hide fear, I think, wonderfully disguised and hidden from yourself and everyone else. Other feelings as well (pause, patient is silent for a minute or two). What do you find yourself thinking?"

Should she simply explain the circumstances and apologize, that is, an ego/superego appeal and invitation to empathy? "I'm sorry to have caused you distress. I know it is a painful time in our work. What happened is that the hour was canceled . . ."

Any one of these responses might be appropriate in different circumstances. Mrs. Jones, for example, who is so volatile and loses control of her rage, might respond best to the feeling of mastery inherent in being able to become calm and work out an accurate explanation. The therapist might then elaborate the conscious transference implications, strengthening the patient's ego by demonstrating her use of displacement as a self-protective device after the surge of emotion has been mastered. The therapist might say first—and while she is in the grip of an intense emotion which she cannot control—"May I speak? Just listen. We see how desperately upset you are, how strong your feelings are. I think there must be a lot under that fierce anger, and it's important. I know." All this in a quiet, soothing but firm voice, repeated however often as necessary.

Then, when Mrs. Jones is calm, the analyst might say something to the effect of: "There were lots of feelings—they were toward me, but perhaps so intense because the roots were in the past—with your mother, perhaps others. But that would have been too scary when you were little, so you had to push them down. Now they erupt at me and at lots of other people—too intense for now, but making sense if we think of the past." The therapist has here invoked benign, empathic authority, has "lent" ego strength, evoked a sense of comfort and protective power, invoked/identified the *conscious* transference and the defensive displacement.

Mr. Smith, on the other hand, ought not to be discouraged from ranting and raving and temporarily abandoning his emotive strictures. For him such loss of control might open doors to his emotions that have been slammed and bolted fast against experiences of what had been overwhelming intensity. In the comfort and support of a safe, accepting and respectfully empathic atmosphere, Mr. Smith can experience, observe, and reflect on his emotions. The analyst is silent; perhaps what occurs is the journey through Freud's (1921) sequence of imitation to identification to empathy, and Mr. Smith can then experience the empathy that his analyst has toward him.

In each of these examples it is clear that the therapist who follows Freud must be somehow able to attend in a way that allows for an empathic, nonjudgemental, absorptive yet intellectual assessment of the masses of material that every session with every patient provides. Whether or not it is possible to sort, evaluate, compare, and understand is variable, of course, and dependent on resistance, skill, knowledge, readiness, judgment, and experience in both patient and analyst.

As examples of the general application of Freud's theory to varied practice, we have here especially cast the cognitive aspects of the therapist's work within the frame of Freud's ideas of id, ego, and superego. It is hard to imagine any therapist who practices not also somehow utilizing topographical concepts. For instance, Freud (1923) referred to the property of "conscious vs. unconscious" as "in the last resort our one beacon light in the darkness of depth psychology" (p. 18; see also editor's note, 1915, p. 165). We also use the role of objects, the processes of narcissism, identificatory processes, psychosexual development, the search for pleasure, and reality testing. Whether or not they are consciously utilized, recognized, and/or explicitly acknowledged as an intellectual substrate, it would seem they are always present in some form in the therapist's vision. Technique depends on what the clinician chooses to emphasize at any given moment; "chooses," implying a conscious, thoughtful, cool judgment, as well as spontaneity and intuition.

All this may somehow communicate an overintellectualized attitude by Freud's followers, especially in the current climate with its emphasis on the inner experience of the analyst, and that inner experience most often not reported with reference to theoretical rationale. But it is important to remember that we do have to make many choices and must have an intellectual orientation as well as an intuitive sensitivity and self-analysis. Sandler (1993) in his summary paper at the Amsterdam Congress of the International Psychoanalytical Association, the theme of which was "From Listening to Interpretation," speaks of

> numbers of maps that we use *but do not know that we are using.* These hidden internal structures, or rules of functioning, are not only cognitive organizations—each of us has also created, in the course of development, a great many internal structures which are not at all so rationally organized, and yet enter into the way in which we organize our individual perception of the world . . . (and) our responses to our analysands' material, but of course they are by a long way not the only elements which enter into the complex processes which occur in the path from listening to interpretation. [p. 1099]

Sandler (1983) has also called attention to the fact that there are public faces and private aspects of our clinical work, and that the private aspect of our technical praxis is only available in part to consciousness. A large part of each analyst's private formulations, he says, are unconscious (and preconscious) part-theories, which are used as the clinical circumstances dictate. However, he speaks (1993) of these pathways by which the patient's mental state is communicated to the analyst, the first of which is "the analyst's straightforward analytic understanding, because of his training, experience and perceptiveness, of the meaning of the patient's communications. *This is not to be underestimated*" (p. 1105, emphasis ours). Sandler indicates, however, that there is a tendency to do so on the part of some important current thinkers on this topic.

Blum (1998), in his Hartmann lecture, speaks of today as "a time of great ferment in psychoanalysis" (in press). He notes the tendency by many analysts to distort and then abandon the model of the objective observer and interpreter, even though today we understand very well that such objectivity can only be optimally productive when coupled with appropriate use of the analyst's subjective experience, sensitivity to his own personality, vulnerabilities, and strengths. The analyst must "make empathic and rational inferences. . . . The 'good enough' analyst retains adequate objectivity about the patient and his/her own subjectivity. . . . [The ideal] is the subjectively objective analyst" (in press).

Since our goals are therapeutic as well as exploratory, it is essential to continue the struggle to understand the nature of the therapeutic effect of psychotherapy based on psychoanalytic principles and the knowledge obtained from exploration. There are, of course, many thoughtful ideas and theories, and—like all other human dynamics—a multiple determination is surely indicated.

We have taken structural theory, that is, the processes of id, ego, and superego function, as an example of one objective organizer that identifies Freud's followers. Within that rubric, what might we hypothesize are the (always interwoven) roles of these different agencies? Why do we try to influence one or another of them at any given time?

One of our most crucial aims is to work through ego processes to widen the sphere of conscious awareness and to overcome obstacles to self-understanding and optimal self-love. When that happens symptoms are alleviated and—albeit with great struggle—character may be modified. Implicit is the involvement of all three intrapsychic agencies, by whatever measure, to facilitate insight, to correct malignant fantasies, catharsis, amelioration and replacement of inadequate and/or inappropriate defenses, and recovery of repressed material, all of which is very familiar to us.

What is less familiar is that Freud (1940) places particular emphasis on the importance of making it possible for the patient "to transfer to us the authority of his super-ego" (p. 181) if we are to achieve a therapeutic result.

This is a thought that does seem to have a resonance with clinical experience. Somehow the patient must be helped to be open to reevaluations of long-held beliefs, especially around moral issues. How can the repressed become tolerable and therefore enter awareness if superego is not relaxed? How can pathological narcissism be transformed if the self is not respected and loved by superego authority? The voices of the inner objects, echoing the pathogenic values, restrictions, condemnations of original superego authority—however well intended—must be muted in favor of a new inner representation: the benign fantasy of the analyst.

Through what agency is this to occur? Superego is not influenced substantially by intellect or by pressure of a dystonic content, that is, exposure to a contradictory system. Therapists know very well that exhortation, explanation, the discourse of reason, the promise of pleasure or the threat of painful consequence simply do not change basic conviction—conscious or unconscious. Ego and superego appeal are weak indeed.

Perhaps it is through the agency of the id that the grounding of superego authority is best understood.

The patient struggles to make his needs known, communicating, however involuntarily, in many ways. The analyst struggles to understand, and then to meet those needs, understanding also that what is wished for by the patient may not be what is really needed. In other words, gratification is not a goal, although it may itself be a need, and if so, appropriately met. A severely troubled patient whose inner object representations are simply too weak to sustain a total separation may need, as well as wish, to be told details about an analyst's absence, the knowledge of which is wanted desperately by another patient whom such information would, in the long run, harm.

Such devotion to meeting real need inevitably powers a transference reaction reflecting a caregiver/early childhood dyad. This will be true, even if it is not consciously acknowledged. Regression is facilitated, not only in the familiar service of the ego (Kris) but also in the service of the id.

We speculate that under these circumstances one of the processes that takes place is an identificatory sequence, repeating the process whereby the superego developed out of the id. It is then the residual id in the superego that allows the impact of new values, ideas, and perceptions. The transference promotes a new balance of structural processes. To Freud's "Where id was, let ego be" (1933, p. 80), we suggest the idea that "where an intransigent superego is, let there be a more malleable id" that identifies with the benign fantasies and trusting observations of the therapeutic intent.

A great deal has been written on the function of identification and empathy in the search for understanding and therapeutic gain. Arlow (1993) speaks to the identification of analyst with analysand, identification as a step on the path toward empathy, and making the point that simple identification leads to sympathy, but empathic comprehension requires a deeper thinking with, rather than thinking about, and is beyond that simple identification. Here again we have Freud's injunction: listening unconscious to unconscious; id to id?

Sandler (1993) quotes Edoardo Weiss (1960) and his concept of resonance duplication, which describes the perception of one person by another by processing not only manifest behavior but also the inner experience of the other. Both authors stress the significance of unconscious (id?) apperceptions. Sandler also elaborates more cogently on the perpetual fluidity of the self-object boundary: "It is this fluctuation which may permit the unconscious process of recurrent primary identification to take place. The bridge provided by such primary identification, incidentally, may be the pathway towards certain forms of learning and to more permanent identification in which the self-representation is unconsciously changed on the basis of an object representation as a model" (p. 1103). This process of a recurrent primary identification is not the result of conscious or unconscious intent on the part of the analysand, but rather the product of the analytic situation and, we suggest, of id information.

All this will be descriptively very familiar to the psychoanalytic clinician who practices using Freud's theoretical ideas. However, we know very well, to our personal and universal sorrow, that there are other circumstances under which human beings seem easily swayed to believe in ways that might have previously seemed dystonic. Is it not possible, however, that those circumstances in some way provide also a relatively easy access to the agency of the id, and perhaps reach to early untamed impulses that render the new behavior actually syntonic?

All this is not to say that thinking in terms of limited sets of constructs was Freud's way or the way of his followers. Rather, we have sought to demonstrate how many ideas first enunciated by Freud continue to inform the practice of emotional healing, even for those whose expressed orientation is cast in other terms. Immediate clinical decisions must always be based on multiple foundations of education and experience, and utilizing the clinician's own theories, whether or not they have ever been codified, whether or not they have ever been articulated. This, too, we share with Freud.

We began with a quotation from Proust that we feel is quite Freudian; we end with a quotation from Freud that we feel is quite Proustian: "We know two kinds of things about what we call our psyche; firstly, its bodily organ and scene of action, the brain . . . , on the other hand our acts of consciousness which are immediate data and cannot be further explained by any sort of description. Everything that lies between is unknown to us, and the data do not include any direct relation between these terminal points of our knowledge" (1940, p. 144).

The scientist and the poet, in their genius, find common ground.

REFERENCES

Adams-Silvan, A. (1993). "To learn the noble game. . . ." The transformation of the listening process into a therapeutic instrument with special reference to analytic memory. *Journal of Clinical Psychoanalysis* 2:513–527.

Arlow, J. (1993). Two discussions of "The Mind of the Analyst" and a response from Madeleine Baranger. *International Journal of Psycho-Analysis* 74:1147–1154.

Bach, S. (1985). *Narcissistic States and the Therapeutic Process*. Northvale, NJ: Jason Aronson.

Blum, H. (1998). An analytic inquiry into intersubjectivity: subjective objectivity. *Journal of Clinical Psychoanalysis* (in press).

Ellman, S. (1991). *Freud's Technique Papers: A Contemporary Perspective*. Northvale, NJ: Jason Aronson.

Freud, S. (1900). The interpretation of dreams. *Standard Edition* 4/5:1–626.

——— (1909). Notes upon a case of obsessional neurosis. *Standard Edition* 10:155–318.

——— (1911a). The handling of dream interpretation. *Standard Edition* 12:91–96.

————— (1911b). Formulations on the two principles of mental functioning. *Standard Edition* 12:218–226.

————— (1912). Recommendations to physicians practising psychoanalysis. *Standard Edition* 12:109–120.

————— (1915). The unconscious. *Standard Edition* 14:161–204.

————— (1923). The ego and the id. *Standard Edition* 19:1–66.

————— (1925). An autobiographical study. *Standard Edition* 20:7–39.

————— (1926). Psychoanalysis. *Standard Edition* 20:261–270.

————— (1933). New introductory lectures. *Standard Edition* 22:3–182.

————— (1940). An outline of psychoanalysis. *Standard Edition* 23:141–207.

Freud, S., and Breuer, J. (1893). On the psychical mechanism of hysterical phenomena: preliminary communication. *Standard Edition* 2:1–19.

————— (1893–1895). Studies on hysteria. *Standard Edition* 2:1–307.

Lewin, B. D. (1955). Dream psychology and the analytic situation. *Psychoanalytic Quarterly* 24:169–199.

Moore, B., and Fine, B. (1990). *Psychoanalytic Terms and Concepts.* New Haven, CT: Yale University Press and the American Psychoanalytic Association.

Nunberg, H., and Federn, E., eds. (1962). *Minutes of the Vienna Psychoanalytic Society,* vol. 1, 1906–1908. New York: International Universities Press.

Sandler, J. (1983). Reflections on some relations between psychoanalytic concepts and psychoanalytic practice. *International Journal of Psycho-Analysis* 64:38–45.

————— (1993). On communication from patient to analyst: not everything is projective identification. *International Journal of Psycho-Analysis* 74:1097–1107.

Sandler, J., Dare, C., and Holder, A. (1973). *The Patient and the Analyst.* New York: International Universities Press.

Schur, M. (1966). *The Id and the Regulatory Principles of Mental Functioning.* New York: International Universities Press.

Slap, J., and Saykin, J. (1984). On the nature and organization of the repressed. *Psychoanalytic Inquiry* 4:107–123.

Stein, M. H. (1965). States of consciousness in the analytic situation: including a note on the traumatic dream. In *Drives, Affects and Behavior,* ed. M. Schur, vol. 2. New York: International Universities Press.

Stewart, W. (1967). *Psychoanalysis: The First Ten Years, 1888–1898.* New York: Macmillan.

Weiss, E. (1960). *The Structure and Dynamics of the Human Mind.* New York: Grune and Stratton.

4

Psychoanalysis and Symbolization: Legacy or Heresy?

Norbert Freedman

The psychoanalytic attitude is a symbolizing attitude. We listen to our patients' stories as signifiers of multiple meanings, and we listen to ourselves from multiple perspectives. Our patients not only deal with drives, self, and objects, but they strive to deal with the symbolization of drives, self, and object relations. What matters, consistently, is the process of translation and transmutation. Psychoanalysis may have been born in the theory of dreams, and matured in the theory of transference and countertransference, but these are all unthinkable without the concept of a process of mediation or transformation. It is a process of linking items of experiences in different spheres of the mind, where one of these items comes to represent the other, a process whereby what is taken as fact— through self-reflection—becomes symbol. Through such a network of mediation, psychoanalytic work accrues, and when such a process is

Note: Appreciation to Sharone Bergner, who, through her imaginative and creative editorial work, has greatly enriched the shape of this manuscript.

throttled, impasse ensues. Hence, it is along lines of symbolization and desymbolization that we can account for psychoanalytic work and psycho-analytic change.

*   *   *   *   *

This discussion may readily appear to be part of the legacy of psychoanalysis, and in that sense might be obvious or redundant, or it may seem to depart from crucial psychoanalytic assumptions, and in that sense flirt with heresy. As is the case in most psychoanalytic discourse, probably both are true. To be sure, such terms as *symbolism, the symbolic,* or *the symbolized* are part and parcel of all psychoanalytic discussions, forming an integral part of the case reports we hear at clinical conferences, but to position the concept of symbolization as the centerpiece for understanding a quality of mind crucial to analytic outcome and process is another matter.

There is little doubt that symbolization as a process of shaping meaning, as a truly psychic process, is thoroughly embedded in the cultural context of nineteenth-century philosophy and belles lettres. Since this was Freud's cultural context, the notion of symbolization surely reaches back to the historical roots of psychoanalysis. It is also true that the idea of symbolism and the symbolic becomes explicit in Freud's writings starting with *The Interpretation of Dreams* (1900) and *The Unconscious* (1915), and I suggest that the crucial distinction between symbolism and symbolization is already reflected in Freud's theoretical distinction between primary pro-cess and secondary process thinking. Herein lies, I believe, the core of the Freudian legacy.

But now, through the evolution of psychoanalytic ideas, things have become more complicated. The term *symbolization,* as it is used with reference to current clinical practice, is a far cry from the symbolism of the turn of the century. Now the word *symbolized* finds itself in the midst of a major paradigm shift, to invoke Kuhn's (1970) concept. These words have become part of the technical and theoretical innovations of the so-called widening scope. Indeed, symbolization as a component of meaning-making has become part of any psychoanalytic enterprise, regardless of denomination. While the term *symbolization* now belongs to our so-called common ground, and has become amenable to empirical study, it is no longer tied to any of the basic assumptions inherent in the original legacy. But then, as we encounter the origins of our thinking, as well as the revisions, we are forced to return to some basic questions. What is it that drives the symbol? And what is it that may foreclose, even annihilate, the construction of symbols? Such questions bring us back to fundamental controversies from our early history.

I suggest that it is this dialectic with and about our basic concepts that is the essence of a contemporary Freudian perspective. It is a dialectic between legacy and—to remain with the terms of Kuhn's elaboration of the development of scientific ideas—heresy. It enables us to find new vistas, and to discern the validity of those early controversies.

*   *   *   *   *

The process of symbol formation—the effort to create personally relevant meanings—lives on in all analytic work today. It has its origins not just in Freud's "Interpretation of Dreams" (1900) or in "The Ego and the Id" (1923) some two decades later, but it can readily be traced to Freud's own sources. The roots of Freud's notions of symbolization have been vividly documented in Ricardo Steiner's impressive essay "In Vienna Veritas" (1994). Here I will make only a few selective comments, sketching the development of those nineteenth-century ideas.

While it is Nietzsche who is usually credited with the discovery of the id, it is in Kant's writing that we find the origins of the ego. He saw imagination as the cornerstone for representing that which is "unrepresentable." To fathom the monster, we need a space in our minds; today we would say a symbolizing space. It was nineteenth-century romanticism's struggle with articulating emotional experience, as voiced by authors such as Novalis and Schlegel (Rauch 1996), that laid a foundation for a crucial aspect of the psychoanalytic process, namely self-reflection. But it was Brentano who added the recognition that emotions are unthinkable without an object of representation, or communication. We always implicitly, if not explicitly, love, hate, or fear someone. Finally, there is Dilthey's intriguing notion of *Nach-Leben*, reliving, which says that the experience or affect that inheres in the object also registers in the subject, the beholder, and it lingers on in consciousness, or perhaps in the preconscious. For Steiner (1995) and the Kleinians, Dilthey's contribution contains the nuclear idea of projective identification registering in the countertransference.

Finally, it is in the work of Ernst Cassirer (1955) that we find a seminal expression of the symbolizing process as a uniquely human attainment. Cassirer was searching for a bridge, some unifying aspect of mind, which allows us to bring together chaos, intuition, and articulated thought. He articulates this unifying idea through the concept of symbolic form, which brings together subjectivity and objectivity. Symbolic form, or the sign, is a container that reflects diversity and particularity while at the same time lending unifying shape.

As this brief sketch suggests, the enduring legacy that Freud has provided for us was framed, if not imprinted, in the Zeitgeist of the nineteenth-century. Still, many features of our current understanding are patently left out of these ideas, many of which are rooted in phenomenology. Excluded is the powerful added understanding of the dynamic unconscious, the explicit recognition of an endogenous motivational structure, and our burgeoning knowledge of infant development, which contributes to our appreciation for how symbolic processes evolve. These are but some of the building blocks that form the basis of the Freudian legacy.

*   *   *   *   *

The quality of thought we call symbolic, in both patient and analyst, is an indispensable part of analytic work. Symbolization is a part of the world of dreams, of fantasy, of symptom formation, of associating and listening, of allowing interpretations to filter into consciousness, and of transference. As Marianne Milner (1952) noted:

> The analytic rule that the patient should try to put all that he is aware of into words, does seem to imply a belief in the importance of symbolization for maturity as well as infancy; it implies the recognition that words are in fact symbols by means of which the world is comprehended. Thus, in the daily battle with our patients over the transference, we are asking them to accept a symbolic relation to the analyst instead of a literal one. [p. 194]

Psychoanalysis, both in its theory and in practice, not only needs symbolization, but, reciprocally, psychoanalysis offers to our understanding of mind a unique interpretation of symbolization. This unique understanding, which has undergone many transformations over the past century, was rooted in Freud's initial perception that symbolizing is located within the system unconscious. It was furthered by Jones's (1916) historic paper, in which he distinguished a core symbolism from symbolization in the wider sense. At its center, symbolism always depends on repression. Jones asserts that what is repressed is symbolized and further, only what is repressed needs to be symbolized. From this starting point, but embracing a wider perspective, Rycroft (1956) offered what I believe to be a unifying definition; for him, the creation of a symbol entails the displacement of an imago of primary interest by an imago of a lesser interest.

This definition has important ingredients. It can be distinguished from the general philosophical or linguistic view of symbolization as the connection between signifier and thing being signified. Here, the linking involves a defense—displacement; it includes the notion of primary interest, which is undoubtedly linked to early bodily experiences; and it involves a shift in the symbolizer's attachment to objects, for what else are the imagos if not wished-for, determined representations of self or object.

While many analysts likely find Rycroft's definition usefully inclusive, it also reflects the fact that the concept of symbolization has undergone dramatic revisions. The clearest extension of the original view is the widening of the range of the concept, which involves the shift from a narrower emphasis on symbol-making that is dominated by primary process, in which it is called symbolism, to an emphasis on its emergence in secondary process as well, in which it is called symbolization. Therein, in this elaboration, lies the progression of the term, from its original legacy to its contemporary extensions. The stages are described in the following sections.

SYMBOLIZATION AS THE CONSTRUCTION OF A BRIDGE

Initially, the line of inquiry was restricted to the focus on the symbolism that is part of the primary process, the symbolism found in dreams, psychosis, fantasy, and art. In such symbolism there is a hallucinatory image, which is often based on bodily sensations finding satisfaction in symbolic representation. This articulation of symbolism contains all the constituents of Freud's early discoveries—from the organizing role of the early body ego to the regulatory role of wish and satisfaction of desire in the effort to structure reality via compromise.

In this last statement lies the beginning of the broader perspective. According to the view described so far, the instigating force for a symbolic structure to arise remains conflict, the need to keep unacceptable wishes out of consciousness. But in symbolism there is a very special kind of compromise formation, whereby condensed or disguised representations are created to fill a gap, to use Rycroft's term. Through the filling of this gap a bridge is created between two spheres of the mind—the unacceptable wish and the perceived actuality. Rycroft recognizes this activity of bridging as belonging to the ego, and it is this aspect of his contribution that sets the stage for the further development of the concept of symbolization.

In the evolving broadened perspective of symbolization, the idea of symbolism was never abolished; it was only subordinated into a broadened context. Symbolism remains a statement of a condensed representation of conflicting wishes. We cannot find a symbol without desire. Otherwise, without desire that motivates the making of a symbol, we would just "go on being," in Winnicott's sense. Symbolism is always a statement of condensed compromise formation, of contradictory or conflictual wishes, of conflict and of conflict resolution. As such, symbolism represents the instigating force or motivation for the development of the symbolizing process. It is a signpost of underlying psychic work.

This idea has important clinical implications. When symbolisms appear in dreams or free associations, they often present themselves in the form of a frozen constellation. The underlying meaning is not accessible to consciousness. In this sense Jones (1916) was right. Symbolism, at first, does depend on repression. When it first appears its meaning may be gleaned by the sensitive clinician, but to the patient the conflict-evoking wishes are not yet known, or owned.

SYMBOLIZATION NOURISHED BY ALLUSION
AND IMAGINATION

In the view of symbolism considered thus far, the connection between two items of experience that are brought together in a symbol was seen as determined by the stark force of a hallucinatory image demanding satisfaction. This deterministic perspective has since evolved, and has become largely replaced by the more contemporary vision of the mediating role of allusion and imagination. The notion of symbol providing an arena for satisfaction is retained, but our original view of the vehicle for such satisfaction—through hallucination—has shifted to a focus on allusion and/or imagination. This shift can be found in the writings of Winnicott (1971) and Milner (1952), and Kubie (1953) in his emphasis on imagination as the connective tissue between various aspects of experience that are linked as meaning is established. With this we return to Kant's idea of the important role of imagination in the construction of meaning.

The arrival at a symbol is no longer seen to be motivated by and dependent solely on that which is repressed, but rather upon a process of mediation between desire and reality. For Milner (1952), the mediating context—the conditions favoring linking—entails both *fantasy*, that is, daydreaming, and *phantasy*, that, is aspects of unconscious mentation. Kubie (1953) invokes an allegorical experience, something that resembles the original trauma but is not *it* in itself, in his effort to explain what motivates and enables the finding of a symbol for previously unsymbolized experience.

In these formulations, repression is seen as partial. The gap between what is desired and that which is acknowledged has widened and the boundaries are blurred. This is especially true of Winnicott's account of the birth of symbolization occurring in transitional space, during that time in development in which the "me" and the "not-me" have not yet been differentiated. Thus, according to this partial-repression view of symbolization, a patient's transition from symbolism to symbolization calls for or involves the creation of an inner psychic space.

SYMBOLIZATION AND THE DIFFERENTIATION OF SUBJECTIVITY

The broadened view of symbolization described so far also implies that the move to symbolization involves a more differentiated experience of wishes, or object relations, and of self; that is, it involves a more differentiated experience of inner life. This perspective on the differentiation of subjectivity is most clearly articulated in Loewald's (1983) definition of the symbolizing process as the linking of one item of experience with another in distinct spheres of the mind, a linking from past to present, fantasy to reality, and so on. This is a linking of highly valued, that is of cathected items, which are the source of analytic symbol formation.

Loewald rejects Jones's idea that unconscious repressed wishes are at the heart of symbolization. In analysis, he notes, when repressed wishes are analyzed, symbolization does not disappear. I might add that while repression might be an instigating force in symbolization, once established, symbolization has its own dynamic force and may flourish. Loewald's understanding of symbol formation, with its emphasis on linking of items of experience in different spheres of the mind, is based on Werner and Kaplan's (1963) thinking regarding the intimate connection that exists between symbolic vehicles and their referents. What is left out is another crucial element of symbol formation—the process of unlinking, or, as the French authors (see, for example, Gibault 1995) call it, uncoupling. When a patient is upset by the angry voice of the analyst as mother's voice, he or she indeed makes a link to the biographical past, but implicitly and explicitly there is a recognition that the analyst is not mother. Otherwise, without this recognition, the patient would be immersed in what Hanna Segal has termed symbolic equation.

Symbolization, then, is an effort toward linking and then also an often strong counterreaction involving uncoupling. It is at this point that we see an inner image that is linked to the present but is not the present, linked to the past but is not the past, an image having dynamic significance in its own right. It is at this juncture that the transition is completed—from symbolism, dominated by primary process, to symbolization, which also involves the processes of qualification and negation. Here is where we see psychoanalytic self-reflection.

The theoretical shift to the notion of symbolizing as a process facilitated by and facilitating the differentiation of subjectivity has important clinical implications. When a patient offers us a symbol, he no longer offers a feeling as a fact, but rather as one of multiple possible perspectives. What else is differentiation if not the apprehension of meanings from multiple perspectives? In this dual process of differentiation of subjectivity—via linking and uncoupling—we can now speak of a triangular symbolizing space, described by the wish, the counter-wish, and the interpreting ego.

SYMBOLIZATION AS A THRUST IN THE DIRECTION OF THE OBJECT

The self-reflective process—especially when the reflection involves emotional experiences—is an event that hardly occurs exclusively within a one-person field. It is deeply embedded in the ambience of the analytic dialogue. Self-reflectiveness is enhanced by—or enabled through—the presence of a listening analyst or a holding environment. Under these conditions there is an expansion of representation—what we've termed the spatialization of the transference. Yet a more specific process may also occur—the patient finds himself in the perception of the other who is reflecting upon him. Finally, however, symbolization becomes motivated by the fact that the very act of self-reflection provides the patient with a vehicle for reaching the analyst-object. As such, the process of symbolization is propelled by the intrinsic wish to connect.

Thus, the appearance of a symbol is not only a way of resolving intrapsychic conflict, nor only a mark of the achievement of more greatly differentiated subjectivity, but it also represents a thrust toward greater object relations, a gesture in the transference. The contribution of Hanna Segal and the Kleinians is that symbolization is part of the depressive position, or, more generally, that symbolization is an expression of concern. It is now unthinkable to us not to consider that the patient who in the "talking cure" offers an analyst a symbolic structure is offering a gift, a gesture, and notably a libidinal one, toward the analyst. Even if this is done partially nonverbally—one is again reminded of Dilthey's notion of *Nach-Leben*—in symbolization, the image that the patient experiences as the thrust toward the object lingers on not only in the consciousness of the patient but also in the consciousness of the analyst. At the same time, the analyst cannot offer the patient a symbol—in the form of interpretations—without also wishing to reach the object. Therefore, symbolization—specifically the social intent of symbolization—always figures heavily in the matrix of the transference and countertransference.

At its best, psychoanalytic treatment is a dialogue between two symbolizers. The patient must absorb the analyst, and so, pari passu, must the analyst absorb what the patient proffers. In the patient's experience the analyst is at first marginalized, perhaps trivialized, then alluded to, and sooner or later the analyst takes center stage, becoming incorporated into issues of primary concern. Hence, the analyst serves as a signifier of analytic work.

The foregoing panorama of views on the symbolic describes contributions made over the last fifty years. It is important to note that these were offered by their authors as distinct, discrete positions on the meaning and scope of the concept. My depiction of these views in succession is meant to suggest that each be seen as addressing a crucial aspect of the process of symbolization, and that, together, they add up to a unified understanding of the concept that reflects the evolution of our field. We now have the scaffolding of the contemporary conceptualization of symbolization that is being offered here.

When a patient offers a symbolic construction during treatment, this act is simultaneously a signifier of intolerable conflict that needs to be bridged; it points to the evocation of allusion and imagery at the periphery of consciousness; it reflects an effort to attain a more differentiated subjectivity; and it is a thrust in the direction of the object, in the context of the transference. The unifying element present in all four of these aspects of symbolization is the notion of spatialization, because in some new way conflicts can now live and breath in a broader, more spatialized perspective. We can thus note that in the transition from the conceptualization of symbolism to formulations of symbolization, symbolization has emerged as a concept that designates a truly transformational activity. To flesh out this type of development more tangibly, let us look at a clinical example.

Early in my career as a therapist I treated a schizophrenic inpatient. He was being threatened with electroshock therapy against his will. Both he and I were determined to "work things through." In one session, after a long silence, he grabbed my arm and startled me with the plea: "Will the bomb kill both of us?" He clearly was alluding to the hydrogen bomb, which was one of the menacing news items of the time. Upon minimal inquiry it became clear that he meant the concrete bomb as well as the symbolic bomb, that is, the fear of being destroyed, his helplessness vis-à-vis the threatening psychiatrist, and his rage at being castrated and annihilated. The bomb functioned as both concrete thing as well as symbol. It became the basis of our reflections over the next several sessions. Sometimes the bomb was treated concretely, as an actuality, and at that time symbolizing space collapsed. But sometimes the bomb became the vehicle to connect to his sense of helplessness, memories of his authoritarian father, or his dread that I might abandon him. But increasingly, and this is the point I wish to stress, the bomb also became both message and missile, directed at me, imploring me.

In its concrete form, the bomb had the quality of a symbolism, a frozen constellation; the meaning was accessible to me but not to him. The bomb was also an allusion to his own helplessness and rage, and sometimes he used his imagination to elaborate upon these previously denied emotions. Sometimes, though rarely, since he was a very disturbed patient, the bomb was interpreted and symbolized: yes, the bomb as symbol was profoundly frightening, and no, we were both safe from the actuality of the bomb. But this dual recognition did not quiet him. The bomb as missile penetrated my consciousness and my reflections and his holding my hand persisted to keep the inner conflict alive. Here, then, we can note the transformation of a concretized image: from symbolism, to allusion, to the beginnings of a self-reflective representation, and to a thrust of all these experiences in the network of transference and countertransference.

So far I have described the evolution of psychoanalytic thinking on the issue of symbolization. The example just cited, however, suggests that the same progression that is evident in our theory can be observed within a single session or over the course of sessions of a psychoanalytic treatment. I have termed this a transformational cycle, which refers to a cycle that begins with a reliance on symbolism dominated by primary process, and evolves to the symbolization of the meanings alluded to in the transference. Elsewhere, I shall elaborate more fully on the constituents of a transformation cycle (which may also be called transference cycle), but here are its main features: A session may open with a frozen constellation, something the patient perceives as fact, often in the form of symbolism. It is a condensed structure fraught with meaning to the observer, or analyst, but not accessible to the patient. Sooner or later allusions or elaborations of the imaginary come to the fore, placing the fact, the frozen constellation, into a new perspective. But then the patient begins to think about thinking (Fonagy 1991), and self-reflectiveness begins. What unfolds now is the process of linking and uncoupling that is initiated by the patient and facilitated by the analyst's interpretation. Finally, self-reflectiveness is recognized as shared reflectiveness that is played out in the intersubjectivity of the two participants. The conflict that was at first frozen and condensed is now alive and symbolized.

Surely, these developments do not necessarily occur in a linear sequence—there is much fluctuation or chaos—as recent developments in complexity theory have taught us. But, while the sequence may vary, reverse itself, or appear chaotic, one may still identify the four essential constituents, which unfold the process of evolution from frozen constellation to symbolization.

In sum, the psychoanalytic understanding of symbolization that is offered here, in contrast to the linguistic or humanistic view of the concept, envisages an evolving and successive process of transformation: a transformation of thought from primary to secondary process, a transformation of desire from condensed and incompatible wishes to the spatialized experiences of contradictory inclinations, a transformation of object relations from a focus on self to an ability to fathom concern. What is created through this process is a network of self-reflective mediation, always sustained by a core motivational structure.

*   *   *   *   *

Two other theorists utilize the concept of symbolization in ways related to, but crucially different from, the contemporary Freudian perspective I am articulating—Lacan and Mitchell. I begin with Lacan, who has written extensively about the symbolic order. For Lacan (1968), the symbolic order discovered by Freud is the unconscious. It is through the deciphering of the language that this order is revealed to us. In his celebration of the unconscious, Lacan eschews the evolution of psychoanalytic ideas not only in Freud's writings during his own lifetime, but of the last century. In this sense, I do consider his thoughts to be heresy, again to invoke Kuhn's distinction.

Space does not permit a fuller discussion, but a critique of Lacan's position is instructive. Let me present a few salient points. First, despite his contribution regarding the "mirror phase" (1949), Lacan's view is a denial of symbolization being a developmental achievement, a perspective we derive from Winnicott's conceptualization of the transitional phase (1971). Another crucial formative aspect of symbolization that is neglected by Lacan is the ongoingness of the capacity to create space that continues throughout life—the process of spatialization, so central to analytic work.

But perhaps the most notably problematic aspect of Lacan's ideas is his assertion that the symbolic is equivalent to the structure of the primary process, or the unconscious. This denies the possibility that symbolic attainment often reflects unconscious, preconscious, even conscious images. Lacan's thinking entails a view of motivation in which everything is predestined rather than evolving.

Now let us turn to another challenge that has a great deal of currency today. In the hands of contemporary relational theorists, symbolization goes through not heresy, but, surely, a significant paradigm shift. While there is considerable variation among relational thinkers, there nonetheless is a common central thrust that characterizes their position. Relational theory stresses the emergence of symbolization in the interchanges between mother and infant, viewing meaning as always inscribed either within the framework of relations to external objects or in relation to the preservation of the self. There is also the recognition of the importance of historical events and the view of the unconscious as involving layers of relative consciousness—in all these ways relational theorists do not suffer from the deficiencies of the Lacanian perspective.

What I take issue with is these theorists' relativism, and here I distinguish between relativization and contextualization. In relativization, all events are deemed to be potentially equivalent. By contrast, contextualization, as I use the term, takes cognizance of a core meaning, a core motivational matrix that, to be sure, undergoes modification in different contexts. It is the absence of a notion of a core endogenous motivational structure for which the relational perspective can be faulted.

Consider, for example, Mitchell's (1988) work in his chapter "Sexuality Without Drive (theory)." In evocative language, Mitchell describes the various ways in which sexual memories, imagery, or representation are always deployed in the service of object relatedness. Sexual fantasies are symbolic vehicles. For the self, they may signify the wish to surrender, dominate, hide, or exhibit, or to flee from intimacy. Sexual excitement and passions may be concealed manifestations of suffocating or annihilating forms of anxiety. Hence—and there is agreement between us about this point—a sexual experience is never merely a discharge event, an elementary release of primary bodily or psychic tension. For Mitchell, all symbolized representations that are met in treatment are condensations of earlier, historically based object relationships. Symbolization thus becomes the process of replaying earlier interactions. What is missing from this account is the integrative and interpretive voice of an ego listening to—and representing—not only relatedness but also endogenous yearnings.

It is instructive to compare Mitchell's account of "sexuality without a drive" with Laplanche and Pontalis' (1968) account of "fantasy and the origins of sexuality." Fantasy is born, they assert, not simply in the opposition between reality and sexual arousal, a kind of reverie. Rather, it is born in the disjunction when sexual excitement is separated from the object. It involves a moment of hallucinatory revival. Laplanche and Pontalis cite the instance of autoeroticism, which is not just the first stage of object relatedness, as is sometimes thought. A drive or wish becomes autoerotic after the loss of the object. It thus involves a transition from a time of before to a time of after. In this way, Laplanche and Pontalis posit a primary object relationship in which drive or wish is created after the experience of disjunction between excitement and the object. Here we have the story of the genesis of unconscious wish and unconscious desire, a story that is of great moment as to how we listen to an analytic hour. We do listen for disjunction, for uncoupling, for the gaps described by Freud, gaps that allow unconscious organizing fantasies to come to the fore.

It may thus be worthwhile to distinguish a relational from an object relations perspective (Ellman, personal communication, 1996), the latter holding to the contextualization of a primary motivational substrate. The general proposition that symbolization calls for continuity, discontinuity, and the recovery of continuity is predicated on the centrality of such a motivational substrate. The gaps or disjunctions define the space in which organizing fantasies can have their play. In this approach, what is meant by organizing fantasies is not just relationship episodes in general, but those, specifically, that are driven by primary emotional structures. These fantasies may then crystallize and become an actuality in shared communication.

We remain indebted to the revisionists. We need Lacan's pounding reminder (echoed by our French colleagues): Where is the unconscious fantasy? We have gained from the relationists' query: Where is the context? These so-called heretic voices have enriched the fabric of analytic thought. Nonetheless, if we were moored to Lacan's vision of *la symbolique*, we would be deprived of the contribution given to us by the accrued knowledge of infant development. At the same time, if we were to rely on the relativism of a relational perspective, we would lose the stabilizing force of coreness in our view of transference, countertransference, and pathogenesis.

*   *   *   *   *

So far, in describing a contemporary Freudian conceptualization of symbolization, I have stressed the importance of a gap, of a disjunction, of moments of discontinuity so crucial for the consolidation of wishes or even passions. But now I wish to speak not of a gap but of a gulf. It is a gulf of meaninglessness, of a paralysis born of confusion, pain, of helplessness, disrupting what Joyce McDougal (1992) has termed the symbolizing chain. It could also be a gulf born of sadism, directing its force at the very network of signification, as is conveyed by Bion's concept of attacks on linking. Thus, our notions of symbolization find their confirmation in the very limits of the process, under those conditions when it appears to be absent. I have termed the process that characterizes such conditions desymbolization.

Symbolization is a network of self-reflective mediation, and in desymbolization this network has collapsed to a zero point. Emotional experiences cannot be named or are throttled, as in alexithymia; there may be endless reporting of daily events presented as concretized or petrified "facts"; the analyst may not be listened to, interpretations not heard, or his/her existence trivialized. The entry into a psychoanalytic dialogue seems barred. It all feels like a motivated event governed by a wish not to know.

In the psychopathology of the twenty-first century manifestations of desymbolization appear to flourish. Some four decades ago Fenichel wrote of depressed patients that they are love addicts. Today addictive phenomena seem to have skyrocketed. Not only is there the addiction to consciousness altering drugs, to dependence on psychopharmacological regulations of thoughts, affects, or volitional behavior, but there is also in our daily life a bombardment with sound bites, sound blasts creating conditions of sensory underload, or overload, dulling the reflective functions—all events that interfere with the symbolic process and with it the self-reflective function.

But surely these issues are not new, and can be found in clinical reports throughout the history of psychoanalysis. One well-known example is Green's (1986) account of the case of the Wolfman, in which he notes that the Wolfman did not wish to know, and so his analysis was marked by the thrust of desymbolization. When desymbolization occurs within the treatment situation, it affects the shape of the transference.

In the psychoanalytic treatment situation the gulf created by desymbolization appears in varied transference contexts. It may appear in three forms—as a transitory negative therapeutic reaction notably occurring at moments of analytic advance (Rosenfeld 1987), as part of the reactivation of a traumatic episode in infancy (Lasky 1993), and as part of a frozen, chronic character structure. The distinct ways in which these frozen constellations appear and are resolved in the clinical situation will be detailed in a forthcoming publication. The analytic literature is replete with clinical examples and interesting conceptualizations of such impasses.

It is only after the resumption of the symbolizing process that we learn about the motivational base of that which is defended against. This recognition is a mark not only of the understanding of pathogenesis, but also of its reversal. Each of these configurations has its own pathway toward repair; there may be an unexpected libidinal encounter in the transference, there may be a reorganizing form of symbolic enactment, or there may be a trust-evoking confrontation proffered by the analyst. Each of these is a thrust in the direction of a more libidinal experience of a spatialized transference. Nonetheless, it is fair to say that instances of desymbolization are, in one form or another, attacks on linking as well as a disavowal of the dependency on the symbolizing object relationship (in this connection, note also Bass's [1997] interpretation of concreteness as a phenomenon of desymbolization). The analyst often works with an intuitive hunch, but will not know fully until the crisis is over. The impasse is resolved, that is transformed, through a reentry into a new spatialized context.

Earlier, in my account of how symbols are created, I suggested that a gap must be allowed to form so that a desire for linking can be implemented. In instances of impasse we see the working of the destructive desire as it exerts its impact over longer periods of time, forming not merely a gap but a gulf of meaninglessness or turmoil. It is a thrust destructive not just against objects and the self, but against the fabric of signification. This locus of attack brings with it its own source of anxiety. One might call it desymbolizing anxiety. There are numerous ways to ward off this danger, and our clinical case literature is filled with poignant examples of desymbolizing patients' attempts to overcome the isolation their attacks on linking bring about, to find tolerable ways to connect.

Thus, the crucial transformational events in psychoanalysis are those that move us from desymbolization to symbolization, from despair to hope, from impasse to interpretation, from being throttled to creating space. It is in the concept of spatialization that, I believe, we find the center of that which leads to analytic change. In the dynamics of the analytic interchange, as we create space in the encounter *between*, we are at the same time also promoting space *within*.

*   *   *   *   *

THE DIALOGUE OF CRATYLUS[1]

Hermogenes, Cratylus, and Socrates gather together to discuss the nature of names, for the knowledge of names is a high thing. Hermogenes opens and says that it is Cratylus who holds that everything has a right name, that the name inheres in the nature of things. A name is not what other people call it by convention but, rather, it has its own voice. There is a kind of inherent correctness in names. Hermogenes, on the other hand, believes that there is no truth in names other than what is dictated by convention. If you give up one name and take a new one, the later name is no more correct than the previous one. And so the controversy continues. Here we find juxtaposed two views on naming, or the origin of language, naming based on arbitrary choice, usage, or context, and, in contrast, naming that is linked to an intrinsic state of being and thus brings up the hypothesis of primal motivation.

Socrates presides like a wise, condescending supervisor lecturing on the nature of the mental process. At first he challenges Hermogenes: names cannot simply be arbitrary signs, for in that way they are univocal and would never extend the range of meaning. Names indeed seem to inhere in the nature of things. A word is true because being is fully absorbed in its meaning. Next, however, Socrates also takes Cratylus to task. Names cannot be just a copy of nature, there must be something arbitrary that leads to their assignment. The image itself must be different from its name. These two things—the image and the name—can be similar but not identical, for then we would need no name at all.

Plato, through the voice of Socrates, evolves a line of thinking that shows that both extreme positions are untenable. His position transcends both views to include that which is intrinsic and that which is arbitrary. Names function to inform us, they give us knowledge, and they help to instruct—shall we say interpret? If a name refers to someone who has changed during his lifetime from an early phase to a later one and yet he holds the same name, there must be something about him that has

---

1. I am indebted to Alain Gibault for alerting me to Cratylus and his relevance to the psychoanalytic understanding of symbolization.

remained constant, even though the name may once have been given as an arbitrary designation. Furthermore, we find a name for that which had not been named before and that which contradicts itself. We name things that are in conflict with each other. In naming we seek not only to designate, but also to realize our intentions, to grasp the essential nature of things. Names point to the dialogue of the soul and logos is the stream that comes out from the mouth. At the end of the dialogue Socrates says to Hermogenes and Cratylus both, "Go, go to the country, and think about these things for a long time."

Naming is at the center of psychoanalytic work. For Fenichel, naming is *it* and something more, and this allusion points toward the very heart of the talking cure. In the evolution of a symbolized transference a name may be found for an emotion previously split off, denied, or not yet recognized. In the spatialization of the transference what takes place is the recognition of unnamed experiences of past or present, experiences in dreams or in fantasies. In the transference-countertransference dialogue, new names are also created. They represent a thrust to grasp an essential experience. All of this collapses in the desymbolized transference. But the evolving process of conquering an inner meaning within the diversity of contexts, which is Freud's legacy, was foreshadowed in Cratylus some 2,000 years ago.

REFERENCES

Bass, A. (1997). The problem of "concreteness." *Psychoanalytic Quarterly* 66(4):642–682.

Cassirer, E. (1955). *The Philosophy of Symbolic Forms, vol. I and II: Language.* New Haven, CT: Yale University Press.

Fonagy, P. (1991). Thinking about thinking. *International Journal of Psycho-Analysis* 72:639–656.

Freud, S. (1900). The interpretation of dreams. *Standard Edition* 4/5:1–626.

——— (1915). The unconscious. *Standard Edition* 14:159–215.

——— (1923). The ego and the id. *Standard Edition* 19:12–59.

Gibault, A. (1995). *Symbolization and its vicissitudes.* Paper presented at the 39th International Congress on Psychoanalysis, San Francisco, July.

Green, A. (1986). *On Private Madness.* London: Hogarth.

Jones, E. (1916). The theory of symbolism. In *Papers on Psychoanalysis*, 5th ed. Baltimore: Williams & Wilkins.

Kubie, L. S. (1953). The distortion of the symbolic process in neurosis and psychosis. *Journal of the American Psychoanalytic Association*, vol. 1.

Kuhn, T. (1970). *The Structure of Scientific Revolutions*. Chicago: University of Chicago Press.

Lacan, J. (1949). The mirror stage as formative of the function of the I as revealed in psychoanalytic experience. In *Ecrits: A Selection*, trans. A. Sheridan. New York: Norton.

———— (1968). *Speech and Language in Psychoanalysis*, trans. Anthony Wilde. Baltimore, London: Johns Hopkins University Press.

Laplanche, J., and Pontalis, J. B. (1968). Fantasy and the origins of sexuality. *International Journal of Psycho-Analysis* 49(1):1–18.

Lasky, R. (1993). *Dynamics of Development and the Therapeutic Process*. Northvale, NJ: Jason Aronson.

Loewald, H. (1983). *Comments on the psychoanalytic concept of symbolism*. Hartmann award lecture at the New York Psychoanalytic Institute and Society, March.

McDougal, J. (1992). *Plea for a Measure of Abnormality*. New York: Brunner/Mazel.

Milner, M. (1952). Aspects of symbolism in comprehension of the not-self. *International Journal of Psycho-Analysis* 33:181–195.

Mitchell, S. (1988). *Relational Concepts in Psychoanalysis*. Cambridge, MA: Harvard University Press.

Rauch, A. (1996). The broken vessel of tradition. *Representation* 53:74–96.

Rosenfeld, H. (1987). *Impasse and Interpretation*. London: Tavistock.

Rycroft, C. (1956). Symbolism and its relation to the primary and secondary process. *International Journal of Psycho-Analysis* 37:469–472.

Steiner, R. (1994). "In Vienna Veritas . . ." *International Journal of Psycho-Analysis* 76:511–583.

———— (1995). *A personal appreciation of the cultural and theoretical implications of Hanna Segal's approach to creativity and aesthetics*. Paper presented at the British Psychoanalytic Association, London.

Werner, H., and Kaplan, B. (1963). *Symbol Formation*. New York: Wiley.

Winnicott, D. W. (1971). *Playing and Reality*. London: Tavistock.

5

On the Place of Self-Reflection in the Psychoanalytic Process

Stanley Grand

Contemporary Freudian psychoanalysis is currently undergoing ferment as it seeks to integrate a variety of competing theoretical perspectives. Insights coming not only from Kleinian, Winnicottian, and Kohutian perspectives at varying distances from the classical paradigm, but also from intersubjective (Stolorow et al. 1987) and interactive (Renik 1993) perspectives emanating from within its paradigm, have challenged some basic assumptions of our classical theory and technique of therapeutic action. Indeed, it is mainly from these latter perspectives that many contemporary controversies spring, and it is concern about these controversies that prompt us to reconsider what we mean when we refer to classical technique.

What is it that distinguishes the classical analytic mode of psychoanalytic action from the many alternate modes of action that have emerged since our clinical interests have turned to patients in the widening scope? Controversy around this issue of what is analytic in our various versions of psychoanalysis has stimulated some to search for common ground (Wallerstein 1988, 1990) between competing paradigms rather than accentuate the differences that might be present among them. Or, as Leo Rangell (1996) has done, direct themselves specifically to the question of what makes a treatment analytic, rather than asking what makes a procedure, or a technique, depart from psychoanalysis. While all of this may ultimately be for the good, I am impressed by Paniagua's (1995) recently voiced concern with Wallerstein's perspective when he asks, "If we have common ground, how come we do such different things?" (p. 359).

While contemporary classical psychoanalysis has been enriched by many and diverse currents emanating from various clinical and theoretical sources, the emphasis of this theory on the ameliorative effects of interpretively generated insight is determined by a theory of pathogenesis that views psychopathology as a result of unconscious intrapsychic conflict. Our technique aims to expand our conscious awareness of such deeply hidden conflict so as to aid us in its control. Clearly, focus on the centrality of a particular technical aspect of a complex clinical process is always determined by the particular theory of pathogenesis that informs one's clinical work, and other theories holding different assumptions about pathogenesis do focus on different technical approaches in their search for ameliorative factors.

It is an unfortunate fact that in psychoanalysis we do not as yet possess criteria for assessing the validity or relative merit of any of these theories of pathogenesis, and thus, no one theory can claim to be definitive on scientific grounds. Couch (1995) has recently cautioned, therefore, that the shift to our current pluralistic world of psychoanalysis, in light of this lack of empirical validation of theoretical assumptions, places us in great danger that

> new ideas remain speculative part theories not integrated with past foundations, and new techniques remain "technical fashions" imposed as the new "correctness" on communities of analysts who are prone to assume that something "modern" is better, where better is only conformity to a new fashion with no convincing evidence of greater therapeutic success. [p. 153]

Indeed, both Paniagua (1995) and Brenner (1995) underline this problem when they remind us that since different technical approaches generate different therapeutic processes, and different therapeutic processes generate different outcome consequences, even the most rudimentary efforts to study the comparative merit of different analytic approaches are seriously compromised.

Thus, the sorts of methodological critiques that presently abound in our field are, by their very nature, only stylistic preferences, and opinions about the superiority of one theory of therapeutic action as opposed to another are mainly value statements rather than facts. Our best recourse, in such a situation, then, is to stay closely attuned to the way our particular theory of pathogenesis and its associated technique and mode of therapeutic action are related to the clinical data at hand. Methodological critiques, then, could be more meaningfully directed toward the adequacy of the links between pathogenesis and technical mode of action, so that the relationship of these aspects of the analytic process to one another and to clinical outcome could be established. It is to the purpose of clearly articulating such links within our classical theory of technique that I wish to direct this chapter, which addresses what I believe to be an important aspect of the classical psychoanalytic mode of therapeutic action: the place of self-reflection in contemporary Freudian psychoanalysis. Such a focus provides a useful perspective from which to distinguish the classical form of analytic treatment from those forms of treatment that use internalization mechanisms as their predominant mode of therapeutic action.

What is it that is claimed to be essential to the classical view of the analytic process? In 1952 Anna Freud suggested that a procedure has the right to be called psychoanalysis if it recognizes and works with two processes in the patient's mind: transference and resistance. To this Rangell (1996) has recently added a specific focus on the intrapsychic, the unconscious, and the conflictual. While such suggestions are useful for clearly establishing the domain of psychoanalytic investigation, they tell us little about the nature of the actual process itself. These key elements of the theory help define a focus for our efforts to pursue our analytic goals, that is, our attempt to achieve a more durable and better balanced structuralization of the patient's mind. But how must we engage our patients in order to ensure that this pursuit takes the form of an *analytic* process, as distinct from other forms of therapeutic process? What are the essential characteristics of the particularly unique kind of dyadic process that we call psychoanalysis?

Freud's own view of pathogenesis and therapeutic action helps in addressing some of these very important questions. Freud's evolving theories of the mind and neurosogenesis, characterized by the shift from the goal of making the unconscious conscious to the more sophisticated effort to replace id discharge with ego control, defined hierarchical models of mental functioning by which more primitive, primary organizations of the mind were subordinated to a higher, secondary level of mental organization and control. Within both of these models of the mind (Gill 1963) psychopathology was seen to reflect either a failure in the development of such higher level organizations, or, if organized, a failure in the capacity of these organizations to subordinate the less evolved modes of mental discharge. Conflict between the aims of these disparate levels of the organization of the mind, that is, between rational thought and impulsive discharge, was seen as a major cause of character deformation and symptomatic state. Freud's evolving approach to the analysis and ultimate resolution of such conflictual tendencies was to develop a technique and mode of action that was consistent with his theoretical view of how the mind worked. For Freud this meant that the technique and mode of therapeutic action would be directed toward raising primitive impulse discharge to a higher, more abstract level. That is, that rational thought should replace unrestrained impulsive discharge. Words and ideas were to bind the discharge of impulsive action and raise it to a higher, more efficient level of controlled expression. Psychoanalysis was the result of this undertaking, and self-understanding, in place of abreaction, was to become the hallmark of Freud's approach to the resolution of unconscious intrapsychic conflict.

Clinically, Freud's momentous shift from hypnosis and the pressure technique to the technique of free association reflected his abiding belief in the value of conscious self-regulation as the fundamental ameliorative factor in the psychoanalytic mode of cure. Hypnosis and the pressure technique, which bypassed the intentionality of consciousness, were discarded by Freud in favor of a technique which enlisted the patient's volition. This shift to a treatment form emphasizing volitional self-regulation and integration has remained central to the development of classical psychoanalytic technique since that time. Freud's focus on the patient's associations, and his shift to the technique of interpreting the patient's resistances to the emergence of underlying, unacceptable transference wishes, resulted in a new and startling technique for raising primitive mental organizations to a level that could be integrated into consciousness, a technique in which self-understanding would be mobilized in the service of self-regulation and self-control over unconscious mental conflict (cf. Coltrera 1981).

Thus, a new integrative technique evolved over time—one that was not only, as Arlow (Panel 1983) suggested, a more effective mode of objectifying mental experience, but one that aimed to engage early infantile trauma in the immediacy of the transference situation. Its purpose, as Lawrence Friedman (1991) suggests, was no longer primarily the recovery of repressed memories, but instead an opportunity for reexperiencing early relationship scenarios in the immediacy of transference reality. Now the analyst as listener and interpreter participated mainly to facilitate the emergence of this internal intrapsychic world into the treatment process. Interpretation, in this more modern sense, thus becomes directed toward the anxieties that stimulate resistances to the full exploration and integration of the meanings of the enacted transferential relationship (Busch 1995, Coltrera 1981, Gray 1994). This, then, is the unique kind of dialogue between two individuals that we call psychoanalytic, a dialogue with the potential for activating early imagoes in dramatic enactments within the analytic space, and one that requires of the patient a degree of objectification by which therapeutic meaning and significance can be derived and integrated.

Thus, from Freud's most fundamental clinical concerns, articulated throughout his technical papers (1911, 1912a,b, 1913, 1914, 1915), to current concerns with the interpretation of the resistances and defenses against the acknowledgment of unconscious wishes and fantasies, classical analysts have focused on increasing the patient's capacity to engage in the process of self-reflection on transference experience. In this effort, the analyst is viewed, as Dunn (1995) has suggested, as a facilitator to the emerging mental life of the patient, rather than as an active participant in constructing the psychic data and process of treatment, an intersubjective view having its origins in the active treatments of Ferenczi and Rank (1925) and its more current representations in the work of Renik (1993) and Hoffman (1991). Thus, Freud's theory of neurosogenesis and the particular unique and novel mode of psychoanalytic action that he originated, and that has evolved in our classical technique, places the process of engaging self-reflection on transference experience at the center of our various technical efforts to attain analytic goals. This is not to say that in our day-to-day work we ignore the full range of our patients' thoughts and feelings about all aspects of their lives both within and outside the transference. It is only to say that the struggle to resolve the resistance to reflecting upon underlying transference fantasies lies at the heart of our analytic work.

CLINICAL ILLUSTRATIONS

Dr. M. began his analysis with a series of objections to the use of the couch. He felt it was demeaning to him to lie on the couch unable to see me since that put me in a "one up" position on two scores: first, I could see him while he could not see me; and second, that my sitting up while he lay on the couch elevated me above him and he didn't feel that was a fair way to begin a collaboration. His objections were strenuously expressed and so we agreed to work in the vis-à-vis position for the time being in order to see if we might better understand his objections and the reasons behind them. While he felt his objections were straightforward and unnecessary to analyze, he was also aware that he might be mistaken, and therefore, in the interests of analytic progress, he would not object to discussing them with me.

Several months of treatment in the vis-à-vis position revealed a number of general issues related to fears of being controlled by me, as well as an intellectual consideration of the possibility that he might feel more vulnerable to me on the couch than he would feel in the face-to-face position where he could prepare for a possible attack. Some working through of these issues both in and outside of the transference led him to the understanding that his fears and anxieties about being controlled had been present throughout his remembered life, and had indeed determined his choice of medical specialty as a radiologist, where he could deal with pictures rather than with real people. However, none of this interpretive work on elements of the transference appeared to touch him emotionally, and his resistance to using the couch persisted.

Throughout the subsequent discussions of these issues Dr. M. frequently would look at the couch and even speculate that he might be more comfortable talking about his fears if he didn't have to look at me. On one of these occasions, sensing a greater readiness to use the couch, I motioned toward it in a way that invited Dr. M. to use it. He hesitated a moment, got up from his chair, and with a flourish of bravado flung himself on the couch. He lay there silently for many minutes. As fate would have it, this silence was suddenly broken by an abrupt and forceful knocking at the consultation room door. Before I could investigate this matter, Dr. M. jumped up from his position on the couch and leaped across the room to his former position in the chair. Upon returning from my investigation of the inopportune disruption I commented to Dr. M. that the suddenness of his movement back to the chair felt to me like someone in fear of being caught at something he shouldn't be doing. In response to this comment Dr. M. hesitantly revealed that at the moment of the knocking he had a frightening feeling of being a little boy, followed by a memory connected to this feeling of how, as a child, he would routinely join his mother to read with her in her bed while his father would be watching TV in the downstairs living room. His enjoyment of these intimate times with his mother were marred only by the fear that he would be caught by his father. He would wait until he heard his father's footsteps on the stairway and then leap from his mother's bed to his own room before his father caught him. The knock on my door had revived the whole situation in vivid detail. Interpretation of this enactment in the transference now seemed to make the patient's conflicts about using the couch understandable and particularly compelling for him. The fear of being caught by his father in his mother's bed, which underlay his resistance to using the couch, also suggested that his decision to move from the chair to the couch involved an intensification of his sexualization of the transference, an explanation that was subsequently to be confirmed in the analytic work.

Dr. M. used the couch regularly following this enactment and recall of his early experience, and the recognition that certain aspects of his anxieties about using the couch involved his fear of being caught by his father in mother's bed. This understanding deepened his transference experience and facilitated self-reflective analytic work beyond the avoidance, denial, and intellectualization characterizing the earlier phase of our work, and led to a more complete understanding of his need to sexualize his relationship with me. However, while his tendency to action was reduced, it remained a notable part of his analytic experience. For several years further into the analysis Dr. M. would routinely be 10 or so minutes late to his sessions and could never seem to be able to pay his bill in a timely fashion. Indeed, this tendency to blatantly enact his resistances to reflecting upon his anal sadism persisted throughout much of this patient's treatment.

Dr. M.'s tendencies to action, together with his intellectual defenses and rigid character structure, combined synergistically into a formidable configuration of defense/resistance, which impeded emotionally meaningful self-reflective work. With such rigidly integrated structures in place, resistances operated to delay his awareness of his progressively deepening transference experience. Whereas the preliminary work of clarifying the nature and purposes of this patient's enactments and defenses resulted in intellectual understandings of some of the fears and anxieties that underlay his resistance to the analytic process, with time an intensification of erotic feelings occurred that compelled their enactment directly in the transference. Once these feelings were brought into the immediacy of the transference situation, interpretations of them were experienced with a sense of conviction not available otherwise.

The deepening and enactment of the transference in relation to me seemed, then, to ultimately enable the resolution of Dr. M.'s resistance to emotionally compelling self-reflective work on his underlying fantasy. Without this enactment self-understanding remained simply intellectual and noncompelling. But further, and most importantly, it was the integrity of Dr. M.'s ego that enabled him to use this self-reflective work to more fully explore and integrate the meanings that his enacted transferential relationship with me had for him. Without this ability to distinguish his enactment as a transference experience it would have remained simply a concrete and real experience for him. Thus, it was in this ability to self-reflect, in the context of the ego's capacity to distinguish real from unreal (Steingart 1983) experience, that interpretation of transference enactments function to effectively potentiate the analytic process.

While it is certainly the case that we currently view the analytic situation and process as complex, entailing the activation and working through not only of highly structuralized intrapsychic conflicts, but of an array of earlier preconflictual developmental issues as well, it is also the case that what is unique about the contemporary classical situation and process is that it attempts, insofar as it is possible, to work through these early issues by means of the same technique (i.e., interpretation) and mode of action (i.e., self-reflection) useful for the developmentally more advanced cases. Thus process, not content, defines this mode of action. To the extent, then, that a self-reflective mode of action engenders self-understanding of transference experience, the treatment remains primarily within the classical paradigm. To the extent that transference is used to replace life experience, this paradigm is modified, since classical psychoanalysis attempts to remain close to its original goal of expanding the patient's capacity for conscious self-regulation and control. Therefore, to the extent that patients traumatized by early caregiving experiences require a treatment form by which the internalization of new objects becomes the predominant mode of therapeutic action, the classical paradigm is altered into what Leo Stone (1954) originally termed a modified analysis. Whether such a term is still useful or not, it does highlight a subtle shift in the action mode of the dyadic situation, a shift denoting a distinctly less self-regulating process, which I believe is worth noting (cf. Gray 1994). The following clinical material is presented to illustrate this distinction.

Mrs. J. entered analysis depressed and frustrated by her relationship with her husband and his family, all of whom lived closely together in the same apartment building. Her complaint was that although she gave generously of her time and energies to everyone in the family, no one gave to her. She self-righteously denounced her husband for his indifference to her and viewed herself as a martyr, all alone in this world with no support from anyone. Asking for help was humiliating for Mrs. J., her formula being "if he doesn't know what I need, then there's no point needing anything from him." Session after session was filled with an unremitting series of complaints against her husband and his family about daily slights and frustrations. Attempts to explore her feelings of frustration and aloneness, as well as preliminary efforts to draw her attention to the possibility that she might be experiencing similar feelings in the transference, were either ignored or rejected outright. Even empathy with her upset feelings was rejected since acknowledging such feelings seemed to be experienced by her as a sign of her neediness. Only empathic resonance with her frustration and upset at her husband for his indifference were tolerated. However, she interpreted my empathy as an acceptance of the validity of her experiences and took it to be a signal for increased anger and self-justificatory complaining. Thus, empathic resonance with her complaint was experienced by her as empowering, and efforts to interest her in reflecting on these experiences, both in and outside of the transference, made her feel angry and misunderstood. If I didn't understand what she was feeling and why, there was no point in discussing her feelings with me. At such times I was experienced unconsciously as the ungiving husband.

Despite these moments of felt rejection an immediate positive idealizing transference developed, and under its influence Mrs. J. felt empowered to begin to express some needfulness toward her husband, which seemed to relieve her depression and sense of hopeless frustration in the marriage. She and her husband planned a trip to Venice as a sort of second honeymoon, and after six months of treatment the couple left on a three-week vacation. Mrs. J. seemed very happy and attributed all her happiness to me.

On her return home the patient was informed of having earned a large sum of money from a business investment she had independently made. This financial success caused my patient to become upset once again as she struggled with the competitive feelings she felt had been evoked in her husband. Her depression returned, and now her small fortune became the center of her complaints. Long months of angry denials of the wish to use the money for herself or her children followed, and much guilt and self-recrimination were expressed as she considered the consequences of having so much money. She angrily swore she would never use it for herself. Once again the relationship with the husband began to disintegrate. Now, however, complaints began to focus more clearly on sexual matters: complaints that her husband never loved her, never satisfied her sexual wishes, that he was revolted by her "bad complexion," that he would not have sex with her because of not wanting to touch her. Her anger and frustration with her husband grew intense. In addition, much of this was also played out in the transference in the form of subtle provocations to get me to confirm her ugliness and lack of sexual attraction. But my efforts to help her reflect upon her provocativeness were rejected as being unsympathetic to her pain and need to "know the truth" about herself. During those moments she allowed her demandingness of me to be revealed, she was unable to distinguish her fantasy distortions of our relationship from the reality that ours was a treatment relationship. Clearly, during such moments I was experienced as the ungiving and rejecting husband.

Despite these periods of frustration and upset with me, the idealizing transference continued, throughout this lengthy analysis, to provide Mrs. J. with pleasure and was her main source of stability and strength. It seemed that access to me was all that she wanted, and her resistance to seeing how she split me, the "good object," from her husband, the "bad object," persisted and was intractable.

Whatever other purposes her complaints about her life had served, Mrs. J.'s resistance to dealing with her neediness in the transference operated as the most powerful obstacle to the development and deepening of a self-reflective analytic process. Her efforts to externalize her struggle by preserving me in an idealized state, while all others were to be condemned for their cruelty and lack of concern, served to continually deflect her attention to external reality and away from self-reflection on her inner world, a process that was itself a major threat to her self-esteem. Thus, the resistances and defenses that characterized the treatment from the beginning seemed to have become chronic.

Clearly, then, Mrs. J.'s ability to self-reflect on transference experience was never fully established throughout this long and arduous treatment. The illusory omnipotence and power that she obtained through her externalizations and idealization of me continued to be major sources of her strength and stability, giving way only periodically to an irritable awareness of their role in denying her neediness and vulnerability. Thus, much of the treatment of Mrs. J. retained the quality of a psychotherapy and could never be transformed fully into an analysis proper. This is not to say that the treatment did not evolve, but only to indicate that the particular process that did develop was different from an analytic process. The patient's self-reflective work on her transference experience was always severely constrained by her narcissistic vulnerabilities. In this sense the treatment never seemed to become analytic with respect to the emergence of a self-rewarding search for knowledge about her internal world. Rather, this aspect of the process remained predominantly at the level of her initial resistances.

For Mrs. J., enactments in the transference defined a real relationship with me that she could neither reflect upon nor allow to be understood as symbolic of core conflictual issues. In the area of her transference experience her fear of self-revelation interfered with the acknowledgment of her distortions of our relationship since such acknowledgment exposed, and made real, her vulnerability and shame. This contrasts with Dr. M., for whom interpretation of transference enactments led to a deepening of transference experience and self-knowledge, and of the analytic process itself.

In Mrs. J., as well as in another patient described below, action sequences were not enactments in the same sense that they were in Dr. M., for whom action was symbolic and stood for a specific dynamic fantasy of oedipal victory and fear of castration. Rather, action in Mrs. J. was concrete and nonsymbolic insofar as the patient was unable to transcend its immediate effects and was unable to use it for self-understanding. Thus, interpretation of the patient's complaints as a repetition of an early childhood dynamic vis-à-vis a significant object was not useful to her but was experienced only as another rejection at the hands of yet one more unresponsive parental figure. Similarly, in the patient to follow, an interpretation of his severe regressive behavior as symbolic of his infantile longing for merger with mother could not be helpful since the patient had actually become, in his internal reality, an infant who could not take distance from his felt experience.

In this sense, then, there is a difference between patients who can use interpretive work on preoedipal infantile longings informatively, that is, for self-understanding, and those who require an actual response from the analyst that conforms with their infantile internal reality, that is, their wish for actual caregiving. In the former case analysis is possible in a more or less classical manner despite the presence of a predominantly infantile character, whereas in the latter case, a psychotherapeutic, that is, ameliorative approach is necessary since interpretation and insight are relatively useless.

In cases like Mrs. J.'s, in which self-esteem issues predominate, and resistance is mobilized against self-revelation and its attendant feelings of anxiety, deep vulnerability, and shame, interpretive efforts in the transference only increase the patient's fear of exposure. The necessary therapeutic accommodation to this fearful response forces a shift from the interpretive mode toward empathic resonance with the patient's experience, eventuating in a process similar to a corrective emotional experience with internalization as the predominant mode of therapeutic action (Gray 1994). For example, early in Mrs. J.'s treatment, when complaints about the difficulties of her life were so central, only my attention to the painfully real quality of her felt rejections could be registered and tolerated, and

necessarily took precedence over interpretations of her underlying conflicted dependency wishes. Since anything I would say was experienced by
her concretely in the transference, that is, in terms of whether it made her
feel accepted or feel rejected, it was not possible for her to use interpretive
work informatively. Indeed, my interventions were almost totally controlled
by Mrs. J.'s sensitivities, and only limited empathic resonance with her
complaints would be tolerated. While interpretations became tolerable
later in treatment, great care was always needed to phrase such interventions in ways that could be acceptable to her.

Clearly, then, ego supportive measures are necessary in the treatment
of patients like Mrs. J. Such patients exhibit more primitive levels of ego
integration, and great difficulty in distinguishing the real from the fantasy
aspects of the transference situation. If such patients can be helped to
sustain the treatment through its early phase, it is often possible to deepen
the treatment, over time, into a circumscribed self-reflective process, and,
in some favorable cases, into a fully interpretive psychoanalysis. That is, a
shift can be effected by which the predominantly internalizing mode of
action tilts gradually toward a more self-reflective process.

In ideal terms, then, it would appear that the engagement of a
predominantly unmodified analytic process requires the active participation of a patient who not only has the capacity for engaging in self-
reflection on transference experience, but also shares with the analyst what
Gehrie (1993) has recently described as analytic, as opposed to therapeutic, goals, that is, a willingness and capacity to forgo immediate relief in the
service of a more thorough understanding of one's unconscious mental
life. Clearly, not all analyses meet this ideal, nor are all patients suitable to
undergo such unmodified analyses. In the extreme, analysis may not be
possible at all. The following clinical material illustrates this point.

Mr. Y. came for analysis obsessed with the painful and overwhelming
thought that he had died emotionally. He claimed he could not feel
anything anymore, and worried intensely that he would never be
capable of having what he called a "real relationship" with another
person. Mainly, he was concerned that he could not feel love, and was
pained by the idea that he could not hope to ever experience the
pleasure of a loving relationship with a woman. Concretely, this was
expressed in his sexual functioning, where he was anorgasmic, al-

though potent. Try as he might, he could not satisfy himself during coitus, and this was a source of great frustration for him.

Mr. Y. began the analysis complaining that he could not understand how talking about himself was going to change how he felt. Nevertheless, he spent many sessions describing in great detail the painful loneliness and boredom of his life and his daily activities at work as a civil engineer. Relatively soon after the start of treatment, the sense of urgency with which he had begun his work subsided. He seemed to have settled into a monotonous and affectless monologue that had an endless repetitive quality about it. The general effect of his communicative style was to create a feeling of emotional flatness during sessions, and this resulted in a sense of boredom for me. After several months of treatment I called attention to his emotional distance and isolation during the sessions and asked if this was something he was aware of feeling. He seemed pleased that I had noticed this about him but was unable to associate to it, nor provide any explanation for it. However, he experienced my comment as a validation of his complaint about his life, and was pleased that finally someone had understood him. He appeared to be truly grateful for my recognition of his plight.

However, rather than being reassured by my having understood him, Mr. Y. began to experience increasing levels of anxiety. It was as if my comments about his distance and isolation had provoked some deep fear in him. He now began to describe feelings of anxiety upon awakening from sleep in the morning but was unable to explain these feelings except to connect them to apprehensions about his ability to work. As the weeks went by depressive thoughts about his 4 year old son, from a previous unsuccessful marriage, began to occupy his mind, and guilt for having abandoned the boy to his depressed mother became intense. A regressive process was under way and it was clear that Mr. Y. was feeling both incapable of controlling it as well as frightened that the analysis was causing it.

In the ensuing months Mr. Y. regressed rapidly to a state of infantile helpless dependency. Now, nothing I would say to him soothed his fears and overwhelmed feelings. Even the sound of my voice was painful to him. His dilemma, as I understood it at the time, was that he both needed my reassurance but could accept nothing from me. He accused me of having trapped him in an impossible situation; a treatment that he could neither leave nor continue. He would sit up to look at me, as if to reassure himself that I was still there, but turn away from me in anger when it became clear that I could not take away his upset feelings. The intensity of this "transference psychosis" (Little 1958) lasted for several months as the patient struggled with the terror of his intense feelings. It was during this time that the patient first requested, and then, when I attempted to explore his request, demanded that I allow him to sit up. Interpretations of his experience of being controlled by me, and the ambivalent longings for merger that gave rise to these feelings, seemed useless. In an angry rage at me Mr. Y. left his place on the couch and sat facing me. Gradually, following this dramatic action, his fears appeared to subside.

With the reduction of his anxiety, Mr. Y. once again resumed his monotonous and relatively affectless monologue about his daily life and work routines with which the pre-regressed phase of our work had begun. Attempts to engage Mr. Y. in an effort to understand his regressive and rageful reactions to me, in relation to his feeling understood by me, were met with polite acknowledgment but did not serve to generate any curiosity in him about the meanings that this regressive episode might have for him. In other words, his improvement seemed to be independent of anything I might have said to him, and seemed to be more a function of the sense of control he achieved from sitting up in the vis-à-vis position.

Regressive cycles such as this one recurred many times over the subsequent course of Mr. Y.'s treatment. Each intensification of transference feelings resulted in a regression to anxious and painful states of helpless neediness and rage at me for my inability to help him overcome his feelings. Interpretations of the transferential meanings of these regressed states were not helpful for him, nor did they facilitate efforts to self-reflect. For him, at such times, words were truly not enough to reverse the regressive movement. What did seem to be helpful was my continual availability, as well as my firm, but concerned confrontations of these self-destructive, masochistic regressions, which provided him with the support and organizing structure he seemed to need to sustain himself through these painful episodes. It also seemed to me that despite the fact that Mr. Y. gained little understanding of the meaning of these regressions, he did achieve a sense of ego strengthening from the fact of having survived them and the intense pain they caused him. Although such cycles recurred repeatedly, they were to become less dramatic throughout Mr. Y.'s treatment. While it was clear that much of the cycling was in response to projections and reintrojections of rage stimulated by his conflicted wish for merger with me, it was also clear that interpretive efforts to help him understand the origin of these painfully conflicted merger wishes would frequently have to be secondary to the preservation of this patient's fragile sense of reality.

For patients like Mr. Y., the failure to distinguish the real from the unreal aspects of the treatment relationship concretize the transference in such a total way that the capacity to reflect on transference experience is lost for much of the time. This concretization of transference experience precludes consistent analytic work, and transforms the treatment process into an ego supportive one in which transference enactments need to be carefully managed. For Mr. Y., resistance to the analytic process was enacted in the form of a severe regression to infantile dependency, and resulted in the rapid development of overwhelming feelings of helplessness, with intense longings for comfort and reassurance. Although the treatment relationship with me was sustained, it became, of necessity, a psychothera- peutically protective relationship that postponed the analytic understand- ing of Mr. Y.'s underlying wishes for merger indefinitely.

Thus, it was the weakness of the Mr. Y.'s ego itself, as distinguished from vulnerable self-esteem, such as was the case with Mrs. J., that inter- fered with his reflecting upon the transference experience. Because of the pervasive failure in distinguishing real from unreal experience, such patients require therapeutic supports from the analyst that go beyond the technically neutral stance of a psychoanalysis, and concessions with respect to the abstinence principle are necessary in order to sustain the treatment. While Mr. Y.'s overwhelming rage made it necessary for him to suffer the pain of severe regression, psychotherapeutic management of this regres- sion enabled him to remain in treatment. Although his capacity to self-reflect continues to be problematic, we both remain hopeful that he may someday overcome his frightening pull to regressive merger.

CONCLUDING REMARKS

While self-reflection has always been a prominent aspect and goal of psychoanalytic work, I believe its powerful impact on the establishment and ultimate shape of this work has not been sufficiently appreciated. Indeed, when coupled with its role in the acknowledgment and working through of transference experience, it becomes a major dynamism powering the analytic process itself. Considered in relation to the ego, it is similar to, but goes beyond, Sterba's (1934) conception of the patient's capacity to split the ego into an observing and experiencing portion, and it is closely related to Gray's (1994) conception of the patient's ability to assess unconscious content through the ego's capacity for close process analysis. From a developmental perspective, it is similar to Main's (1991) conception of metacognitive capacity, that is, the ability to "understand the merely representational nature of their own (and others') thinking" (p. 128), as well as Fonagy's (1996) reflective self, that is, "the clarity of the individual's representation of the mental states of others as well as the representation of their own mental state" (p. 74). From my own perspective, self-reflection on transference experience is most clearly identified with the effort to work through the repetition compulsion, and in this sense is necessarily involved in the resolution of the core of the patient's neurosis. As such, it is linked to Freud's (1937) deep appreciation for the fact that the neurosis could only be defeated in the presence of the transference object.

Gehrie (1993) attributes central importance to self-reflection in his conception of what he has called the "envelope of analytic experience."

The envelope of analytic experience is that space or range of subjective experience within which a state of analyzability is intact, and therefore, the patient is amenable to the expectable oscillation between experiencing and abstraction from the experience which functions as the fulcrum of the analytic process. It is the space in which an analysand is able effectively to maintain the distinction between transference experience and analytic reality, even at the height of the repetition compulsion. . . . Should this envelope of limits be exceeded . . . then the experience quotient of transference must be reduced in favor of understanding by means of interpretation, until the crucial distinction is once again manageable in the mind of the analysand. The overall aim is the crucial balance of experience that characterizes the existence of a state of analyzability. [p. 1101]

The envelope of analytic experience is, for Gehrie, an "enabling context" (p. 1100) that offers the analysand the optimal opportunity to develop the capacity to maintain analytic goals, even if not clearly present at the outset of a treatment. It is an environment in which the capacity to understand and reflect is organized, possibly for the first time.

While this capacity to achieve a balance between experience and abstraction varies over time in all patients, and indeed, may vary greatly in many, such a capacity is crucial to the patient's analyzability, since transference experience alone is not transformational. As Gherie indicates, all experience, including the corrective emotional kind, is processed through the filters of character and transference "regardless of the beneficence of a new object." "New experience must evolve," Gehrie says, "into an opportunity for further work, and not simply cognitive work, but emotional work which consists of reprocessing of transference organized subjective experience" (p. 1092).

The three patients I have described here illustrate specific types of analytic difficulty often encountered in our efforts to facilitate the kind of "reprocessing of transference organized subjective experience" which Gehrie considers essential for the achievement of analytic goals. Each patient defends him- or herself in distinctive ways against the anxiety generated by his/her unique transference experience. Dr. M., for example, whose character structure was rigidly integrated, defended against the anxiety of making his unconscious transference fantasy conscious by acting out. Thus, his rigid character structure and his acting out were synergistically organized for the purpose of maintaining repression. Self-reflection remained relatively sterile and affectless until his unconscious transference fantasy emerged directly in the treatment situation. But, in Mrs. J.'s case, where self-esteem issues predominated, anxiety seemed to be generated by the experience of the transference itself. Thus, the treatment press toward the emergence of transference feelings appeared to stimulate much shame and humiliation in her, since it raised her awareness of her own neediness. Her resistances and defenses were, therefore, mobilized to protect herself from the vulnerability she might have experienced in becoming aware of her own imperfectibility. Finally, in the case of Mr. Y., where ego integrity appeared to be the main issue, anxiety was generated by the wish/fear of his transferentially organized tendencies to merge with me. Defenses and resistances were mobilized to protect his vulnerable ego from the experience of dissolution, an experience made more difficult for him by the projection of his merger wishes, which were stimulated by my empathic understanding of his plight. Severe regression and rage at me for not being helpful were the result. Under such conditions self-reflection was not available to him as an ego resource, since his rage and regression to a state of infantile helplessness precluded it. Furthermore, since giving up his rage would have increased his sense of ego vulnerability, he was dynamically impelled to hold onto the very thing that destroyed his capacity to self-reflect. Thus, words and ideas were ineffective for dealing with Mr. Y.'s catastrophic regression, and the use of other technical modalities became necessary. In such cases, efforts to reprocess transference organized subjective experience are highly problematic.

Taken together, then, these three cases reveal a progression toward increasing vulnerability to disorganizing anxiety and a tendency toward increasing use of externalization as a major defense against it. Whereas Dr. M. was capable of using self-reflection to overcome his resistances to the reprocessing of transference experience, Mrs. J. was only relatively able to do so. Mr. Y. found this task to be beyond his capacities for much of his treatment experience. From this perspective, then, self-reflection, as a core aspect of the ego's functioning, is clearly dependent on the structural integrity of the patient's ego. As was shown here, it may become subject to destablization by either drive or superego pressures, which limit its availability for analytic work.

As a process serving the analytic goals that we strive for, self-reflection is dependent on our own emotional receptivity, technical expertise, and the creative tactfulness that we bring to the analytic situation in order to help patients with the difficult task of reprocessing transference organized subjective experience. To the extent, then, that patients entering analytic treatment come with ego impairments and compromised capacities for symbolization, objectification, boundary formation, and controlled regression, technique must be creatively adjusted, insofar as our own emotional capacities permit, in ways that take account of these impairments, so that difficulties with the engagement of self-reflection on transference experience may be overcome. When, however, despite our best efforts, such impairments cannot be overcome, then treatments other than psychoanalysis become the treatments of choice.

Finally, it is this capacity to bring transference experience under the ego's watchful, self-reflective eye that, for me, defines the central organizing process that is the analytic process. And, it is the balance between the emotionally charged experience of the transference and such self-reflective functioning that ensures that this analytic process is not simply a cognitive process but an emotionally charged one as well. This, after all, is what Freud (1914) was referring to when he said that "one cannot overcome an enemy who is absent or not within range" (p. 152).

REFERENCES

Brenner, C. (1995). Some remarks on psychoanalytic technique. *Journal of the American Psychoanalytic Association* 4:413–428.

Busch, F. (1995). *The Ego at the Center of Clinical Technique.* Northvale, NJ: Jason Aronson.

Coltrera, J. T. (1981). On the nature of interpretation: epistemology as practice. In *Clinical Psychoanalysis,* ed. S. Orgel and B. D. Fine, pp. 83–127. New York: Jason Aronson.

Couch, A. S. (1995). Anna Freud's adult psychoanalytic technique: a defense of classical analysis. *International Journal of Psycho-Analysis* 76:53–171.

Dunn, J. (1995). Intersubjectivity in psychoanalysis: a critical review. *International Journal of Psycho-Analysis.* 76:723–738.

Ferenczi, S., and Rank, O. (1925). *The Development of Psychoanalysis.* New York: Nervous and Mental Disease Publishing.

Fonagy, P. (1996). The significance of the development of metacognitive control over mental representations in parenting and infant development. *Journal of Clinical Psychoanalysis* 5:67–86.

Freud, A. (1952). The mutual influences in the development of the ego and the id. *Psychoanalytic Study of the Child* 7:42–50. New York: International Universities Press.

Freud, S. (1911). Papers on technique. *Standard Edition* 12:85–96.

——— (1912a). The dynamics of transference. *Standard Edition* 12:97–108.

——— (1912b). Recommendations to physicians practicing psycho-analysis. *Standard Edition* 12:109–120.

——— (1913). On beginning treatment. *Standard Edition* 12:121–144.

——— (1914). Remembering, repeating, and working through. *Standard Edition* 12:145–156.

——— (1915). Observations on transference love. *Standard Edition* 12:157–171.

——— (1937). Analysis terminable and interminable. *Standard Edition* 23:209–253.

Friedman, L. (1991). A reading of Freud's papers on technique. *Psychoanalytic Quarterly* 60:564–595.

Gehrie, M. (1993). Psychoanalytic technique and the development of the capacity to reflect. *Journal of the American Psychoanalytic Association* 41:1083–1111.

Gill, M. (1963). Topography and systems in psychoanalytic theory. *Psychological Issues* Monograph 10.

Gray, P. (1994). *The Ego and the Analysis of Defense.* Northvale, NJ: Jason Aronson.

Hoffman, I. Z. (1991). Discussion: towards a social constructivist's view of the psychoanalytic situation. *Psychoanalytic Dialogues* 1:74–105.

Little, M. I. (1958). On delusional transference (transference psychosis). *International Journal of Psycho-Analysis* 39:134–138.

Main, M. (1991). Metacognitive knowledge, metacognitive monitoring, and singular vs. multiple models of attachment: findings and directions for future research. In *Attachment Across the Life Cycle,* ed. P. Harris, J. Stevenson-Hinde, and C. Parkes, pp. 127–159. New York: Routledge.

Panel. (1983). Interpretation: toward a contemporary understanding of the term. *Journal of the American Psychoanalytic Association* 31:237–245.

Paniagua, C. (1995). Common ground, uncommon methods. *International Journal of Psycho-Analysis* 76:357–371.

Rangell, L. (1996). The "analytic" in psychoanalytic treatment: how analysis works. *Psychoanalytic Inquiry* 16(2):140–166.

Renik, O. (1993). Analytic interaction: conceptualizing technique in the light of the analyst's irreducible subjectivity. *Psychoanalytic Quarterly* 62:553–571.

Steingart, I. (1983). *Pathological Play in Borderline and Narcissistic Personalities.* New York: Spectrum.

Sterba, R. (1934). The fate of the ego in analytic therapy. *International Journal of Psycho-Analysis* 15:117–126.

Stolorow, R., Brandchaft, B., and Atwood, G. (1987). *Psychoanalytic Treatment. An Intersubjective Approach.* Hillsdale, NJ: Analytic Press.

Stone, L. (1954). The widening scope of indications for psychoanalysis. *Journal of the American Psychoanalytic Association* 2:567–594.

Wallerstein, R. S. (1988). One psychoanalysis or many? *International Journal of Psycho-Analysis* 69:5–21.

——— (1990). Psychoanalysis: the common ground. *International Journal of Psycho-Analysis* 71:3–20.

PART III

CHANGING PERSPECTIVES
ON THE THERAPEUTIC
RELATIONSHIP

Overview of Controversies

Jane Tucker

How do Freudians today understand transference, and how do contemporary ideas on the analyst–patient relationship in psychoanalysis fit into Freudian thought? Our conceptualizations of the therapeutic dyad and its role in technique have evolved considerably since Freud's encounter with Anna O's professed love for Breuer.

Freud at first saw transference as a disruption in the treatment, in that it interfered with free association and the recovery of memories. It was with his treatment of Dora (conducted in 1900, published in 1905) that he became aware of transference as an "inevitable necessity" (p. 116) that allows the patient the "conviction of the validity of the connections" (p. 117) made in an analysis. In a postscript to that paper he defined transference as new editions of the impulses that are aroused during the progress of the analysis but are seen not as belonging to the past but as applying to the physician. From that point on this fundamental clinical concept began to be recognized as a crucial component of analytic treatment. Freud subsequently added to the concept (1912, 1914, 1915), and by 1920 (with the publication of "Beyond the Pleasure Principle") transference had become a proven vehicle for exploring the vicissitudes of human passion.

Three types of transference were delineated by Freud (1912): erotic transference (the displacement of love from an object in the past), unobjectionable transference, and negative transference. Transference to the analyst was considered a form of erotic transference; the unobjectionable transference was seen as conscious and as a subtype of erotic transference.

In Freud's thinking there was always a certain tension between analyzing transference and attempting to recover memories. He could see that patients were obliged to repeat repressed material as a contemporary experience, but he seemed to wish that they could remember these experiences instead. (For a discussion of this point see Ellman 1991, passim.) As for countertransference, it was a topic he addressed only a few times (1910, 1915).

Many analysts since Freud (some during his lifetime) have defined transference more broadly than he did and have questioned whether the treatment relationship is primary as an agent of change in analysis or only a route to what is primary—the reconstruction of the past. And important issues have been raised about whether transference is influenced mainly by occurrences in the relationship or by the compulsion to repeat.

Several developments have contributed to generate such concerns, and to render them more than academic. Philosophical and cultural attitudes concerning status have brought scrutiny to analytic authority in its ability to evoke so dramatically the enduring power of the parental embrace, and thus to induce experiences of inequality. And recognition of the immensity of psychoanalytic intimacy has led to explorations of the effect of the process on both participants. But principally the questions about the nature and function of the treatment relationship have been derived from a confluence of two developments: research into infancy and childhood and the efforts to treat nonpsychotic but deeply troubled patients using the psychoanalytic method—the situation referred to, following Stone (1954), in the short-hand phrase "widening scope." The treatment of such individuals, who often feel in need of long episodes of communion—rather than communication—with the analyst, effected changes in our understanding of therapeutic action in the psychoanalytic situation; the work with them led to conceptual expansion and reformulations, including reevaluations of such technical positions as neutrality, abstinence, and anonymity.

The contributions of such theorists as Winnicott (1958, 1965) and Balint (1968) were fundamental in advancing an understanding of how the analyst's activity needs to be related to the developmental requirements of the patient. Those ideas were significantly extended by Loewald (1960), whose concept of the treatment as making possible the development of a new object relationship broadened considerably our knowledge about the role of the analyst. It was not that the analyst was to provide any extra-analytic corrective emotional experience, but rather that the analyst was recognized by Loewald as creating an environment that goes beyond technical skill in its ability to further the treatment. Loewald's idea of the new object relationship was that it served as a background relationship and was separate from the transference.

A significant addition to these ideas came from a 1984 paper in which Grunes introduced the concept of the therapeutic object relationship and sealed the place of this construct in psychoanalysis. The definition of this concept is "a situation of primal intimacy between patient and analyst which contains both an illusional (transference) and real aspect [and] . . . involving a special type of empathic permeability of boundaries between analyst and patient" (1984, p. 131); that definition will be quoted again in the chapters in this part of the book.

From Grunes's perspective, interpretation is a crucial agent for therapeutic change—without the differentiation provided through verbal interpretation the reorganization of experience wouldn't come about— but there is a relationship demand factor in treatment that cannot be met by interpretation alone; particularly with the more regressed patient, the therapeutic object relationship is a primary facilitator of change. The analyst in the therapeutic object relationship is objective but not neutral, according to Grunes; however he has not found that the forms of need satisfaction that are met symbolically in the therapeutic object relationship—needs for empathy and communication—interfere with "the therapeutic tension level needed for free association and fantasy formation" (1984, p. 139).

The concept of the therapeutic object relationship offered a clinical and theoretical unification between relationship and transference. "It should be clear," noted Grunes in mapping the operating principles of this configuration, "that in the kind of relationship I have been describing, analyst and patient are not pausing for a detour into a real relationship and then getting back to the serious business of analytic treatment. They are ipso facto in a special illusional and real relationship which is part of the very process of analysis itself" (1984, p. 136).

The following chapters, by Drs. Mark Grunes, Helen Gediman, and Irving Steingart, show how some contemporary Freudians understand transference and what they think about related issues of enactment, intersubjectivity, and the place of such technical positions as neutrality, abstinence, and anonymity in psychoanalytic treatment. They do not always agree.

In Chapter 6, Grunes expands his description of the therapeutic object relationship "as a crystallization of a contemporary Freudian perspective that has as its aim the integration of drives, self, ego, and object relations within the context of developmental psychoanalysis." He defines that form of psychoanalysis in contrast to the contemporary classical structural view and puts to rest some issues regarding abstinence, neutrality, and anonymity: "In this setting occasional personal, explicit self-disclosures do occur," he tells us, "and yet they are in a way incidental to the mostly tacit, intensely mutual self-disclosure that is also built into this analytic process."

Grunes describes an "emotional force field of primal intimacy" that provides a context within which the expansion of consciousness by means of the interpretation of unconscious experience can take place. He also describes how this contributes to the analyst's own psychic vitalization. He explains, too, how he has come to find the concept of the therapeutic object relationship applicable to all patients, not only to those with notable developmental deficits.

Gediman, in Chapter 7, points to the austerity of early characterizations of technique and catches in clinical vignettes the texture of how the "real" and the transferential are woven together and how a skillful contemporary analyst uses the real and the entrancing surface to work toward an understanding of past and present unconscious meanings. She explains that incidents are "hot" and "real" because they are alive in the transference, and she shows how real events impart a tone of authentic urgency to treatment. Gediman believes that certain interactions may facilitate the therapeutic enterprise. It is in the service of authenticity that she thinks analysts may legitimately be self-disclosing, as a means of advancing analysis of the transference. She emphasizes that for a contemporary Freudian the deciding factor is whether something is in the interest of the patient. And while she considers that psychoanalytic treatment is a joint venture, she reminds us of how and why Freudians attribute a greater degree of authority to the analyst than to the patient.

In Chapter 8, Steingart takes up the topics of intersubjectivity, the repetition compulsion, transference and countertransference, and some ideas about the psychic reality of the self. Although he believes that the personality of the analyst inevitably influences the treatment, Steingart, unlike Grunes and Gediman, does not grant the treatment relationship a mutative status in the production of knowledge, development, and change. For him the emphasis is on intrapsychic reality and the analysand's "conflict-derived, fantasy-informed repetition compulsion," with its whisper of a story constantly renewed. Intrapsychic reality may be shaped or enabled by intersubjectivity, but it is not created by this.

It is the analysis of repetition more than the working method of the analyst that Steingart credits for effecting growth. Transference is important in that it offers a window onto fantasy; the therapeutic relationship is emotionally arranged to enable the repetition compulsion to be experienced and subjected to analysis.

Steingart and Gediman are in apparent disagreement, too, about the ideas of Renik (1995) concerning the value of analyst–patient interactions; Steingart does not find convincing the notion that such actions advance interpretive understanding.

The controversy about the mutative effect of the treatment relationship has been an enduring one in psychoanalysis. Yet if it divides these writers, there are certainly other ideas they hold in common. All agree on the force of the repetition compulsion and on the necessity for interpretation; all agree that what might seem to be extra-analytic realities cannot be so regarded, that rather it is the relationship of these events to the unconscious that makes them powerful; all agree that transference and countertransference are not—or should not be—equal in their occurrence, and that the analyst–patient relationship is a nonsymmetrical one, in which it is the prerogative of the analysand to be the object of the endeavor.

Those are some of the positions that mark a contemporary Freudian perspective, and in the course of setting them out, the three chapters show much about what it is that makes being a psychoanalyst such an interesting and satisfying—if often unsettling—occupation.

REFERENCES

Balint, M. (1968). *The Basic Fault: Therapeutic Aspects of Regression.* New York: Brunner/Mazel.

Ellman, S. J. (1991). *Freud's Technique Papers: A Contemporary Perspective.* Northvale, NJ: Jason Aronson.

Freud, S. (1905). Fragment of an analysis of a case of hysteria. *Standard Edition* 7:7–122.

——— (1910). Future prospects of psycho-analytic therapy. *Standard Edition* 11:141–151.

——— (1912). The dynamics of transference. *Standard Edition* 12:97–120.

——— (1914). Remembering, repeating, and working through (further recommendations on the technique of psycho-analysis II). *Standard Edition* 12:145–156.

——— (1915). Observations on transference love (further recommendations on the technique of psycho-analysis III). *Standard Edition* 12:159–170.

——— (1920). Beyond the pleasure principle. *Standard Edition* 18:7–64.

Grunes, M. (1984). The therapeutic object relationship. *Psychoanalytic Review* 71:123–143.

Loewald, H. (1960). On the therapeutic action of psychoanalysis. *International Journal of Psycho-Analysis* 41:16–33.

Renik, O. (1995). The ideal of the anonymous analyst and the problem of self-disclosure. *Psychoanalytic Quarterly* 54:466–495.

Stone, L. (1954). The widening scope of indications for psychoanalysis. *Journal of the American Psychoanalytic Association* 2:567–594.

Winnicott, D. W. (1958). *Collected Papers: Through Paediatrics to Psycho-analysis.* New York: Basic Books.

——— (1965). *The Maturational Processes and the Facilitating Environment.* New York: International Universities Press.

6

The Therapeutic Object
Relationship—II

Mark Grunes

Some years ago I published a paper entitled "The Therapeutic Object Relationship" (Grunes 1984). At that time I advanced the idea that "within the category of more regressive pathology the patient's structural impairment, and depleted and archaic object relations, create a relationship demand factor in treatment which cannot be met by interpretation alone" (p. 123).

It seems useful at this point to retrospectively review the therapeutic object relationship. Its major feature was viewed as a mutually interpenetrative emotional force field of empathic permeability and primal intimacy between analyst and patient. This force field does not develop spontaneously. It comes about mainly for two reasons. The first is the analyst's comprehensive interpretive skill at all levels of ego and instinctual development, particularly those that are more archaic and involve the various and conflictual dual unities and emotional unifications with a maternal presence. The second factor in the development of the force field of empathic permeability is the analyst's emotional and therapeutic position of deep interest, devotion, love, and respect for the patient's individuation first systematically described by Loewald (1960). It is this analytic position and its interpretive implementation that leads Jonathan Lear (1990) to describe the analytic process as a special form of love. Steingart (1995) has also recently described the evolution of real love between analyst and patient, in their mutual love of truth and reality, as a major force in the analytic process.

Within the force field of analytic intimacy the growth forces of the patient's adult ego as well as certain early developmental imperatives become operative. The progressive force field of primal intimacy also occurs in part because of the patient's intense and real, as well as illusional transferential, attachment to the analyst as a new developmental object. The intense love and hate generated in the trials of a resumption of self and ego development become a major driving force of the analysis as the patient reaches progressively higher levels of emotional unification with and separateness from the analyst. The expansion of the patient's consciousness with the exposure of unconscious experience occurs by means of the differentials of verbal interpretation. The emotional force field and interpretation, adjusted to the patient's ego tolerance, cannot exist without one another. In fact they reciprocally define one another. Finally, in a similar sense of reciprocal definition, the therapeutic object relationship is constituted by the analytic process itself. It is not a more real or more human time-out or supportive detour from the analysis itself.

In this chapter I utilize the concept of the therapeutic object relationship as a crystallization of one contemporary Freudian perspective that has as its aim the integration of drives, self, ego, and object relations within the context of what I call developmental psychoanalysis. After discussing some further aspects of the therapeutic object relationship I will focus on some contrasts in the developmental outlooks of Freud and Winnicott that are pertinent to the therapeutic object relationship and to the correlate matter of the integration of intrapsychic and interpsychic perspectives. I will conclude with a contrast between a developmental psychoanalysis and the branch of contemporary Freudian practice that can be called contemporary classical structural theory of technique and therapeutic action.

In my original paper (Grunes 1984) I emphasized the special pertinence of the therapeutic object relationship for the more regressed patient. Since that time I have come to believe that the concept of the therapeutic object relationship is quite applicable to the analytic treatment of all patients, although its operation becomes more explicit in the treatment of the more disturbed patient. The change in my point of view came about largely because my clinical experience and that of others brought into question the idea of the good neurotic patient. I do not mean that levels of more and less serious psychopathology have disappeared. But more and more it does seem that all neurotic patients over the whole course of treatment, or in certain phases, evidence such features as condensations of oedipal and preoedipal dynamic and structural conflict, narcissistic ego vulnerabilities, significant pregenital fixation, primitive anxieties and defenses, and some degree of early, cumulative environmental trauma.

In a major sense the nature of the treatment relationship is a function of the analyst's capacity to vary his choice of interpretive level with the patient's ego tolerances, from more classical resistance analysis, to empathic subjectivity, to interpretive skill and knowledgeability in areas of early ego pathology. The analyst's choice of the developmental level of the content of interpretation is a substantial part of the reality of his therapeutic relationship with the patient. It is a real factor in how well understood, cared and provided for, guided, supported, and respected the patient will feel. The analyst needs to be able to vary the developmental content level of interpretation from early dependence and maternal dual unity, to the fiercely willful, anally influenced, separational thrusts of the rapprochement period, to the parricidal separations from authority and incandescent erotic attachments of the oedipal period. The treatment relationship is also a function of the analyst's psychic arrangement of himself in relation to the patient's ego tolerances, whether he or she can be a self object, a container, a holding environment, or a separate otherness. To put these matters in another form, the interpretive stance may vary from no interpretation at all, to empathic location inside the boundaries of the patient's perspective, to transitional emotional positions in which the analyst is partly inside the patient's subjective perspective and partly outside as separate object and objective observer, to a more fully defined otherness who is available for the rageful collisions that can be enacted at such times, but are developmentally needed by the patient.

My position has been that it is better for the treatment relationship to become as consciously systematic for the analyst as is possible within the limits of the preservation of spontaneity. When the real treatment relationship is a conscious and accepted part of treatment, it is much more likely to be integral to the analytic process itself. It then becomes unnecessary to graft a relationship factor onto the treatment such as a therapeutic alliance, a real relationship, or a human relationship. (When did the analytic process become *non*-human?) With grafted-on treatment relationships the analysis of pathological transference becomes oppressive and requires some other relationship or parameter as a respite from the analysis proper. I described certain central aspects of this problem in psychoanalytic technique in my earlier paper (Grunes 1984):

> The matter I am describing here is at issue in several papers by Greenson (1965, 1969, 1971, 1972). The way in which Greenson dichotomizes the real from the transference relationship results in the assignment of the deepest intensities of analyst–patient interaction to the pathological transference. The reality of the relationship, on the other hand, is consigned to a kind of upper-level, rational and conscious friendly helpfulness. The result, I believe, is that the transference analysis becomes overburdened by the patient's sense of an endless reductionism to the past and to pathology. I believe that Greenson's dichotomy makes the analytic work oppressive. The patient comes to feel that his nonrational intensities are pathological errors, and he is left with a sense of dubious adaptation to a pallid version of reality—the isolated instances of friendly and rational "realness" in the treatment. [p. 138]

The affective core of the therapeutic object relationship is the primal intimacy of the empathically permeable, emotional force field between patient and analyst. This primal intimacy, with its nonerotic libidinal bond, carries the entire analysis. It is graphically pictured by Loewald (1970):

> In contrast to physics or biology, for instance, psychoanalytic knowledge and explanation depend not so much on the difference between the processes obtaining in the scientist and those obtaining in his subject, but on their similarity and inter-relatedness. It is a commonplace that introspection and empathy are essential tools of psychoanalysis and that we can analyze others only so far as we have been analyzed ourselves, and understand ourselves. To this there is the corollary: we understand ourselves psychoanalytically by seeing our-

selves as others (objectivating introspection), and our self-understanding is greatly enhanced by analyzing others. . . . This is not only because in the external other we can see ourselves more clearly, but also because in this concentrated, in this specially focused and heightened field of forces, the analyst's intrapsychic field gains in vitality and vivid outline. The analysand in this respect can be compared to the child who—if he can allow himself that freedom—scrutinizes with his unconscious antennae the parent's motivations and moods and in this way may contribute—if the parent or analyst allows himself that freedom—to the latter's self awareness. Internal communication, on which self-understanding is based, and communication with another organization of the same rank of reality—the psychic reality of another individual—are inextricably interwoven. [pp. 47–48]

In my earlier paper I had not quite grasped, at a deeper level, the powerful gratification for the analyst, captured so well in Loewald's sentence: "In this concentrated, in this specially focused and heightened field of forces, the analyst's intrapsychic field gains in vitality and vivid outline." It is this mutual process in its contribution to the analyst's psychic vitalization and growth that enables him to love his work and gradually his patient who makes such work possible. It is the process of emotional interpenetration in addition to transference that also moves the patient to love the analyst and the treatment process itself, and that brings such concentrated vitality to his or her life.

A patient once said to me, "When I hear you start to talk, to grope around in yourself, putting the idea together, it's enormously exciting. I mean I feel alive. I feel I could run around the room." It was much later that I realized the patient was experiencing me groping around in the him that was also inside of me, and most likely was himself groping around in the me that was also inside of him.

The interpsychic force field between patient and analyst goes a long way to putting to rest, I believe, a number of perennial, thorny issues within the theory of technique. Mainly these issues are equality between patient and analyst, abstinence and gratification for both analyst and patient, the analyst's emotional neutrality and emotional participation, and anonymity of and self disclosure by the analyst.

The analyst's participation in the force field is emotional, by necessity.

This does not mean that it is impulsive, undisciplined, reckless, or intemperate.

If analyst and patient can allow themselves to be available to each other, they gain vivid emotional knowledge of each other. In this setting occasional personal, explicit self-disclosures do occur, and yet they are in a way incidental to the mostly tacit, intensely mutual self-disclosure that is also built in to this type of analytic process.

Freudian clinical theory constitutes the history and foundation of the concept of the therapeutic object relationship. I have already mentioned two contemporary Freudian viewpoints, which I have called contemporary classical structural theory and developmental psychoanalysis. The first follows a line of development from Freud's early ego concept identified mainly with defense, consciousness, reality relations, and the external world. The line then proceeds to the classical ego psychology of Heinz Hartmann (1939, 1964) and David Rapaport (1967).

Classical ego psychology viewed the ego as an impersonal apparatus, primarily involved in adaptation to external reality, powered by nonlibidinal neutralized and sublimated energy and autonomous from the drives. Contemporary classical structural theory of therapeutic action and technique is descended from classical ego psychology, but varies in its degree of incorporation of object relations and developmental views.

The second line of development proceeds from Freud's use of the term *ego* as self rather than structure, his awareness of the role of object relations in ego formation ("the shadow of the object has fallen upon the ego" [1917, p. 249]), and in his attribution of libido to the ego in his concept of eros. It is here that Freud seemed to be saying that a theory of love could not be derived from a theory of sex, although there could not be a theory of love without a theory of sex. This line of development then moves to American developmental ego psychology between 1940 and 1975 and is identified with Margaret Mahler (1968, Mahler et al. 1975), Edith Jacobson (1964, 1971), and Phyllis Greenacre (1971). All three developed psychologies of the self and of object relations, and were concerned with infant and early childhood development and the maternal environment. Later developments in this evolution expanded emphases on the self and object relations while retaining and modifying the centrality of instinctual drives and intrapsychic conflict. Winnicott (1965a,b, 1975), Loewald (1980), Balint (1965, 1968), and McDougall (1980), among others, represent this direction, which I am calling developmental psychoanalysis.

Contemporary classical structural theory emphasizes primary narcissism, opposition between the claims of reality and the instinctually driven wishes of childhood, the frustration and renunciative requirements of reality, distinction between primary and secondary process, and the role of ego delay, regulation, and control in the process of adaptation.

The second view, which I am calling developmental psychoanalysis, attempts integrations of drive relations and object relations, preoedipal and oedipal relations, and self and ego concepts. It emphasizes primary object relationship as well as primary narcissism, and the good-enough environmental mother as external reality, not principally in opposition to the child's wishfulness. A developmental psychoanalysis also emphasizes transitional unification between primary and secondary process, and the evolving role of pleasurable, transitional unifications between self and external reality in the process of adaptation.

These transitional perspectives serve to introduce certain contrasts between Freud's early ego and drive psychology and Winnicott's views on individual development.[1]

Winnicott (1960) begins with the assumption of a primary unity between the baby and the external world, not with primary narcissism in primary antagonism to the external world and reality. The good-enough early dual unity and the good-enough disillusionment of the illusion of oneness, which is what weaning is really all about, will determine whether the baby's or the young child's reality is a friendly one or a hateful one. The child may deal adaptively with premature and insensitive resolutions between inside and outside, between self and other, but the adaptation will be obsessional and mechanical, reality will not feel enjoyable, and it will never feel as if it had been created by the child itself. (Clearly all of these matters, however complex, have great pertinence to a treatment relationship.)

Winnicott provides us with insight into how the love of reality and otherness comes about. Freud speaks of the hard and painful necessity to accept and adapt to reality. Developmental truth is some combination of both views. But the second without the first can defeat the child's and the patient's wish to reach out to external reality. Freud's reality is the strict father; Winnicott's is the breast that is there when it is needed. The

---

1. I am indebted to the late Susan Deri for clarification of these contrasts between the work of Freud and Winnicott.

Freudian mother is the object of instinctual hunger; Winnicott's is the holding environmental mother. Freud and Winnicott had different views of the possibility and desirability of combinations of opposites, particularly aspects of external and internal reality. Freud focused on the most effective methods of distinguishing between the two; Winnicott took great pleasure in discovering harmonies between the two. These harmonies were the basis of Winnicott's transitional space in which inside and outside, imagination and reality, the "me" and the "not-me" can be separate and yet inter-penetrated. This is what Winnicott meant by transitional space. This is a space of ego-relatedness between self and other, a libidinal place that need not be instinctually excited, and it is the location of tenderness and affection that need not be derived from sublimated instinct or neutralized energy. This is the libidinized interpenetrative self-other space, which, in my view, sustains the analytic process.

What I have called contemporary developmental psychoanalysis dif-fers from contemporary classical structural theory of therapeutic action and technique. I will use the therapeutic object relationship as a focus for this comparison.

Boesky (1988), Brenner (1985), and Gray (1973, 1982) are good representatives of the contemporary classical structural view. They empha-size oedipal level conflict resolution and exclude any technique of struc-tural change from the analytic process. In Boesky's words, "The building of psychic structure is better left to nature" (p. 310). All three writers attempt to exclude internalization of the analyst as part of the treatment process. They consider the reality of the therapeutic relationship between analyst and patient to be an undesirable, suggestive influence that derives its therapeutic results from the hypnotic action associated with technique in the early history of psychoanalysis. All three attempt to reduce as much as possible the analyst's function as empathic, participant observer. Blum (1986) cites Brenner as stating, "eighty years of psychoanalytic data gathering from free association have repeatedly demonstrated that empa-thy is regularly subject to falsification, self deception and disguise" (p. 315). All three emphasize the analyst's role as an external, objective, natural science observer. The opposition between the analyst's objective view and the patient's subjectivity constitute the basic unit of treatment—analysis of resistance against the emergence into consciousness of id derivatives.

The developmental model of therapeutic action goes as far back as Freud, who considered the patient's positive transference to be the driving force of the analysis. Freud used transference here in the sense of an attachment to the person of the analyst rather than in the sense of transference distortion. In a 1906 letter to Jung, Freud wrote, "I have kept to myself some things . . . or presented them in such a way that only the initiate recognizes . . . analysis is actually a cure through love" (1974, pp. 12–13). Some comments of Freud's in a 1910 letter to Ferenczi also seem to reflect his belief that a libidinal treatment relationship is a part of the process of analysis. Writing of the patient's exposure of transference love and the need to be loved, Freud writes, "He [the patient] has shed a skin and leaves it for the analyst. God forbid that he should now be naked without a skin" (Jones 1955, p. 447). It is only in the context of an emotionally intense force field between patient and analyst that Freud assumed the adversarial relationship of resistance analysis could be sustained.

In England the developmental approach was articulated by Winnicott (1965a) and Balint (1968)—Winnicott, in his concepts of maternal failure, analytic regression to dependence, and the analyst's symbolic provision in a holding environment; Balint, in his concepts of benign regression, the new beginning, and an analytically appropriate manner of meeting certain, nondefensive, affiliative, and separational object needs exposed by the regression.

In this country the focus on the separation-individuation paradigm in the analytic treatment relationship of adults by Mahler (1968) and her associates; the primal transference and physicianly care and concern of Stone (1961); the basic transference of Greenacre (1971); Edith Jacobson's (1971) awareness of the importance of the analyst as a real libidinal object, especially in depression, and perhaps most specifically as I have already indicated; Loewald's (1960) conception of the analyst as a new object in the resumption of ego development—all contributed to a developmental paradigm in a context of interpretation and insight.

Paul Gray's (1982) version of the contemporary, classical structural paradigm of therapeutic process is a good representation of the general model and contains many contrasts to the developmental paradigm. He describes the therapeutic action of psychoanalysis as a learning process, a cognitive process in which the major ingredient of therapeutic action is the patient's mental comprehension of the analyst's observations of his ego and id. Gray describes the analyst's role and basic emotional position, and the most desirable ultimate perception of it by the patient, as one of "kindly, scientific neutrality." "The analyst," he says, "must invite the analysand to use his observing ego to share the analyst's perception of the data." Gray views developmental paradigms such as the one I have defined as providing "parental roles which share a reliance on interpersonal influence" (p. 645). There is no reason to believe that Gray's treatment relationship of "kindly, scientific neutrality" is any less parental than the developmental paradigm. It may simply constitute a different kind of parent.

The absence within the contemporary classical model—at least of the particular variety I am describing—of variation of interpretive level and stance, as well as the absence of the deeper libidinal collaboration of a therapeutic object relationship, it seems to me, especially at times of ego weakness, deeper regression, and defused aggression, leave the patient too vulnerable to a sense of threatening isolation and self disorganization. At these times adherence to the contemporary classical model often compels recourse to psychotherapeutic parameters, or causes iatrogenic psychic pain and severe resistance.

In conclusion, I have presented a contemporary Freudian psychoanalytic perspective, which I have called developmental psychoanalysis. I have used the concept of the therapeutic object relationship as a crystallization of central aspects of technique and therapeutic action in such a developmental psychoanalysis, which I have contrasted with contemporary classical theory of technique and therapeutic action.

REFERENCES

Balint, M. (1965). *Primary Love and Psychoanalytic Technique*, revised ed. London: Tavistock.
——— (1968). *The Basic Fault: Therapeutic Aspects of Regression*. London: Tavistock.
Blum, H. (1986). Countertransference and the theory of technique: discussion. *Journal of the American Psychoanalytic Association* 34:309–328.
Boesky, D. (1988). Comments on the structural theory of technique. *International Journal of Psycho-Analysis* 69:303–316.
Brenner, C. (1985). Countertransference as compromise formation. *Psychoanalytic Quarterly* 54:155–163.
Freud, S. (1917). Mourning and melancholia. *Standard Edition* 14:239–258.
——— (1974). *The Freud/Jung Letters*, ed. W. McGuire, trans. R. Mannheim and R. F. C. Hull. Bollingen Series 94. Princeton, NJ: Princeton University Press.

Gray, P. (1973). Psychoanalytic technique and the ego's capacity for viewing intrapsychic conflict. *Journal of the American Psychoanalytic Association* 21:474–494.

——— (1982). "Developmental lag" in the evolution of technique for psychoanalysis of neurotic conflict. *Journal of the American Psychoanalytic Association* 30:621–656.

Greenacre, P. (1971). *Emotional Growth: Psychoanalytic Studies of the Gifted and a Great Variety of Other Individuals*, vols. I and II. New York: International Universities Press.

Greenson, R. R. (1965). The working alliance and the transference neurosis. *Psychoanalytic Quarterly* 34:155–181.

——— (1969). The nontransference relationship in the psychoanalytic situation. *International Journal of Psycho-Analysis* 50:27–39.

——— (1971). The real relationship between the patient and the psychoanalyst. In *Explorations in Psychoanalysis*, pp. 425–440. New York: International Universities Press.

——— (1972). Beyond transference and interpretation. *International Journal of Psycho-Analysis* 53:213–217.

Grunes, M. (1984). The therapeutic object relationship. *Psychoanalytic Review* 71:123–143.

Hartmann, H. (1939). *Ego Psychology and the Problem of Adaptation*. New York: International Universities Press, 1958.

——— (1964). *Essays on Ego Psychology*. New York: International Universities Press.

Jacobson, E. (1964). *The Self and the Object World*. New York: International Universities Press.

——— (1971). *Depression: Comparative Studies of Normal, Neurotic, and Psychotic Conditions*. New York: International Universities Press.

Jones, E. (1955). *The Life and Work of Sigmund Freud*, vol. 2. London: Hogarth.

Lear, J. (1990). *Love and Its Place in Nature: A Philosophical Interpretation of Freudian Psychoanalysis*. New York: Farrar, Straus, & Giroux.

Loewald, H. (1960). On the therapeutic action of psycho-analysis. *International Journal of Psycho-Analysis* 41:16–33.

——— (1970). Psychoanalytic theory and the psychoanalytic process. *Psychoanalytic Study of The Child* 25:45–68. New York: International Universities Press.

——— (1980). *Papers on Psychoanalysis*. New Haven, CT and London: Yale University Press.

Mahler, M. S. (1969). *On Human Symbiosis and the Vicissitudes of Individuation*. New York: International Universities Press.

Mahler, M. S., Pine, F., and Bergman, A. (1975). *The Psychological Birth of the Human Infant*. New York: Basic Books.

McDougall, J. (1980). *Plea for a Measure of Abnormality*. New York: International Universities Press.

Rapaport, D. (1967). *The Collected Papers of David Rapaport*, ed. M. M. Gill. New York: Basic Books.

Steingart, I. (1995). *A Thing Apart: Love and Reality in the Therapeutic Partnership.* Northvale, NJ: Jason Aronson.

Stone, L. (1961). *The Psychoanalytic Situation.* New York: International Universities Press.

Winnicott, D. W. (1960). The theory of the parent–infant relationship. In *The Maturational Processes and the Facilitating Environment.* New York: International Universities Press, 1965.

——— (1965a). *The Maturational Processes and the Facilitating Environment.* New York: International Universities Press.

——— (1965b). *Playing and Reality.* London: Tavistock; New York: Basic Books.

——— (1975). *Through Paediatrics to Psycho-analysis.* London: Hogarth; New York: Basic Books.

The Therapeutic Action in the Real, Transferential, and Therapeutic Object Relationship

Helen K. Gediman

There is a basic assumption that the dichotomy of transference and real is arbitrary, false, misleading, and fundamentally out of synch with Freudian psychoanalysis today. That false dichotomy assumes that the therapeutic action of psychoanalytic treatment is based solely on the technique of interpretation of intrapsychic conflict. However, our present understanding of the therapeutic action of psychoanalysis has evolved significantly into a more broadly based, multiperspectival approach to the psychoanalytic treatment of a widening scope of patients.

I once had occasion to consult with a woman whose analysis was stalemated. The analyst, apparently concerned with the degree of his patient's pathology, had decided it was important to be very "real." The patient feared she was not being analyzed. Being real meant to him doing something extra-analytic or nonanalytic. He revealed such personal information as the kind of car he drove, the names of his children, and his favorite restaurants and vacation spots. I suggested to the patient that her analyst's self-disclosures seemed to have made her worry that her analyst thought she was a fragile patient and that she needed a real relationship with him because he believed she could not withstand the rigors of analytic work. By rigors, I had in mind the three cardinal hallmarks: neutrality, abstinence, and anonymity. I later had occasion to speak with the analyst who agreed that this was indeed his rationale. Was the analyst's choice of the contents of his self-disclosure, which by definition always involves some modification of the principle of anonymity as we once understood it, a travesty of what is meant as a "real relationship"? I think so. That slippage in an understanding of the real relationship was not unique to him and led me to organize this chapter around a central question: How do we maintain the analytic attitude with its usual safeguards of neutrality, abstinence, and anonymity, and also honor the modifications that have evolved with those steady refinements and progression of our understanding of the way the mind works and in our analytic technique that characterize Freudian psychoanalysis today?

When we speak of the real relationship and the therapeutic action from the point of view of contemporary Freudian psychoanalysis, obviously we are not advocating telling the patient what kind of car we drive, where we take our vacations, whether or not we are married, or how many children we have. The value of the concept of the real relationship does not center on feeding a patient herring, as Freud (1909) did to the "Rat Man." It is not typified by letting a patient use the telephone in an emergency. It is not limited to such emergency actions as that of an analyst lending a patient money to get her car out of a parking garage on the day the patient was mugged. These are all real occurrences; however, they are extra-analytic. Events such as these have the potential for real repercussions on how the analysis will progress, because they are responded to by the analysand as meaningful events that stimulate conscious and unconscious fantasies, conflicts, and other psychic events, including real emotionally charged interaction patterns with the analyst that are often highly analyzable. When we speak of the real relationship, what we all, I expect, are limiting ourselves to is a real relationship that is part and parcel of and often indistinguishable from the therapeutic relationship, that impacts significantly on the transference, and that is a crucial part of the therapeutic action of psychoanalysis. Loewald (1960) and then Grunes (1984) pioneered the evolving historical context from which this basic position derives. To highlight the essence of the position, I shall present some clinical material and then discuss four main technical areas that touch on new ways of looking at neutrality, abstinence, and anonymity. These are the areas of technique, self-disclosures by the analyst, intersubjectivity, and interaction.

PROCESS FROM SELECTED SESSIONS

I have chosen two different series of sessions with one analysand, Ms. D., occurring over the course of several weeks, to illustrate how a "real" event, not intrinsic to the analytic process, led to repercussions and to other "real" events that subsequently became intrinsic to the process. These latter events involved interactions that centered on the transference-countertransference, became part and parcel of the therapeutic relationship, and contributed significantly to the quality of the object relationship with my patient and to the therapeutic action of the analysis that I was conducting. These accounts of process are consistent with the major point made by Grunes (1984): "Analyst and patient are not pausing for a detour into a real relationship and then getting back to the serious business of analytic treatment. They are ipso facto in a special illusional and real relationship which is part of the very process of analysis itself" (p. 136).

First Series of Sessions

In the vignettes to follow, there was indeed a "real" component to the interaction, that is, real in the sense that it wasn't what usually happens, and was determined by extra-analytic conditions—the weather and my buzzer system. Just to mention these factors renders them minute and pedestrian, hardly approaching the real factors in the relationship that have seemed to others to be so significant. However, these events had repercussions leading to interactions within the analysis that were far more important and touched directly on the therapeutic action with this patient.

Shortly after Ms. D.'s return from a ten-day vacation, a real incident served to highlight the real and how it may be employed therapeutically. It also highlighted how the therapeutic has very real aspects. There is something intrinsic to the therapeutic process that is very real and alive and it is this very realness in the therapeutic interaction that is indispensable to the therapeutic action of psychoanalysis. Loewald (1960) and

Grunes (1984) thought that in what constitutes the therapeutic action, the analyst does very little that is real outside of what the analyst normally does in conducting an analysis. Both distinguished their positions, as I would distinguish mine, from those who employ an extra-analytic corrective emotional experience as a new real experience in an effort to effect new change. The idea of a real relationship that transcends the therapeutic is not a useful way of looking at therapeutic action. My view is also in line with Strachey's (1934) ideas on the therapeutic action and the mutative interpretation: the interpretations that produce real change are those that are directed to something that is "hot" and "real" in the ongoing transference. The two incidents I am about to review qualify as real and alive not simply because they were spurred on by extra-analytic realities, but because they were affectively hot in the transference. The first was the patient's phone call to me at my home, not my office, on the evening before her first scheduled postvacation appointment in which she said she would be unable to make the appointment because a blizzard forced her plane to land in another city. She called me at home again the next evening, still delayed in the distant city, to tell me she would call as soon as she got back to schedule an extra appointment if I had the time.

The first session after the vacation was a regularly scheduled working session when the "real" did not enter in. I am using the word *real* in quotation marks to illustrate, once again, how I think the distinction between real and therapeutic is arbitrary, misleading, and confusing. The second meeting after her vacation was a double session (easy to do on a snowbound day) and the first of two specially scheduled make-up sessions. That double session had ended with her saying "I'll see you tomorrow morning" (a regularly scheduled session) and I said, "Yes, at 9:00, I'm sorry, 8:15," to which she responded, "Tomorrow's is at 8:15, Friday's extra one is at 9:00." I had arrived at my office for the third session after the vacation break, the second specially scheduled makeup session, just before 7:45. At 8:15 I had not yet heard the buzz on the handset of my intercom system. In that sense, the session was characterized by a "real" incident. Ms. D. was almost never late and usually considerably early, so I was concerned that the snow conditions were making navigating through the city quite difficult. Yet this patient certainly would have left plenty of extra time. At 8:33 the buzzer on the handset rang, she announced herself, and I buzzed her in. She stormed into the room, looking at me wrathfully and said, "Where were you when I buzzed at 7:50? And I buzzed you again at 8:10."

I told her that I was right here in my chair. "You couldn't have come in the building or I would have seen you. I was on the sofa in the lobby the whole time." She was clearly confused, but I was not. I had noticed from time to time that my buzzer did not always ring loudly. Sometimes I only heard a barely audible "ping," and I was meaning to have the system checked out. I felt bad that I had been postponing that chore, and told her that sometimes it was hard to hear the buzzer, and I had noticed that that was particularly true if the button outside the door was pressed too lightly and didn't make the proper connection. Undaunted, and undoubtedly defensive, I then suggested to her that if she ever buzzes and does not get an answer, she should press the bell on the door that is not connected to the buzzer system. I make this suggestion to all patients, because sometimes, when they come early and ring, I am not in my consulting room but somewhere else in the suite—the kitchen, the bathroom, or my partner's consulting room. She reminded me later that I had suggested that to her, too. I apologized to her for the inconvenience.

During this session, less than twenty minutes in length, the patient at first did not know what to do. "Is this a session or not?" She then got off the couch and stomped toward the door as though to leave and I said, "Sit down, please." Her anger, clearly directed at me, soon turned back around upon herself. "I'm so stupid. I should have pushed the doorbell harder." Then, "As I was sitting out in your lobby, I had the thought that something must have happened to you, but today is my birthday and I felt abandoned. I felt that way, even though I know it was absurd. And now that the situation is clear, I still am so furious. It doesn't make any sense but that's how I feel." I made use of this material in the usual way, interpreting how old feelings can surface in these conditions even though rationally they do not appear justified. It is important to note that I claimed full responsibility for the buzzer problem. The system was not perfect. She contrasted her reaction to that of being stranded in the faraway city for three days, saying that she was calm and untroubled by that act of fate, knowing it was not anyone's fault and nothing bad would come of the delay. I pointed out how it was important for her to blame someone, and even though I claimed responsibility, she had to maintain that it was her fault. I was aware that I had not yet touched on her longing to be with me while she was on vacation, when she returned, and now, waiting for me. The closest I could get was to refer to the possibility that she may have had the idea that I had not been thinking of her at just the time when she was most eager to see me, and so she then turned her longing into fury, and then the fury at me was turned around into anger at herself for making a mistake, for not being perfect. "That's how it always was. When my mother turned away from me, I had to find out what I was doing wrong to get her back. I actually thought you got the time mixed up, that you thought today was at nine and tomorrow at 8:15." I said: "And then you had to be the little girl taking charge of things, knowing more and better than the mother who makes mistakes." In this and other ways, the aborted session turned something in the extra-analytic "real" relationship to something analytically real in the transference and in the therapeutic interaction. In a calculated violation of the rule of abstinence, I offered to extend the next session to make up for the time we had missed today—another "real" action on my part with implications for the real therapeutic object relationship.

During the next of this series of sessions, she told of a string of mishaps—events at her office that she was not there to take charge of as she usually would; more plane delays, and so on. She told me the reason she did not call my office, but called me instead at home the night she knew she was stranded was because she did not know if I checked my office answering machine from home, and did not even know if one could do so. I told her it was clear that she wanted to make contact with me, but feared that I might not care enough to check on her whereabouts by calling my machine. She was focusing instead on her failing to be as conscientious as she felt she should be, mainly because she believed and presumably wished, unconsciously, that she had intruded on me. She was also afraid of intruding on my patients if she had called the office. I noted how she always got angry when there were telephone-ringing intrusions on her sessions. So there were the more obvious themes of reproaching herself and me, which really seemed to be covering up her desire to make contact after a frustrating and lonely separation.

As for the real, the therapeutic, and the transference relationship, real analytic events were set off by her analytically meaningful call to me at my home. There was also the extra-analytically real issue of my door buzzer. Either there was a mechanical failure, and/or she did not press hard enough. She got a real, nonanonymous response from me about my concern about my patients, for I assured her I checked my machine for messages regularly on weekends. This was said for the purpose of calling her attention to how untrustful she was of anyone except herself to take care of her properly. I had also offered her extra time, which she accepted.

I had scheduled an extra appointment, and apologized for the buzzer problem.

I told a little anecdote to her, of how her response to coming home reminded me of how little children when separated from their mothers due to trips or illness, long to be with mother and eagerly await the reunion. But as soon as they are reunited, instead of being happy they turn angry and reproach mother. I told her that that was what I thought was being repeated when she was so angry with me that I was not there on time after her return. She said, "So, I'm really having a reaction to my mother and not to you." She was clearly ambivalent about the possibility that I might attribute her unplanned affective responsivity simply to displaced transference. She made clear her discomfort that I might be inauthenticating her response, distancing it from the aliveness in the here-and-now transference or from the real relationship that included all the volatile, stormy, and intimate events that had really transpired between her and me. Those real events that had occurred outside the expected therapeutic frame, that started by chance with the blizzard, and that then spiraled into all sorts of unusual unpredictable ramifications and real responses to me and from me in the real and transferential analytic relationship, had set a brand-new tone in the treatment, centering on a set of interactions that were clearly analyzable. Ms. D. searched for a phrase to characterize this new relationship precisely. She settled on "real, but not quite real, perhaps artificial," or "only transference." This sounds a lot like Winnicott's (1951) transitional space—the transference being real and not real at the same time. This patient was troubled if she did not know all the "rules" of treatment. The rules helped her feel in control of things by offering her guidelines about how to be on good behavior and how to do what she was supposed to do in this process. She was an angry perfectionistic child in gleeful combat with her maternal counterpart. Anxiety and rage emerged when real events that transcended the expectable structure of the analytic situation—the fundamental rule, the neutrality, abstinence, and anonymity that define the analytic situation—took her by surprise. The new and unpredicted tone in our relationship lent a sense of authentic urgency, providing the analytic "hot spots" that define the optimal setting for interpretations of the interface of the real and the transferential in the therapeutic object relationship. I cared to listen, I accommodated her, I reassured her—all real. But I also calmly interpreted her projection of her perfectionism and need for nonintrusion onto me. The therapeutic action indeed included the interface of the real with the transference. It is not a matter of one or the other.

Before going on to the second series of sessions, it would be helpful to review the way Grunes (1984) fleshes out aspects of that interface as one theoretical context for understanding the treatment I am reporting. There has been, outside of contemporary Freudian analysis, too arbitrary a distinction made between the real relationship, the transference, and the therapeutic object relationship. Grunes bases his argument on the problematic nature of the continuing, excessive dichotomy in the psychoanalytic literature between the transference and the actuality of the treatment relationship. Particularly among the more regressed, or as we now like to say, "widening-scope" patients, there is a "relationship demand factor in the treatment which cannot be met by interpretation alone" (p. 123). I would extend this idea to neurotic patients as well. They also require a therapeutic object relationship, perhaps with different emphases than Grunes has advocated for the more disturbed. Grunes uses the term *therapeutic object relationship* interchangeably with such terms as *analyst–patient relationship* and *therapeutic interaction.* He characterizes it as a situation of primal intimacy between patient and analyst that contains both an illusional or transference and a real aspect. The intimacy involves a special type of empathic permeability of boundaries between analyst and patient. "One very early form of the primal transference would involve the pleasure . . . of self-definition through feeling focused upon by mother and focusing upon her focusing upon him" (p. 138). That relationship, which is a parent–child analogue, is the matrix of change in which interpretation and analysis of transference occur. Most important, the relationship between the transference and the actualities of the analyst's own real presence through his or her empathy, interactions, and even certain disclosures—this combined real and transference relation—is organically related to psychoanalytic treatment in the first place and does not constitute a parameter to be analyzed (see Eissler 1953). Grunes's (1984) and Loewald's (1960) focus on interactions and notions of reciprocal, symbolic-creative communication, and Renik's (1995) recent advocacy of disclosing to the patient his way of thinking insofar as it is relevant to the joint venture of analytic work, are all congruent with the hallmark of Freudian psychoanalysis today: in the way we interact and in what we disclose, the patient is always at the center.

Second Series of Sessions

Within days of returning from *my* vacation in Mexico and a break of nearly two weeks, an additional incident occurred that heightened the feelings that had emerged during *her* vacation when she became stranded and sorely needed to contact me. I apparently had some viral condition, jet lag, Mexican sleeping sickness, call it whatever, which led to sporadic fatigue and sleepiness for about two weeks. One morning, I actually dozed off during my first session of the day, which was the session that preceded Ms. D.'s. This was the first time I had ever had the experience of falling asleep, or at least of entering this particular, and highly atypical for me, altered state of consciousness during a session. The patient I was with, not Ms. D., noticed something wrong, remarked that I looked unsteady on my feet and somewhat faint, and said she felt reluctant to talk about her own troubling matters when I looked to be so clearly under the weather. I remember struggling very hard to stay awake during this session, but all my willpower and determination would not allow me to do that. To my great surprise, I was brought back with a jolt when I heard my first patient of the day say, "I think I should leave now." We had actually run over by 10 minutes. Perhaps I should have canceled my next session, the one with Ms. D. But since I had not as yet fully realized the extent of my indisposition, I proceeded on with my work, assuming, falsely, as it turned out, that my usual alertness and energy level would be restored in short order.

Ms. D. was in the waiting room, and when I went to meet her, she looked extremely troubled. She lay down on the couch and said, "When I was in the waiting room and you didn't come out on time I thought you died." She had thought of calling my son whose name she knew from her prior researches into my real life, but did not have his address. She had also forgotten the address of my office, so she thought it would be useless to call 911 for help. She had thus remained paralyzed to do anything about saving me, like calling the police or someone who knew how to do CPR. She had the idea that I was dying of a heart attack as her mother had a few years ago. Mother was then exactly the same age as she knew me to be, having looked up my birth date in a library archive earlier in the treatment. In response to my inquiry, she said she had not thought to have my doorman call 911. She simply thought I had died and she could do nothing about it. To my surprise and dismay, I was still in the grip of this strange fatigue and dozed off for brief moments periodically during this session.

During my next session with Ms. D., when I truly had regained most of my normal energy level, she said she had worried quite a bit on the day of the previous session when I was late to meet her and when she thought I might have died. My hair had not look combed, and I looked disheveled and out of character, as her mother did on the morning she had her heart attack and died. On that morning, just shortly before Ms. D. started treatment with me, she heard strange sounds emerging from her parents' bedroom that frightened her, but neither she nor her father did anything about it, such as calling 911. She now believes that the sounds were the death rattle, but at the time had mistaken them for sexual moans and therefore did not enter the room to check on her mother's condition and possibly save her life. She had been angry at her father for not calling the police. She was angry at herself for not learning CPR. Any of these moves might have been able to save her mother, a selfless person who did very little to take care of herself. Ms. D. told me I'd better go see a doctor right away. I said, "You seemed paralyzed to do anything then, just as you felt paralyzed to do anything to save me when you thought I might be either dead or dying."

In a deliberate discarding of the ideal of anonymity, I decided to tell the patient that I had originally had jet lag and then developed fatigue, which my doctor told me sounded like a viral infection, caught from recirculated air in the jet plane, and that the symptoms should let up entirely within another week. I also told her I felt well enough to work right now. As I rethink the incident at this present time, it would have been best if I had also told her that in retrospect, I realized it might have been better if I had canceled our session on the day I had dozed off with my first patient and let her know that I needed to check out my condition with a physician immediately.[1] Like Renik (1995), I believe that the question is not *whether* to disclose, but how to *manage* the unavoidable condition of constant disclosure. I shared that bit of reality about my medical diagnosis with her because it seemed cruel, heartless, and untherapeutic or antitherapeutic simply to deal at that moment with the fantasies in the transference. The analytic "hot spot" of my dozing off, a critical or pivotal moment in the analysis, eventually would provide ample opportunity for mutative interpretation. As it turned out, my action, or enactment, if you will, was in tune

---

1. I am grateful to Dr. Irving Steingart for his help on this issue.

with her thinking: she did not want to talk about her strong feelings for me as simply a replica of those experienced in connection with her mother's death because then I would brush them off as transference. I said, "You want to be sure that I also understand that you care personally about me — that there was something alive and present going on in your concern for me that was not just a repetition of your ambivalent feelings at the time of your mother's death." That turned out to be a very helpful intervention, but the patient still could not get the sexualized "death rattle" sounds in her mother's bedroom out of her ears during our session. If only she had paid more attention, she would have brought mother to the hospital and saved her life. But it wasn't right to barge into her mother's bedroom while father was there when she heard sounds that she did not heed or do anything about at the time, becoming similarly paralyzed then as now when she thought it wasn't right to barge into my office or even knock on the door with another patient in there. Doing the right thing became more important than saving the life of selfless people like her mother, or me. I was selfless because I showed up to help her when I was sick. This self-lessness is also typical of the patient's own self-representation, in which she often disregards her own well-being by sacrificing autonomy in doing what is right for herself in the interests of doing the right thing for an "other." Needless to say, there is a big reaction formation element in this pattern, for her own self-interests are often put first, as they were in her failing to take action in "rescuing" me when she thought I might be dying.

Shortly thereafter, she had pains in her abdomen, for which she refused to see a physician for fear he would think she was being hypochondriacal. "I'm actually envisioning a fast and painful death from cancer." Suicidal thoughts frequently masked ambivalent and murderous feelings. She had a dream, remembering only the fragment, "You died in your chair." It was the anniversary of her mother's death. I said, "There's a connection between wanting to rejoin the dead and your thoughts about your mother's death and mine." There was a real person in Ms. D.'s life, G., offering possibilities for real contact, but with me she could remain in the safe world of fantasized transference objects. The night before the dream of my dying in my chair, she had read, for the second time, Freud's (1915) paper, "Observations on Transference-Love." Her profession is as far removed from psychoanalysis as any could be. She thought she could maintain her self-sufficiency by reading about transference, a sort of enactment, rather than asking me directly about what I meant when I said that thoughts of joining her mother through death at just the time when the possibility for a real and lasting relationship were opening up for her were connected with thoughts about me—some longing to be with me if I had died. What was going on with G., and now with me since the day of my indisposition, had become all too real and bewildering. I said, "You have been trying desperately through reading the dead Freud's words on transference love to avoid the real live aspects of your relationships with G. and with me."

Was my telling her of my jet lag and fatigue gratuitous? I do not think so. She was relieved to hear I was basically fine. But that didn't stop her from fantasizing about my death. From her point of view, I turned out to be fallible, imperfect, falling asleep during a session—contemptible enough to justify her suicidal fantasies. My disclosure was irrelevant from that point of view, for this issue would have come up in any event. But my disclosure in this instance, and in the instance of telling her I check my machine to keep my patients as a focus of my attention during a weather emergency, did matter from the point of view of restoring authenticity and aliveness to our relationship as a backdrop for the analysis of the transference. Without that authentic counterpoint, she could more easily experience the analysis as make-believe. Rendering the treatment game-like could convert it into a perpetual analysis at the expense of growth, development, and meaningful analysis of the transference. The transference would have been forced out of that optimal transitional space between play or fantasy and of reality. In this instance, it could take on a malignant character and derail the treatment. Aliveness in the real relationship as a backdrop for authentic transference analysis often requires us to drop temporarily the analysis of repetitions and of unconscious fantasies, particularly those based on projections in the transference. We might say, for example, when a patient distorts the meaning of what we do, "That was not my intention." That sort of disclosure brings in a note of authenticity to the analysis that makes it more than the sterile game it too easily can become. One often hears from patients about to slam the door on treatment, "Don't play mind-fucking games with me." In the less neurotic and more "widening-scope" patients, such disclosures may prevent a regressive transference from disrupting and ruining the process.

COMMENTARY

The classic adherence to the analytic ideals of neutrality, abstinence, and anonymity, have, in Freudian psychoanalysis today, been abandoned in their original and rigid forms in favor of the evolved contemporary technique that I shall now discuss under four main rubrics: (1) the therapeutic action consists of more than the simple technique of interpretation leading to conflict resolution via interpretations; (2) disclosure in a departure from the ideal of anonymity is inevitable; (3) intersubjectivity, in a Freudian frame, implies a degree of asymmetricality that keeps the patient at the center and does not diminish the authority of the analyst; (4) interaction between patient and analyst is crucial to the therapeutic action.

Technique: Beyond Neutrality, Abstinence, and Anonymity

Arlow and Brenner (1990) have made the point repeatedly in their recent work that the psychoanalytic process itself consists only of technique, and the technique consists exclusively of imparting insight via the interpretation of conflict and compromise formation. This particular and limited technique, they say, constitutes the therapeutic action of psychoanalysis. Their view is oversimplified, because in fact the technique and the therapeutic action encompass more than the interpretation of conflict— and the unconscious processes that inevitably enter in—by consistently applied technique in a standard analytic situation. There have always been analysts who regard the psychoanalytic process as something other than, or in addition to, or as transcending that technique. Technique, in the view being critiqued, is limited to the dynamic interactions of the patient's conflicts and the analyst's technical interventions. What I wish to emphasize is that interpretations of conflict within the transference matrix are not worth their salt unless they refer to real experiences within the here-and-now relationship. The psychoanalytic process and its therapeutic action are far more than synonymous with changes brought about simply, as Arlow and Brenner would have it, by consistently applied technique in a standard analytic situation, and by the analyst's interpretations, alone. It is not that the standard technique has changed, or that the analyst does anything radically different. It is just that more, and more complex, things happen than analysts working simply out of older traditions have acknowledged.

In a panel presented at the Columbia Association for Psychoanalytic Medicine (1996), "Change Within the Analyst," the participants, Jacobs, Kernberg, and Renik, agreed that what makes analysis work goes beyond uniform application of standard technique. They addressed the issue of changes in our basic attitudes toward the once sanctified values of neutrality, abstinence, and anonymity. Kernberg rightly maintained that technical neutrality no longer refers to the analyst being simply a blank screen or a reflecting mirror of the patient's projections. Neutrality is not disgruntled indifference but is an objective, concerned stance about the patient's problems, requiring a position equidistant between the contradictory forces operating in the patient's mind. Renik (1996), even more recently, speaks of the "perils of neutrality" as including not just the fallacy of the analyst as blank screen, but also the undesirability of remaining equidistant between contradictory forces. There indeed has been a tradition among many Freudian analysts of opposing the patient's harsh superego by vigorously disagreeing with the patient's irrational self-criticisms. The Columbia panel understood correctly that interpretations may, in and of themselves, be gratifying, and in that regard, they rightly called into question the analytic ideal of abstinence. Loewald (1960), Stone (1954), and others have always thought that gratifications for both parties in the dyad were inherent in the standard method. Furthermore, many have discovered that there are also gratifications in the new analytic object relationship. Chused (1996), in her work on abstinence and the therapeutic action, argues for maintaining the idea, not the ideal, of abstinence. She expands on the traditional notion, and sees abstinence as a means of providing a special, new context in which the patient gains informative experiences about how he or she needs to make new objects into old ones. In other words, abstinence, so conceived, provides conditions for the patient to learn about transference. Analysts are no longer timid about gratifying the patient by interpretation and by real interactions intrinsic to the process—interactions that are not simply a mutually indulgent pink tea, but ones that encourage the advancement of the process and promote growth in the patient. And since disclosure of aspects of the analyst's personality is inevitable to one degree or another, modifications in our ideal of anonymity are required. As originally conceptualized and applied, the stances of abstinence, anonymity, and neutrality could and often did become stereotypical and dehumanizing, and not necessarily the basic constituents of the analytic attitude and the therapeutic action. Any rigid adherence to these stances could actually squelch the possibilities for alive, real, authentic, interactive, relational work, deadening its contents in keeping with certain revered but outmoded traditions of the past.

There seemed to be an interesting consensus among the Columbia panelists that when we place exclusive emphasis on these values in their original context only, without regard to the subtleties of our impact on our patients, we are identifying with the rigidities of our analytic ancestors, sometimes in the extreme, as with the aggressor. The participants believed, as do I, that it would be best at this juncture in the history of our profession not to get bogged down in our introductory teaching with the technical aspects of neutrality, abstinence, and anonymity, in their historically antiquated contexts, but to start candidates' education with where we stand today in regard to our evolved technique. Curricula should then move back to the historical origin of the concepts, and then move back on forward to our present rationales for modifying them, from the less to the more real, authentic, and engaged.

Disclosure

Where do Freudian analysts today stand on the issue of disclosure? Renik's (1995) view that the analyst disclose his or her own reality in order to increase the self-awareness of the other person is a wise guideline to follow. He articulates and communicates everything that in his view will help the patient understand where the analyst thinks he or she is coming from and trying to go with the patient: "I propose that it is useful for the analyst consistently to try to make sure that his or her analytic activity is understood as fully as possible by the patient. . . . An analyst should aim for comprehensibility, not inscrutability. I am not advocating imposing one's thinking upon a patient, but I am suggesting that one's thinking should be made available" (p. 482). It is difficult to dispute the view that total and complete anonymity is a myth that encourages idealization of the analyst and distorts technical neutrality, for even the analyst's way of formulating interpretations give clues about his or her personality. Technical neutrality is eminently compatible with a full exploration of the patient's realistic and unrealistic perceptions of the analyst. Our acts of disclosing do not purport to enhance our exhibitionism, or narcissism, or masochism, but only to benefit the patient. In Freudian analysis today, the principle of disclosure does not serve to enhance some extra-analytic real relationship, although the patient often fantasizes that it does, and those fantasies must be taken up and analyzed. This approach to disclosure is a relevant aspect of the real relationship for contemporary Freudian psychoanalysis: in the way we interact, and in what we disclose, the patient is always at the center.

Intersubjectivity

What is critical to the Freudian position on intersubjectivity, as contrasted with my understanding of the relational view, is a more asymmetric view of transference and countertransference influences. Freudians attribute a greater degree of authority to the analyst than to the patient. This topic is center stage now, as in Brenner's (1996) paper spearheading an issue in the *Psychoanalytic Quarterly* devoted to the topic. The paper was presented originally at a meeting of the New York Psychoanalytic Society, at which Steven Mitchell was the discussant. Mitchell argued against Brenner's defense of the position that we should attribute greater authority to the analyst than to the patient. Brenner's position, he said, ignored the relational school's assumption of intersubjectivity in which neither of the two parties, analyst or analysand, has a better hold on *the* truth. If that is the position of the relational school, then it is entirely constructionistic, and ignores the interminglings of objective and psychic realities. Those espousing an extreme symmetrical view of intersubjectivity would dispense entirely with the concepts of technical neutrality, anonymity, and abstinence, rather than modifying them in accordance with contemporary developments in our understanding of technique.

In his critique of the relational position on intersubjectivity, Kernberg (1996) points out the dangers of too much symmetry in transference and countertransference analysis: "An analyst's excessive concern with the effects of authority on the patient—with the patient's 'vulnerability' to any viewpoint different from the patient's own—may bring about a masochistic submission to the patient's pathology and a loss of the psychoanalytic perspective, rather than the analytic resolution of the origins of this vulnerability as a defense" (pp. 147–148). Since there should not and cannot be, if the analyst is well analyzed and well trained, a constant symmetry of countertransference and transference, too much communication of the analyst's values and reality colludes with a vulnerable side and prevent analysis of the patient. Although the realities of the transference and the therapeutic and the real relationship do get explored, they are not disclosed indiscriminately.

Interaction

The most mutative thing that happens in the psychoanalytic process, and that is on a par with the interpretation of conflict, relates to the significant and inevitable interactions between patient and analyst that ultimately lead to structural change and personal development. By structural change, Loewald (1960), who was ahead of his time in grasping the importance of therapeutic interactions, meant aspects of ego development, which he assumed are resumed in the therapeutic process in psychoanalysis. This ego development is contingent on the relationship with a new object—the analyst—that, in turn, derives from the earliest mother–child dyad. But he did not suggest any new modifications in technique. He simply argued for a different way of understanding the role of interactions and object relations, which he wished to integrate into the Freudian mainstream, long before others had the foresight to do, as central to therapeutic change—to the therapeutic action.

I now skip three decades to address one of the newest and most creative contributions to this area, that suggested by Wilson and Weinstein (1996). They borrow the concept of the zone of proximal development (ZPD) from Vygotsky (1978) to refer to important interactions in the optimal interpersonal context of psychoanalysis that is outside of but works in tandem with the transference. Mutual influences between analyst and analysand are inevitable, and interactions are inevitable and desirable, and must be recognized for what they, as real relationships, contribute to the therapeutic action of psychoanalysis. Consider, for example, Grunes (1984), who zeroed in on a specific quality of desirable mutuality in his characterization of the therapeutic object relationship as a mutually interpenetrative emotional force field of empathic permeability and primal intimacy between analyst and patient.

The precursors of the ZPD concept are the unobjectionable positive transference, the therapeutic alliance, and the holding environment. The ZPD construct "supersedes the false dichotomization of the real relationship and the transference" (Wilson and Weinstein 1996, p. 173), and provides for a multileveled view of transference and the interactive role of the analyst. It builds on Bird's (1972) notion that later transference is built on powerful dyadic interactions, similar to but not necessarily identical to earliest object relations. ZPD is a present-day extension of Loewald's germinal ideas that the analyst not only interprets transference distortions but conveys a new reality that the analysand internalizes, because it explicates how mutative interpretations are internalized.

The ZPD is particularly important in sustaining the buffeting of transference. The analyst strives to be inside the ZPD but outside of the transference of the analytic work, and not to be the oft-caricatured blank screen of personal indifference. The ZPD involves ordinary discourse for the purpose of clarification of meanings in the context of real related interactions, and is often more important than transference analysis, especially in early volatile stretches that need to be tempered by meaningful analytic dialogue, when it is particularly important to sustain the therapeutic action. Perhaps we could usefully regard my remarks to Ms. D. about my viral condition as a timely positioning of discourse within the ZPD.

While we are accustomed to thinking of volatile stretches of work with the widening scope patient, I have learned that we encounter them in all patients, because all patients at one time or another require some version of a therapeutic object relationship to guarantee the therapeutic action of good technical interpretations of intrapsychic conflict inside and outside of the transference. Real dialogue—not a deliberately manipulated corrective emotional experience, not giving up analytic authority while being seduced into accepting that transference and countertransference have symmetrical status—provides the interactive context that brings to life the latent potential of the intrapsychic. The new object relationship is real and grows from real interactions that are part and parcel of the transference and its interpretation. Ergo, transference promotes rather than opposes a real relationship. That is how Freudian analysts think today about the transference and the real relationship. What is different in Freudian psychoanalysis today, from the way it was and from other approaches, is not an essentially new technique. One need only consult Fenichel's (1941) magnificent small volume on technique for an appreciation of the enduring legacies that still inform the bread-and-butter part of our daily work. What is different is an essentially new appreciation that has evolved over the years of the realness of transference-countertransference and other interactions that promote new growth and development in a new relationship with the analyst and with significant others. This argument, so basic to contemporary Freudian psychoanalysis, is predicated on the idea that the analyst as simply a reflecting mirror in the reactivation of the infantile neurosis in the crystallization and resolution of the transference is an outmoded notion. Even when the analyst does function abstinently and as a neutral mirror, that very functioning creates certain interactions and inspires fantasies that must be analyzed, and prompts new integrative and, as Chused (1996) notes, informative experiences that constitute a new object relationship. Loewald (1960) said that by the very act of analyzing transference distortions, the analyst becomes available to the patient as a truly new object, but not by providing a corrective emotional experience. The newness consists of the patient's rediscovery of early paths of object relations. This rediscovery then leads to new ways of relating to objects and of being oneself. Here is the crux: infantile and contemporary object may be united into one. Any real relationship also involves a transfer of past and present unconscious images onto present-day objects. This context for real dialogue in tandem with the transference, while the analyst maintains authority in a nonsymmetrical basic real relationship, is the hallmark of Freudian psychoanalysis today.

REFERENCES

Arlow, J. A., and Brenner, C. (1990). The psychoanalytic process. *Psychoanalytic Quarterly* 59:678–692.

Bird, B. (1972). Notes on transference: universal phenomenon and hardest part of analysis. *Journal of the American Psychoanalytic Association* 20:267–301.

Brenner, C. (1996). The nature of knowledge and the limits of authority. *Psychoanalytic Quarterly* 65:21–31.

Chused, J. F. (1996). Abstinence and informative experience. *Journal of the American Psychoanalytic Association* 44:1047–1071.

Eissler, K. (1953). The effect of the structure of the ego on psychoanalytic technique. *Journal of the American Psychoanalytic Association* 1:104–143.

Fenichel, O. (1941). *The Problems of Psychoanalytic Technique.* New York: Psychoanalytic Quarterly.

Freud, S. (1909). Notes upon a case of obsessional neurosis. *Standard Edition* 10:153–318.

———— (1915). Observations on transference-love. *Standard Edition* 12:157–171.

Grunes, M. (1984). The therapeutic object relationship. *Psychoanalytic Review* 71:123–143.

Kernberg, O. (1996). The analyst's authority in the psychoanalytic situation. *Psychoanalytic Quarterly* 55:137–157.

Loewald, H. (1960). On the therapeutic action of psychoanalysis. *International Journal of Psycho-Analysis* 41:16–33.

Panel (1996). *Change Within the Analyst.* Participants: Theodore Jacobs, Otto Kernberg, and Owen Renik. Presented at the meeting of the Association for Psychoanalytic Medicine, New York, March.

Renik, O. (1995). The ideal of the anonymous analyst and the problem of self-disclosure. *Psychoanalytic Quarterly* 54:466–495.

——— (1996). The perils of neutrality. *Psychoanalytic Quarterly* 65:495–517.

Stone, L. (1954). The widening scope of indications for psychoanalysis. *Journal of the American Psychoanalytic Association* 2:567–594.

Strachey, J. (1934). The nature of the therapeutic action of psycho-analysis. *International Journal of Psycho-Analysis* 15:127–159.

Wilson, A., and Weinstein, L. (1996). The transference and the zone of proximal development. *Journal of the American Psychoanalytic Association* 44:167–200.

Winnicott, D. W. (1951). Transitional objects and transitional phenomena. In *Collected Papers: Through Paediatrics to Psycho-analysis*, pp. 229–242. New York: Basic Books, 1958.

Vygotsky, L. (1978). *Mind in Society. The Development of the Higher Psychological Processes.* Cambridge, MA: Harvard University Press.

8

A Contemporary–Classical Freudian Views the Current Conceptual Scene

Irving Steingart

My use of the term *contemporary–classical* may seem odd and even oxymoronic. Yet what I intend to lay out is a viewpoint that appreciates our current emphasis on intersubjectivity and countertransference but that, at the same time, retains the classic Freudian perspective on psychic reality as a foundational intrapsychic construct. I intend to comment on the following topics: (1) intersubjectivity in the context of the repetition compulsion; (2) transference and countertransference in the context of intersubjectivity; and (3) self in the context of one's psychic reality, with a brief reference to dynamics related to one's experience of time.

While my first two points may sound like conceptual porridge or, worse still, irredeemably glib terminology, I believe this reflects the current theoretical ferment within psychoanalysis. It is impossible to present my own contemporary Freudian conception of the psychoanalytic relationship outside the context of an extraordinarily pluralistic scene that contains many confusing and haphazard conceptualizations.

To more clearly explicate my own praxis, I draw on the innovative and cogent work of Irwin Hoffman (1983, 1992a,b). Hoffman's unique approach can be construed as a midline position between someone like Levenson (1972), who eschews any conception of a fictive transference in favor of an exclusive reference to the actual relationship with the analyst, and someone like myself, who still centers my conduct about the intrapsychic nature of the analysand's fictive transference, despite my recognition of the inevitable impact of real aspects of my personality on the shape or even occurrence of such transference (Steingart 1995). Although calling Hoffman "midline" does not do justice to the complexity of his thinking, my point is simply to use the clarity of his writing and his candid presentation of his clinical work as a point of departure for elaborating my own position with respect to intersubjectivity, the therapeutic object relationship, role responsiveness, enactment, and the use of the self.

Intersubjectivity represents our most general notion about any relationship between two people. A psychoanalytic relationship, of whatever theoretical persuasion, is an unusual relationship, not found in ordinary life (Schafer 1983). What is unique about the analytic relationship, from a contemporary–classical Freudian perspective, is that it highlights and examines the analysand's conflict driven, fantasy informed, extraordinarily stereotyped, repetition compulsion.

The shape and even the possible occurrence of aspects of the analysand's repetition compulsion are enabled—or not—by both the personality and the working method of the analyst. Freud (1912) recognized this in his first paper on technique. While the precise description of this repetition compulsion is seamlessly taken up by the language of one's own theory, every theoretical orientation that exists in our literature conceives, in one way or another, of an analysand's repetition compulsion (Steingart 1995). And, to the extent a repetition compulsion is enabled by a psychoanalysis, every theoretical persuasion presumes, in one way or another, that the therapeutic relationship has become *emotionally arranged* so as to make this possible (Steingart 1995). But, if this is so, then it is also maintained, in one way or another, that the analyst's mental state becomes emotionally arranged so as to foster the flourishing of the analysand's repetition compulsion (Beres and Arlow 1974, Hoffman 1992a,b, Levenson 1972).

To the extent that the analysand's repetition compulsion becomes the experiential subject matter of the treatment relationship, however conceived, one is finding in my view a so-called one-person psychology in the very midst of intersubjectivity. For a contemporary–classical Freudian, there are other, perhaps easier, ways to make a case for a one-person psychology—symptoms providing one clear illustration. I will later present a remarkable clinical example of a self-in-conflict that further substantiates this concept. But having come to my point in this way will help us to consider transference and countertransference in the context of intersubjectivity.

Annie Reich (1960) argued that transference and countertransference cannot conceptually consume the entire analytic relationship. This is true, but irrelevant. If all that happened between analysand and analyst was transference and countertransference, then all that took place in the analysis would be endless repetition compulsion. The question is whether we believe that every aspect of an analysand's transference engages the analyst's mentality in countertransference of one sort or another. Paula Heimann (1960) understands this to be the case. She states, "Along with . . . evenly hovering attention . . . [the analyst] needs a freely roused emotional sensibility so as to perceive and follow closely . . . [the] patient's emotional movements and unconscious fantasies" (p. 10). She goes on to talk about how, if an analyst's "tools are in good working order" (p. 10), the analyst must be "sustaining his [or her] feelings" (p. 12), resulting therapeutically in the analyst's feelings being used only for "understanding his [or her] patient" (p. 12).

I cite Heimann (1960) in some detail because of the importance she attaches to the concepts *unconscious fantasies, sustaining* feelings, and only *understanding* the analysand. With regard to this last point about the analyst using his or her feelings only to understand, Heimann is very clear. If the analyst expresses countertransference feelings to the analysand, or enacts such feelings in some way, then the analyst is no more useful to the analysand than, as Heimann puts it, "any Tom, Dick, or Harry" (1960, p. 13). It is only in an analytic relationship that the analysand "exclusively and consistently . . . [has the] *prerogative* to be the object of research into reasons and meanings" (p. 13).

These words—"object of research"—may seem cold and unfeeling. But Loewald (1960), speaking to the "therapeutic action of psychoanalysis," emphasizes how the analysand's coming to possess such a "prerogative" (Heimann 1960) entails a unique kind of love that the analyst has for the analysand. Indeed, the therapeutic action of psychoanalysis lies in the inseparable fusion of such a love with the insights it makes possible.

Elsewhere (Steingart 1995) I have elaborated this love as involving a love of the analysand's mind and any experience the analysand produces with his or her mind. Here, in the context of describing a contemporary–classical Freudian point of view, I would like to emphasize the analysand's production of fantasy. I will return to this point shortly when I draw upon Hoffman's (1996) work, using it to elucidate what I take to be a significant negative consequence of Hoffman's current recommendation for clinical practice.

Before doing this, I believe I can now succinctly express my views about transference and countertransference in the context of intersubjectivity. As I see it, two prevailing conceptions exist. Sandler (1976) credits Heimann (1950) with originating the idea that countertransference functions as a valuable source of information for the analyst regarding what is dynamically relevant at a given moment for interpretation. Because it does not interfere with the analyst's capacity and desire to try only to understand the analysand, it will not necessarily lead the analyst to interpret. However, Heimann (1960) does talk about how an analyst's "tools" may not be in "working" order. This could cause the analyst to verbally express or enact some feeling. Such analyst expressed or enacted affect may not be relevant for the analysand to feel understood and may not further free associational expression of intrapsychic conflict. In any event, Heimann (1960) believes that all analyst affect that is "freely roused" by the analysand's transference should be construed as countertransference, whether a useful tool or not.

I do not agree. The alternative perspective is stated by Beres and Arlow (1974) and is rooted in Freud (especially 1912). Rather than viewing countertransference as an experiential source of information requiring the analyst's "sustaining" (Heimann 1960) his or her feelings, Beres and Arlow (1974) talk about empathy operating as a "signal." "The affect experienced by the therapist we suggest is in the nature of a signal affect, a momentary identification with the patient which leads to . . . awareness" (1974, p. 35). They define this as a special sort of awareness that enables an interpretation that comes into the analyst's mind "in the form of a free association" (p. 28). Beres and Arlow provide a vivid example of how such empathy-as-a-signal can involve a shared fantasy, with affect and fantasy complementing each other.

However, Beres and Arlow (1974) in their examination of empathy use Racker's (1968) framework of "concordant" and "complementary" identifications, which leads them, I believe, to an erroneous conclusion like that of Heimann (1950, 1960). Empathy mediated by a concordant identification is a simple, one might say, natural process. The analyst identifies with the analysand-as-agent who is having a certain experience. This is not countertransference of any sort. On the other hand, empathy produced by a complementary identification involves the analyst identifying with the object of the analysand's agency. For example, I may feel myself belittled by the analysand or identify with someone else who is belittled. In such a case, Beres and Arlow explain, "Empathic understanding of the patient is much more complicated than simply the sharing of affects . . . [with the] patient" (p. 39). Indeed, it is, and Racker (1968) himself incisively describes this complication:

> The complementary identifications are closely connected with the destiny of the concordant identifications. . . . It is clear that rejection of a part or tendency in the analyst himself, his aggressiveness, for instance may lead to a rejection of the patient's aggressiveness (whereby this concordant identification fails). . . . [This] leads to a greater complementary identification with the patient's . . . object towards which . . . [the patient's] aggressive impulse is directed. [p. 135]

But what Racker (1968) is here describing is how it is psychic conflict in the analyst that is always involved in complementary identification, which then is best understood as a type of countertransference. We can imagine the analyst's difficulty in maintaining a concordant identification with an analysand such as the Marquis de Sade, who is describing in a cold-blooded manner some horrible sadistic perversion. (The Marquis, let us say, is required to be in analysis to avoid imprisonment.) The analyst's own likely conflict in identifying with such brutal sadism will defensively result in a complementary identification, or countertransference, with the victimized, degraded object of de Sade's attacks. All such complementary identification is always experienced by the ego as passively suffered, rather than as empathy in which the analyst feels his or her experience to be simply and naturally "enriched" (Freud 1921). However, even in this de Sade example, if the analyst manages to "sustain" (Heimann 1960) the feelings engendered by such a complementary identification-as-victim, then this countertransference can be only a rich, experiential source of information. Thus, it is clinically and theoretically self-evident why countertransference is always—potentially—extraordinarily informative about the prevailing clinical process.

I cannot emphasize strongly enough my belief that these two characterizations of the analyst's mental state constitute a real difference, which makes for different intersubjective sensibilities. For me, as a contemporary–classical Freudian, the significant contribution of Heimann (1950, 1960), and those who have built upon her work, such as Racker (1968), is the realization that there are two kinds of optimal intersubjectivity—one involving the analyst in what remains only a useful countertransference versus one resulting in the analyst's experiencing an empathic signal. This distinction is to be regarded as descriptive rather than prescriptive. Either kind of intersubjectivity can work analytically, and there is some irony here. Just as Freud (e.g., 1937) was not able to conceive of any sort of countertransference as enabling a productive psychoanalysis, some Freudian analysts now believe (e.g., Jacobs 1991, Renik 1993a,b) if an analyst does not become aware of (hopefully productive) countertransference, that analyst *must* be deceiving himself or herself and the treatment will be subject to some unproductive consequence. I believe both views are conceptually extremist and incorrect.

For me, these two kinds of analyst mentality that can support an analysis—what Heimann (1960) means by "sustaining" countertransference feelings and what Beres and Arlow (1974) mean by empathy as a "signal" experience—are subjectively so different that it makes no sense to call them by the same name, be it countertransference or empathy. What seems most likely to me is that these represent two kinds of analyst "work style" (Steingart 1995, Winnicott 1949) and issue from the analyst's personality, from the kind of person he or she really is or is not. This makes for two very different kinds of intersubjectivity, and undoubtedly has something to do with an analysand's working better with one analyst than with another.

There is one final development in our ideas about transference-countertransference in the context of intersubjectivity, that, if not originated by Joseph Sandler (1976), is for me best articulated by him: "Parallel to the 'free-floating attention' of the analyst is what I would like to call his [or her] free-floating . . . [role] responsiveness" (p. 45). So now, in addition to Heimann's (1960) "freely roused emotional sensibility" (p. 10), we have the possibility of analyst enactment. I say "possibility" because, as I read Sandler (1976), he suggests only a potential that such analyst responsiveness will result in an enactment. Role responsiveness, then, also can function as a "signal" (Beres and Arlow 1974), similar to the analyst's affect, and what occurs, again, is an association by the analyst that can be useful for interpretation. Hence, everything I have just said about contemporary Freudian practice with regard to an analyst's affect becoming in some way countertransferential applies in the same way to the analyst's role responsiveness.

Owen Renik (1993a,b) is noteworthy in advancing a contrary position. Following on Sandler's (1976) idea of analyst role responsiveness, he argues that an analyst's interpretative understanding is the outcome of having taken some countertransferential action that is dynamically congruent in some way with the analysand having taken some transferential action. Although Renik (1993a,b) believes that he and Sandler (1976) agree here, I think this is incorrect. Sandler contrasts how an analysand may "report rather than enact" (p. 45), and how "the analyst may be able to 'hold' his response . . . as a reaction of his own which he perceives" (p. 44). In addition, when Sandler invokes the idea of "enact," he is clearly referring to something different than the analysand's overall behavior in the transference. For Renik, however, all behavior in the analytic dyad, other than what is referred to as the working alliance (e.g., Rangell 1993), is construed as action. This includes the characterization not only of silence but of verbalization as action. Consequently, Renik's thesis concerning the ubiquity of countertransferential action becomes semantically true, albeit far from empirically convincing. Moreover, Renik argues his case on the basis of a James-Lange theory of emotion that has long been considered seriously flawed (Mandler 1975, and, of course, Freud 1926).

In any event, whatever position a contemporary Freudian takes about the inevitability of countertransferential affect and enactment, there remains an important consensus as I read the current literature: It is still believed to be best *not* to express with words to the analysand the analyst's countertransference emotion or enactment. At least, this is considered normative and desirable.

Hoffman (1992a,b) considers that it is both normative and desirable for analyst enactment to occur, and for the analyst to express with words to the analysand what has taken place within himself or herself and in the interaction. A recent example provided by Hoffman (1996) involves his saying yes to his analysand's question about whether he would be interested in looking at some videotapes of a TV series that involved a character's sessions with his therapist. The sessions had to do with an adult man's inability to communicate his feelings to his father. I do not question Hoffman's agreement to look at the videos. I have described elsewhere (Steingart 1983, 1995) how such circumstances can productively enter an analysis. Specifically, such an enactment by the patient can be treated as a free association, and an analyst's acceptance of this enactment functions initially like listening to a verbal association. Nonetheless, sooner or later I would want to understand with the analysand his associations about the video material, why he felt it important that I look at it, and why in this circumstance it did not suffice for him only to tell me with words and feelings about his experiences with the TV program.

But Hoffman (1996) does something additional, in keeping with his theory that there exists a productive tension between the fictive transference and the analyst's involvement as "important and consequential in its own right" (p. 114). Hoffman (1996) "chatted" with the analysand about "various aspects" of the video, "mulled over" (pp. 128–129) with the analysand whether a possibility existed for some reconciliation with his own father, and agreed with the analysand that such was not the case. This I would not do, although Hoffman is perfectly correct that my not doing so would have its own real impact on the treatment relationship, which would be transferentially experienced in one way or another.

It is curious to me that Hoffman, in considering the potential consequences had he acted otherwise, cites a possible transference experience of "grief," but not hatred, even though the analysand was a son of Holocaust survivors. Also, it is not at all my experience that a later analysis of the patient's need for the enactment will "suck the life out of the experience" (Hoffman 1996, p. 128). To the contrary, an interpretative appreciation of why words were not enough can further enrich the experience. Further, and this is something Hoffman understands, his practice really impacts the clinical process so that "to some extent free association . . . as the central focus of analytic attention . . . is replaced . . . with the free emergence of multiple transference-countertransference scenarios" (p. 113). I believe that Hoffman minimizes the crucial effect of this downplaying of free association. But equally important for a contemporary–classical Freudian is that the opportunity for analysand fantasy, especially increasingly fantastic fantasy, is curtailed. Does this make for a different therapeutics, because such fantasy brings with it a kind of centering of the analysand in his or her intrapsychic reality that is not possible with Hoffman's praxis? I believe it does (Steingart 1995). But given the lamentable situation of psychoanalysis and its institutes (Holzman 1976), it is very unlikely we will ever see systematic research devoted to such a topic. Hoffman himself, as someone who has engaged in psychoanalytic process research (Hoffman and Gill 1988), is unusual in this regard.

I offer a striking clinical example in support of my position.

For a former analysand, the use of fantasy, especially the special shape and more fantastic quality of dream imagery, was very important for a productive analysis. What often occurred with regard to her free associations was that any comment by me would be experienced as dangerously intrusive. Even if I were simply to point out what seemed to me to be a manifest theme in her associations that would be obvious to anyone, she would feel I was taking over the analysis and enslaving her. Eventually she associated this experience with me to her mother's "famous whistle." She was called in from play as a child by her mother's whistle and the piercing loudness of this sound could be heard throughout the neighborhood. She remembered battles with her mother, that extended into latency, over her refusal to eat certain foods, to the point that she would be required to sit several hours at the dinner table to finish her meal. She remembered that she would never give in and her mother would finally send her to her room.

In the context of her dream imagery, and her associations to the material, things between us were usually very different. With her dreams, she and I could be in a collegial relationship. This was because, to begin with, her dream experiences were felt to be her productions.

Another important aspect of her transference had to do with her father, whose intellect she greatly admired both when she was a child and now as an adult. However, as a child, she never felt well connected to her father, and she longed for, but felt she never obtained, either a clinically healthy parental enjoyment of her feminine sexuality or a recognition of her intellect. One transference dream involved me with my penis on her buttocks. Because there was some reason to believe that I had AIDS, she was anxious that I would penetrate her. I did penetrate, and I did have AIDS, so I could not be trusted. She associated to AIDS an irony connected to some comments I had made in the previous hour that she had found helpful. My comments had concerned the care of her father who was then aged and somewhat infirm. It was deadly dangerous and annihilating to feel that I was helpful.

I cite this transference dream because it illustrates how transference, at least for this contemporary–classical Freudian, is not the be all and end all. Transference experiences, optimally, are a window into increasingly fantastic fantasy, although how much this will be so will vary from one analysis to another. Again, does this perspective toward one-person psychology in the midst of intersubjectivity make a difference? I believe it does.

But what is this difference? It has to do with the foundational, classical Freudian concept of psychic reality. Freud's (1916) canonical idea of an intrapsychic psychic reality as "decisive" is, in my opinion, still rock bottom. It is why Freudians practice with an emphasis on free association, fantasy formation, a normative nonrevelation of countertransference, and so forth. Everything is designed to maximize the opportunity for expression of the analysand's psychic reality. But Freud and any contemporary–classical Freudian analyst also understand that one's psychic reality always has some connection to what Freud (1939) called "material reality," which should not be understood to refer, naively, only and literally to physical substance. It includes the mental. In the psychoanalytic relationship, the analysand's material reality importantly includes the personality of the analyst. This involves the analyst's psychic reality, which inexorably will shape, and even enable or inhibit, the expression of the analysand's psychic reality.

An example of this can be found in child development. By now, we are all familiar with the varied mutual regulations that go on between infant and caregiver (Stern 1985). Assuming circumstances in which regulations are assessed to be optimal, and thus conducive to healthy internalization and development, a Freudian nevertheless believes that somewhere in the first year of life the infant in some manner constructs what Freud (1915) called a "purified pleasure ego." This is a psychic reality in which outside is all bad, painful experience, and inside is all good, pleasurable experience. Klein (1975) added the useful idea of a paranoid sensibility to this bad, painful outside. None of this downplays in the least a determining influence of the factual status of observable mutual regulations. This material reality (Freud 1939) includes as well the psychic reality of the caregiver. All of this, in part, determines whether this inside-good/outside-bad psychic reality represents an initial, healthy differentiation of experience that will be followed by other, more complex psychic realities.

The point is that the phenomenology of this infant's psychic reality cannot be inferred in some straight line way from the factual status of observable mutual regulations (Beebe and Lachmann 1988). A Freudian believes that an infant's mind—indeed a human mind at any age—is simply too generative, as well as too sensitive to the psychic reality of significant others, for such concrete and unilateral inference making. This entire perspective overlaps with what analysts (May et al. 1958) informed by existential philosophy mean by a "being-in-the-world" who alone is responsible for the world he or she creates.

The question that remains is this: Do Freudian analysts like Renik (1993a,b), who believe the center of emanation of analysand psychic reality is located in the intersubjective flux of transference–countertransference, foster a clinical process in which the analysand's free associations are significantly diminished, as compared to Freudian analysts who still work with the idea of an intrapsychic emanation? If so, there would be, I believe, a different sensibility with regard to increasingly fantastic fantasy formation, the sense of analysand agency, and the experience of change in analysis (see especially Rangell 1993 on "will"). My own position is that the analysand's psychic reality is inevitably shaped, or even enabled or impeded, but not created in its essentials by the intersubjective flux (Steingart 1995). Most importantly, every version of a productive analytic process must have a heuristic with regard to a belief in reality, or at least, as Schafer (1984) puts it, a working conception of reality. This necessity is embedded in the idea of a therapeutic alliance (Rangell 1993)—indeed in the very notion of analysis (psycho*analysis*). Analyst and analysand must have some agreement about what there is to analyze.

Related matters of agency, insight, and new object relations experience are vividly illustrated in the following experience of the analysand whose AIDS transference dream I just described.

This analysand associatively reported the following remarkable experience: She wanted to make a bowel movement, and she elected to put on some music to help move her bowels. She then developed an experience wherein the music "distracted" her and made it more difficult to move her bowels. Clearly, the analysand was enslaving herself, just as she had felt enslaved by her mother. This time she had no will to do anything but repeat this experience.

I emphasize "she" as it is always a self in conflict with itself. Put another way, I have always regarded (Steingart 1969) the concept of the self relative to our psychic system terms (*id, ego, superego*) to be a "whole" versus "parts-of-the-whole" matter. Freud did not explicitly leave us with such a term, although there is much in his writing that would suggest a need for it (e.g., Freud 1914, Steingart 1969). He did once (Freud 1915) use the term *total ego*, which I think is confusing.

In closing, I offer two more brief considerations about possible dynamics with respect to oneself, one's experience of having a mind and one's experience of time. First, I propose that a development occurs in the anal-rapprochement phase from simple awareness to reflexive self con-sciousness—an experience of there existing with regard to oneself and others an "I" or "me"—which amounts to an emergent sensibility of having a mind. Second, I believe that such a self—and mind—necessitates an existence of one's self *in time* and, moreover, that a body not so organized into a reflexive self-awareness can only experience itself as existing in space. Support exists for such a contention in recent neurobiological research and theorizing (Damasio 1994). To the extent this is true, then all our familiar anal-rapprochement, sadomasochistic dynamics may come to apply to an analysand's possession of his or her own time. This was certainly a productive way of understanding the analysand I have described, and generally, it is a perspective I have found useful in my clinical practice.

REFERENCES

Beebe, B., and Lachmann, F. (1988). The contribution of mother–infant mutual influence to the origins of self and object representations. *Psychoanalytic Psychology* 5:305–339.

Beres, D., and Arlow, J. A. (1974). Fantasy and identification in empathy. *Psychoanalytic Quarterly* 43:26–50.

Damasio, A. R. (1994). *Descartes' Error: Emotion, Reason, and the Human Brain.* New York: Avon.

Freud, S. (1912). Recommendations to physicians practising psychoanalysis. *Standard Edition* 12:109–120.

———— (1914). On narcissism: an introduction. *Standard Edition* 14:67–104.

———— (1915). Instincts and their vicissitudes. *Standard Edition* 14:111–140.

———— (1916–1917). Introductory lectures on psychoanalysis. *Standard Edition* 16:3–461.

———— (1921). Group psychology and the analysis of the ego. *Standard Edition* 18:67–145.

———— (1926). Inhibitions, symptoms and anxiety. *Standard Edition* 20:20–178.

———— (1937). Analysis terminable and interminable. *Standard Edition* 23:216–254.

———— (1939). Moses and monotheism. *Standard Edition* 23:7–140.

Heimann, P. (1950). On countertransference. *International Journal of Psycho-Analysis* 31:81–84.

———— (1960). Countertransference. *British Journal of Medical Psychology* 33:9–15.

Hoffman, I. Z. (1983). The patient as interpreter of the analyst's experience. *Contemporary Psychoanalysis* 19:389–442.

———— (1992a). Expressive participation and psychoanalytic discipline. *Contemporary Psychoanalysis* 28:1–15.

———— (1992b). Some practical implications of a social constructionist view. *Psychoanalytic Dialogue* 2:287–304.

———— (1996). The intimate and ironic authority of the psychoanalyst's presence. *Psychoanalytic Quarterly* 65:102–136.

Hoffman, I. Z., and Gill, M. (1988). Clinical reflections on a coding scheme. *International Journal of Psycho-Analysis* 69:55–64.

Holzman, P. S. (1976). The future of psychoanalysis and its institutes. *Psychoanalytic Quarterly* 45:250–273.

Jacobs, T. J. (1991). *The Use of the Self: Countertransference and Communication in the Analytic Situation.* New York: International Universities Press.

Klein, M. (1975). *Envy and Gratitude and Other Works: 1946–1963.* New York: Delacorte Press/Seymour Lawrence.

Levenson, E. A. (1972). *The Fallacy of Understanding.* New York: Basic Books.

Loewald, H. W. (1960). On the therapeutic action of psychoanalysis. In *Papers on Psychoanalysis*, pp. 221–256. New Haven, CT: Yale University Press.

Mandler, G. (1975). *Mind and Body: Psychology of Emotion and Stress.* New York: Norton.

May, R., Angel, E., and Ellenberger, H. F. (1958). *Existence: A New Dimension in Psychiatry and Psychology.* New York: Basic Books.

Racker, H. (1968). *Transference and Countertransference.* London: Hogarth.

Rangell, L. (1993). The psychoanalytic theory of change. In *Psychic Structure and Psychic Change: Essays in Honor of Robert S. Wallerstein, MD*, ed. M. J. Horowitz, O. F. Kernberg, and E. M. Weinshel, pp. 159–190. Madison, CT: International Universities Press.

Reich, A. (1960). Further remarks on countertransference. In *Annie Reich: Psychoanalytic Contributions*, pp. 271–287. New York: International Universities Press.

Renik, O. (1993a). Countertransference enactment and the psychoanalytic process. In *Psychic Structure and Psychic Change: Essays in Honor of Robert S. Wallerstein, MD*, ed. M. J. Horowitz, O. F. Kernberg, and E. M. Weinshel, pp. 135–158. Madison, CT: International Universities Press.

——— (1993b). Analytic interaction: conceptualization of technique in light of the analyst's irreducible subjectivity. *Psychoanalytic Quarterly* 62:553–571.

Sandler, J. (1976). Countertransference and role responsiveness. *International Journal of Psycho-Analysis* 3:43–48.

Schafer, R. (1983). *The Analytic Attitude.* New York: Basic Books.

——— (1984). Misconceiving historiography and psychoanalysis as art. Discussion of R. E. Geha's "On Psychoanalytic History and the Real Story of Fictitious Lives." *International Forum of Psychoanalysis* 1:363–372.

Steingart, I. (1969). On self, character, and the development of a psychic apparatus. *Psychoanalytic Study of the Child* 24:271–300. New York: International Universities Press.

——— (1983). *Pathological Play in Borderline and Narcissistic Personalities.* New York: Spectrum.

——— (1995). *A Thing Apart, Love and Reality in the Therapeutic Relationship.* Northvale, NJ: Jason Aronson.

Stern, D. (1985). *The Interpersonal World of the Infant.* New York: Basic Books.

Winnicott, D. W. (1949). Hate in the countertransference. In *Through Paediatrics to Psycho-analysis*, pp. 219–228. New York: Basic Books.

PART IV

THE DIFFICULT PATIENT

Overview of Controversies

Elsa First

The difficult patient. Immediately questions arise: Who is the difficult patient? How is he or she difficult, and for whom? The word *difficult* might seem a euphemistic avoidance of diagnostic categories, but it does have the advantage of being clinically based. The difficult patient is one we find difficult to help by means we consider therapeutic.

Psychoanalysis has always had a special relationship with the difficult patient. Starting with Freud, the psychoanalytic method developed in parallel with its understanding of psychic suffering, and the method was defined in terms of its applicability. Freud specified narcissistic conditions and the psychoses as forms of suffering that must be deemed untreatable by the psychoanalytic method of free association and interpretative understanding. Freud's prescient considerations were based on the observation that those patients resembled psychotics in being unable to take an interest in others.[1] Patients with severe narcissistic conditions, in Freud's (1914,

---

1. Etchegoyen (1991) has pointed out that the idea of locating the distinction between neurotic and psychotic in terms of capacity to form relationships with others versus

1933) view, could not be helped by interpretative understanding because they could not form a relationship with the analyst.

Another prescient insight of Freud's was that certain patients could not make use of interpretation, or be helped by communicating their own experience in words, because of difficulties in symbolization. In a fascinating gnomic statement Freud (1911) observed (in the case of Schreber,) "Paranoia decomposes just as hysteria condenses. Or rather, paranoia resolves once more into their elements the products of the condensations and identifications which are effected in the unconscious" (p. 73). That is, to adopt a contemporary Bion (1959)–influenced language, hysteria creates metaphors by making passionate links, whereas paranoia destroys meaning by fragmenting experience into concrete bits. Norbert Freedman's work on desymbolization (Chapter 4) most directly elaborates Freud's point about decomposition of psychological connections in borderline conditions.

Sheldon Bach (Chapter 9) speaks from a sophisticated understanding of the intrinsic interrelatedness between the capacity for symbolization and self and object constancy. Bach incidentally reminds us that meaning can be obliterated not only by a concreteness that sees no alternatives but also by an abstractness that is too fluent in seeing all possible angles.

As psychoanalysis has illuminated the difficult patient, so has the problem of the difficult patient interrogated, challenged, and refined psychoanalytic technique in a dialectic through the decades. The 1930s saw explorations of character disorders and primitive defenses; the 1950s saw the application of psychoanalysis on an experimental basis with psychotics and severely borderline patients by Winnicott (1947, 1954), Bion (1954, 1957), Searles (1963), and Rosenfeld (1947, 1987), among others. The 1960s were characterized by reappraisals of the noninterpretative elements of the treatment situation, which led in turn to new understandings of borderline or narcissistic difficulties in forming usable treatment relationships.

Where are we today? Mark Grunes (Chapter 6) remarks that changes in his point of view

came about largely because my clinical experience and that of others brought into question the idea of the good neurotic patient. I do not

---

"withdrawal of libido" (p. 71) can be traced through papers written by Jung, Abraham, and Ferenczi in the years just prior to Freud's discussion of Schreber.

mean that levels of more and less serious psychopathology have disappeared. But more and more it does seem that all neurotic patients over the whole course of treatment, or in certain phases, evidence such features as condensations of oedipal and preoedipal dynamic and structural conflict, narcissistic ego vulnerabilities, significant pregenital fixation, primitive anxieties and defenses, and some degree of early, cumulative environmental trauma. [this volume, p. 131]

If we agree with Grunes, then every patient is a difficult patient at least some of the time and to some degree, and an authentically searching analysis would need to reach the areas of difficulty in the most intelligently cooperative patient.

There is another pleasant irony in the interplay between psychoanalysis as a practice and the more severe disturbances: Recent outcome studies suggest that psychoanalysis, as practiced by some today, may be the treatment of choice for those severer disturbances that formerly were often considered to be unsuitable for analysis. In a comment on outcome studies, Susan Coates (1998) remarks,

It is beginning to emerge that psychoanalysis with adults may be differentially more effective with *more* seriously disturbed patients, such as severely depressed patients or borderline patients, over the long haul. Here an historical note may be in order. It is to the credit of psychoanalysts, and not other clinicians, that they first identified the type of patients now characterized as borderline. They did so because they observed that there was a class of patients, seemingly presenting as hysterics, for whom analysis, at least as it was then conducted, was *not* suitable. Now it turns out, after several conceptual revolutions within psychoanalysis—in understanding disorders of the self, and the common developmental antecedents of such disorders, and in understanding the special techniques they require in treatment—that it may be just these once thought to be "unanalyzable" patients who may be most helped by psychoanalysis, as compared to briefer and/or less intensive forms of treatment. [pp. 115–116]

Sheldon Bach (Chapter 9) and Andrew Druck (Chapter 11) both represent a contemporary Freudian psychoanalysis in which polarities of

so-called deficit based and conflict based explanations—so often politi-
cized in the past—have been left behind. This is the debate between
"can't" and "won't." The person can't do such and such because he never
got the ingredients for it or won't do it because it would tear him apart or
elicit self-punishment or intolerable anxiety. A deeper understanding of
the object relational context for both so-called structural deficit (can't)
and internal conflict (won't) has led to psychoanalytic stances that bear
both in mind. Similarly, these analysts attend equally to the patient's
growth in insight or self-reflective capacity and growth in the capacity to
tolerate and engage in relationship, including the analytic relationship.

Andrew Druck provides a remarkably thoroughgoing systematic and
creative reexamination of these polarities, showing how the clinical process
reveals their necessary interplay and interpenetration. His extended
clinical example shows a therapist variously weighing all factors in the
balance in a flexible technique. The exposition is finely detailed so that
each reader can engage with the complex issues that enter into judgment
calls in this kind of work.

Sheldon Bach focuses on the question of how to establish and
maintain analytic contact with the difficult patient, which he frames as the
problem of maintaining analytic trust. Focusing on trust leads to the
analyst's ongoing preconscious monitoring of processes of disruption and
repair in the analytic dyad. Bach thereby makes a significant link with
observational studies of mother–infant communication where disruption
and repair has proved an important theme and where it is not the absence
of disruption but the capacity for repair of disruptions and the reestablish-
ment of communicative collaboration and mutuality that have been shown
to have value for healthy development (Beebe et al. 1997, Stern 1971,
1977).

Also new are Bach's suggestions for establishing an initial alliance by
discussing with the patient the patient's own ego-dystonic difficulties in
self-regulation as the patient understands them and has so far tried in
effect to self-medicate.

Difficult patients, Bach stresses, were often the recipients of intermittent cathexis from their early caregivers, and they repeat this not only with
their objects, but in their experience of themselves as only intermittently
alive. (This is a different view of the repetition compulsion invoked by
Lasky.) One detail of Bach's rich presentation deserves underlining. Bach
reports that difficult patients often say, "I never knew what my mother was

thinking or feeling." They are, Bach adds, "telling you that they still can't read how other people think or feel and that they still can't believe that their own feelings are real or legitimate" (this volume, p. 192). For those interested in specifying the means of intergenerational transmission of disturbances of the self, this moment of noncommunication would be important to explore. What is going on in the mother exactly when her feelings vis-à-vis the child cannot be read?

Richard Lasky (Chapter 10) describes a patient who virtually ensures that the analyst cannot be honest with him. Lasky, who has a special interest in the abusive patient, has chosen specimen material from a verbally abusive man in an analysis to exemplify a particularly compelling aspect of resistance to analysis in certain types of difficult patient. (An added difficulty here was that the treatment was mandated, not by courts but by the university system.) Much consideration has been given in the literature to patients who are covertly or subtly sadistic or demeaning, and, perhaps especially in the literature on child patients, to identifying degrees of relatedness or unrelatedness, connected with overtly violent or destructive or cruel behavior. Lasky's patient is not subtle in his attacks, and the analyst finds him explosively unrelated.

Lasky's presentation, unlike the others, is not focused on technique. Rather, he takes up the mandate of exemplifying his variety of contemporary Freudian thought by using this abusive patient to show, in what might be considered an almost pure form, the relative invariance of transference phenomena both inside and outside the analysis, when, in his view, the patient is powerfully under the influence of the repetition compulsion. In this regard, Lasky characterizes the patient's abusiveness as primarily drive-discharge phenomena, denoting by this an unrelatedness to the analyst and the analysis, which he sees as the result of a structural condition. While the other contributors would presumably contextualize this problem differently, considering how the analyst might both tolerate and withstand the attack in a way that could possibly create a situation where eventual self-reflection can take place, Lasky is concerned with helping the patient achieve a more stable mental organization, in which the ego is not constantly disrupted. Verbal abuse can serve many functions including keeping control of the interaction and controlling any potential relatedness. Lasky's patient could also be seen as trying to engage him in a situation of mutual hatred.

The range of chapters in this part of the book illustrates some of the controversy in contemporary psychoanalysis over technique and therapeutic action in relation to countertransference.

We may ask what helps the analyst hold the situation constructively and remain able to think about the patient? Is the analyst more helped by trying to re-find a neutral stance vis-à-vis the patient's dilemmas, reminding himself in effect, "This has very little to do with me"? Or is he or she more helped by taking the view, "Look at what has been re-created here," and appreciating his or her present participation in what has been re-created in the treatment situation? Or both?

Some of the questions stimulated by reading these three chapters in tandem will be considered in Chapter 12.

REFERENCES

Beebe, B., Lachmann, F., and Jaffe, J. (1997). Mother–infant interactive structures and presymbolic self-object representation. *Psychoanalytic Dialogues* 7:133–182.

Bion, W. R. (1954). Notes on the theory of schizophrenia. *International Journal of Psycho-Analysis.* 35:113–118.

——— (1957). Differentiation of the psychotic from the non-psychotic personalities. *International Journal of Psycho-Analysis.* 38:266–275.

——— (1959). Attacks on linking. *International Journal of Psycho-Analysis.* 40:308–315.

Coates, S. (1998). Having a mind of one's own and holding the other in mind: commentary on paper by Peter Fonagy and Mary Target. *Psychoanalytic Dialogues* 8(1):115–148.

Etchegoyen, R. H. (1991). On narcissism: text and context. In *Freud's "On Narcissism: An Introduction,"* ed. J. Sandler, E. Person, and P. Fonagy, pp. 54–74. New Haven, CT and London: Yale University Press.

Freud, S. (1911). Psycho-analytic notes on an autobiographical account of a case of paranoia. *Standard Edition* 12:3–82.

——— (1914). On narcissism: an introduction. *Standard Edition* 14:69–102.

——— (1933). New introductory lectures. *Standard Edition* 22:5–182.

Rosenfeld, H. A. (1947). Analysis of a schizophrenic state with depersonalization. *International Journal of Psycho-Analysis.* 28:130–139.

——— (1987). Appendix: on the treatment of psychotic states by psychoanalysis—an historical approach. In *Impasse and Interpretation,* ed. H. A. Rosenfeld, pp. 281-311. London: Tavistock.

Searles, H. (1963). Transference psychosis in the psychotherapy of chronic schizophrenia. *International Journal of Psycho-Analysis* 44:249–281.

Stern, D. (1971). A micro-analysis of mother–infant interaction: behavior regulating social contact between a mother and her 3½ month old twins. *Journal of the American Academy of Child Psychiatry* 10:501–517.

———— (1977). Missteps in the dance. In *The First Relationship*, pp. 109–128. Cambridge, MA: Harvard University Press.

Winnicott, D. W. (1947). Hate in the counter-transference. *International Journal of Psycho-Analysis* 30. Also in *Through Paediatrics to Psycho-Analysis*, pp. 194–203. New York: Basic Books, 1975.

———— (1954). Metapsychological and clinical aspects of regression within the psycho-analytical set-up. *International Journal of Psycho-Analysis. Through Paediatrics to Psycho-Analysis*, pp. 278–294. New York: Basic Books, 1975.

9

On Treating the Difficult Patient

Sheldon Bach

Perhaps the primary problem in engaging the difficult patient is to build and retain what Ellman (1991) has called analytic trust. These difficult patients have generally lost their faith not only in their caregivers, spouses, and other objects, but also in the world itself as a place of expectable and manageable contingencies. Imagine what it would be like to inhabit a world where you never feel certain that your loved ones will be there when you come home, and not even certain that your home will still be there. Imagine what it is like to turn on your kitchen stove or your car ignition, always half-expecting them to explode. Imagine what it is like to feel that the air you breathe is toxic or that the air supply is running out. These patients have lost their trust not only in people but also in the environment as a reliable place that will hold them safely. So one task we have is to restore this faith, and to rebuild it again and again as it inevitably gets lost in the vicissitudes of the transference.

We do this by making the analytic consulting room a safe and reliable place and by being absolutely truthful with the patient about everything that occurs in this place and that happens between us. Whenever the situation becomes momentarily unreliable, sometimes because we have failed as we inevitably must over the course of years, we recognize this and analyze our own reactions as well as the patient's, for there is no way that a patient who mistrusts everything will trust us at all if we insist on leaving ourselves out of the equation. There is a way of being absolutely straight with the patient without indulging in confessions, apologia, or gross parameters, and this way is different and must be worked out with each individual patient.

I say "worked out" with the patient because, even if the patient is unable to engage in mutual collaboration, as most of these patients at first are not, *we* are always collaborating with them by going along with their vision of reality even when they reject ours. In the transference regression these patients do not really experience themselves as completely separate, and so they cannot believe or coexist with separate psychic realities. The idea that the same reality can be viewed in different ways by different people, and that the patient's *and* the analyst's views can both have truth and legitimacy, is often beyond their emotional comprehension. Thus a true collaboration between two independent people may be impossible, and we must defer to the patient's vision of reality until he becomes able to tolerate our presence and psychic reality in the room with him.

By this means we enter the patient's phenomenal world and begin to build analytic trust, which at first may be more of a trust in the safety of the analytic setup than in us as an object. For in many cases we do not really exist as an object until we make a mistake, or until something happens to make us loom up as a threatening stranger. Such disruptions of the budding narcissistic transference and the therapeutic alliance may result from the patient's impulses or our own ineptness, expressed in a mutual enactment or a projective identification, but they demand immediate understanding and rectification.

Each episode of attempted alliance, disruption of the alliance, and repair raises the mutual trust to a higher level—we have gone through something together and survived it. Each episode of mismatch, disruption, and repair is also an ongoing process of regulation of the dyadic system. I am emphasizing the simultaneous emergence and interplay of mutual trust and mutual regulation in the analytic dyad. What do I mean by mutual regulation?

In the days when psychologists still experimented with conditioning rats, a well-known cartoon showed one rat in a cage telling another; "I've got this guy trained by now—every time I press the lever, he gives me a pellet of food!" The psychologist, of course, felt that he was conditioning or regulating the rat, but indeed they had arrived at a jointly satisfactory state of mutual regulation. They could trust each other to be constant, reliable, mutually satisfying objects. Now this sort of mutual regulation is continually occurring, often without awareness, in the successful mother–infant dyad and also in the successful patient–analyst dyad. The analytic dyad is unusual in the analyst's insistence that dysregulations should ultimately be verbalized and analyzed, not just remedied or glossed over. But since so many of our difficult patients are products of poorly regulated mother–infant dyads or badly regulated family systems, it is not always easy to know how to handle any immediate situation.

Let me be doubly concrete and imagine a situation where a new patient complains of being too hot or too cold in the consulting room and asks that the temperature be regulated. Do we simply comply as social convention demands, do we question and investigate further, or, having checked that the temperature is normal, do we make an interpretation about possible emotional reactions and physiological changes? I suspect there is no cookbook answer to this kind of question, and that the complexities of mutual regulation in the treatment process can be addressed only through the complexities of mutual discussion in the supervision process in which the two parties have learned to trust each other and to speak openly. In this sense, good supervision is similar to good therapy.

But I hope that by now I have made it clear why I feel that analytic trust is based on and grows with successful mutual regulation. The patient arrives to find you always there and mostly on time; his own irregularities of arrival and of thought and emotion are met with temperance and understanding; the couch is always there, the temperature is usually comfortable, and nothing physical ever explodes. Slowly, he begins to develop trust, first in the physical regularities of the analytic holding world, then in the process by which each mismatch is slowly understood and repaired, then in the reliability of the analyst as some kind of part object or self object and, ultimately, in the reliablity of the analyst as a separate whole object.

Meanwhile, we are uncovering and analyzing those regulatory difficulties that most of these patients have even if they don't know it. I am talking about disturbances of breathing, of sleeping, of eating, of bodily

functioning, and of orientation in the world, but I also include disturbances of emotional regulation that are inseparable from the physiological,
for example, dysregulation of affect so that highs and lows are too extreme,
too prolonged, or too rapidly cycled and unpredictable. Above all, I am
referring to a kind of intermittent cathexis of the object (Furman and
Furman 1984) so that object constancy is almost always in question. Many
of these patients have experienced this intermittent cathexis from their
own caregivers, who attended to them only when they were needed as
narcissistic objects. When grown up, they tend not only to repeat this
intermittent cathexis with their own objects but also to experience
themselves as only intermittently alive and coherent; their own self-
constancy is always in question. Of course, regulatory problems like
disturbances in orientation, emotional regulation, or intermittent cathexis
will emerge in the transference anyhow, with the patient either doing it to
you or getting you to do it to him. But since these transference reactions
are so often accompanied by intense rage and other blinding emotions, I
think the analyst is at a great advantage if the subject has already been
raised and discussed in a historical context.

We are talking about people who, because of an early failure of the
environment to fit in with their very unusual temperaments or endowments, or because of an early or cumulative trauma, have not even
developed a trust in the regularities of their physical environment, let
alone their object environment. These early disturbances of mutual
regulation, which, as Schore (1994) has demonstrated, get built into the
developing nervous system, lead inevitably to dysregulation of the drive
economy and to disturbances of object relations.

Although the earliest nonverbal and verbal interactions can profoundly influence brain chemistry and synaptic growth, I believe that later
verbal interactions and mutual regulation can also influence brain chemistry and alter behavior at least as much as psychotropic medications. Over
the course of the first few years infants learn to respond at the symbolic
level as well as at the sensorimotor levels of the mother–infant interaction.
But even adults, and particularly difficult patients, continue to respond at
the sensorimotor-physiological level, precisely because that is where the
earliest mutual regulations went awry. These sensorimotor-physiological
responses frequently manifest themselves in inappropriate or negative
transference reactions or enactments, which are often as hard for the
patient to understand as they are for us. I try in the first sessions with

these patients to get an overview not only of the dynamic picture but also a history of the early dysregulation with which it is entwined. This frequently interests the patient sufficiently so that he may try to fill in the missing data or to verify it on his own initiative. I find that working with this from the very beginning is a big help in dealing with transference disruptions, in understanding and managing them, and in arriving at the better regulated interaction that is the foundation of basic trust.

Naturally, I go along with those patients who refuse to talk about anything but the immediate here and now, but I treat it as a kind of defensive distortion. Normally, past, present and future interconnect and continually retranscribe each other, so that touching a life at any point should connect us with the whole. But with difficult patients it is easier to move the case if one has a handle on both the past and the present.

Since there is little time for theoretical discussion, let me simply state my belief that controversies such as here and now versus then and there, deficit versus conflict, hermeneutics versus science, interpretation versus holding, and other similar shibboleths are often false dichotomies that promote political correctness and keep us from thinking and speaking about what we actually do. I recall that in the not too distant past the fear of employing parameters made a whole generation of analysts talk and act as if the political police were just around the corner. So in the multiplicity of positions about the analyst's stance with the patient, it still seems to me that the best place to be most of the time is as close to the patient's phenomenal world as possible.

Just to put a little flesh on these bones, here is a brief example from a recent consultation.

A competent and experienced analyst presents a young professional woman, attractive and successful, whom he has seen in therapy for three months and who is threatening to quit. The patient complains of her need to attach herself to some man, but when he gets too close she feels obliged to break it off. She divorced her husband after starting an affair with an older man who lived in another country. When this older man phoned her to break off the relationship, she developed frightening somatic symptoms, called the Emergency Medical Service, and threw herself into the arms of the responding ambulance driver who was obliged to hold her and caress her to calm her down. She then had a brief affair with this driver that helped carry her through the period of breakup with the older man. She is able to say that her mother was always nervous and agitated, that the beloved older man was, in her own words, "a fantasy father figure" and that her father used to rub her legs to put her to sleep, but none of this seems to help her or to engage her.

When the therapist takes a long weekend vacation, she goes to a psychic who gives her a piece of rock that makes her feel more calm and secure. Over the weekend she joins a group of Buddhists who meditate and chant. When the therapist tries to connect these enactments with his absence, she appears to find him vaguely amusing and seems unaffected. Shortly thereafter she complains that therapy is boring, is not helping, and makes plans to leave. The therapist repeatedly focuses on her need to attach herself to some man and to break it off when he gets too close, but when this interpretation does not seem to help, he comes for a consultation. Talking with the therapist in the way that I have here helps him find a way into the case. He now remembers that when the patient first went to kindergarten, her mother dropped her off in front of the schoolhouse and she became disoriented and never found her way to the classroom. He remembers that the patient always envied those little girls whose mothers shampooed their hair, because her mother never touched her like that. As the therapist begins to inquire into other areas of self- and mutual regulation, the patient becomes more responsive. As a young woman she felt that she lacked "discipline," and she moved to Germany in the hope that living in Germany might instill some discipline in her. Now he helps her understand that her "lack of discipline" is really an inability to self-regulate, connected to her mother's failures to help her regulate when she was a child. The patient stops talking about leaving and becomes more interested in her history. The treatment is under way.

I have been emphasizing mutual regulatory processes both because they are terribly important with the more disturbed patient and also because we normally don't hear much about them in Freudian theory, where the economic point of view has gone out of fashion. Nevertheless, many of these patients *know* there is something wrong with their regulatory processes but are unable to conceptualize it, and have given themselves explanations such as "I don't have any discipline," "My trouble is I love too much," "I'm disorganized and disoriented and it's genetic," and so on. They are often interested to discover that these lifelong issues may stem from a chronic dysregulation of the dyad or family system, and that self-regulation can be learned.

Approaching these issues from the economic or regulatory side is usually much easier for difficult patients, most of whom have problems with reflective self-awareness and symbolization. The patient who went to see a psychic while her analyst was away could not see any connection between these two events, and would probably have been frightened and fled if she had. But I do believe that talking with her about the stone the psychic gave her and her psychophysiological reactions to its solidity and permanence would have elicited her own feelings of tenuousness and impermanence, which underlie her belief that she lacked discipline. I would then anticipate associations about childhood attempts at self-healing by playing with solid objects or putting herself in situations, like the Buddhist chanting, which gave her a temporary sense of solidity and stability. If she became interested in this, one might track the changes in her feelings of insubstantiality and, only after a long time, begin to relate these to the analyst's physical or emotional absence.

Now even in this oversimplified case vignette, there are so many things going on simultaneously and so many possible theoretical levels and viewpoints that the clinician may well wonder how to sort it out or where to begin. Do we address the patient's complaint that she needs to attach herself to some man but then feels compelled to break it off? The therapist did try to make just such transference interpretations when she threatened to quit, but to no avail. Should we address her affair with the oedipal older man, who calmed her and soothed her like her own father when he used to rub her legs to put her to sleep? She makes these connections herself, because she knows about the Oedipus complex, but they touch nothing in her. Should we deal with her anger at her mother, who abandoned her on her first day at school and presumably never shampooed her lovingly as she imagined other mothers did? Should we interpret her father's leg massages as substitutes for her mother's shampoos? While all these dynamic connections are valid enough, I am reasonably sure that initially they would get nowhere.

If we are only able to listen carefully enough, patients will usually prescribe exactly what is necessary for their healing to begin. In this case, in response to a long weekend break, the patient reacts by finding a hard, permanent, massageable object, and a state of consciousness in which she can feel alone yet surrounded by others. So we know that she is unusually sensitive to separations but is able to deal with them only in a concrete way. She requires a regulatory dyad that will stabilize and solidify both her self-regulation and her analytic trust, yet at the same time she is likely to struggle against those very parameters such as increased frequency and use of the couch that will help the dyad become regulatory. We handle this by remaining phenomenologically close to her concrete use of objects and things in the interests of self-regulation, while at the same time trying to relate them to her earlier history of dysregulation.

Thus, with these patients, we start from the concrete and move to the abstract, we start from the physical and move to the mental and emotional, just as we always start from whatever is self-centered and only gradually move to whatever is object-centered. We do this because their deficiencies of symbolization and self-awareness lead them to communicate impulsively by enactments that are sometimes unintelligible and often uninterpretable. They respond at this behavioral and sensorimotor level because their basic mistrust and ongoing dysregulation have prevented them from developing the kind of separateness and transitional space, the impulse control, the symbolic abilities, and the degree of self-reflection that would be prerequisite for the use of classical analytic technique.

One might say that classical technique assumes a large degree of shared reality between analyst and patient, an assumption that usually does not hold with the difficult patient. One way that children learn about reality is by reading their mother's face and learning that she has a mind and feelings that are sometimes the same as theirs and sometimes different. Ideally, they learn that their own feelings and their mother's feelings both have reality and legitimacy. But when difficult patients say, "I never knew what my mother was thinking or feeling," they are telling you that they still can't read how other people think or feel and that they still can't believe that their own feelings are real or legitimate.

Caregivers convey reality by legitimizing the child's emotions and thoughts. If the mother's face conveys one meaning and her metacommunication in a different modality conveys another meaning, then the child may not become schizophrenic but he is likely to become a difficult patient. Problems of reality are tremendously amplified in the psychoanalytic situation, not only because of the potential conflict between the psychic realities of patient and analyst but also because of the many different levels of reality on which the treatment exists. Do the patient and analyst really love each other or really want to kill each other, or is it only metaphorical? At times it certainly feels real enough to both participants. Ideally, the analyst can move freely between levels of reality and encompass the metaphor, but the difficult patient, who could never read his mother's face and be sure of reality, has big problems achieving this.

In the psychoanalytic situation this often emerges as an underlying sadomasochistic struggle over whose version of reality should be accepted. Freud (1915) speaks of "women of elemental passionateness" who treat transference love as real love and "refuse to accept the psychical in place of the material" (pp. 166–167). But one cannot interpret the transference, which is a metaphor, to a patient whose mental organization is unable to accommodate the symbolism of metaphor. In practice this means that such patients will confuse or confabulate what should be transferential and symbolic issues with real issues of love or death, and will struggle with the analyst as if he were in fact refusing to love them or trying to rape or kill them. The patient I discussed had a very real fear of her own "elemental passionateness," which was one reason she was so hesitant to allow herself to become deeply involved in treatment.

These patients are unable to understand that the same reality can be viewed in different ways by different people and that their point of view and the analyst's point of view can both have reality and legitimacy. This is because of their great difficulty shifting between levels of meaning, symbolism, and reality, but it is precisely at these shifts or transitions between levels, contexts, and frameworks that most transference disruptions occur and also that the greatest potential for change emerges (Bach 1994).

The patient who, in response to a weekend break, goes to a psychic and gets a rock to calm her, would very likely have become angry and upset had the analyst continued to insist on the connection between these two events. I believe that to conceptualize this as denial is misleading. She would have experienced the analyst's insistent interpretations just as she experienced her mother's dropping her off outside the schoolhouse, as a dysregulation and a desertion. She would have become confused and disoriented and would have felt lost. This confusion, which is a mental disorientation at transitions between levels of symbolism and contextual frameworks, may often be expressed or paralleled by a physical disorientation at transitions between places and events.

In treatment we hold the patient in the analytic framework, and a good deal of our effort goes toward maintaining and adjusting that framework, which the patient is constantly probing in order to test the levels of reality and learn how much he can trust us. Through enactments and counterenactments, through projective identifications that are contained and metabolized, through constructions and interpretations and through the vicissitudes of the transference, a transitional space develops in which confusion, ambiguity, and separation can be tolerated and explored. This feels to the patient very much as if, instead of being dropped off outside the school, the analyst had instead taken her by the hand and accompanied her into the classroom.

Eventually, a psychoanalytic space develops that is able to contain two whole, autonomous individuals who are capable of loving and hating each other and of trying to deal with each other's psychic realities. By then the patient's language and verbal behavior will truly be linked to his sensorimotor and nonverbal behavior and the analyst's interpretations will be heard not as boundary violations or contradictory communications, but as potentially helpful contributions. But by then, of course, the treatment is almost over.

One may well ask, as indeed this book's editor, Dr. Carolyn Ellman, did ask me, "So what's Freudian about that?" Upon reflection, one of the things that seems Freudian to me is that I was trained as a Freudian analyst and still believe that the classical method is the paradigm we strive for with the ideal analytic patient. The modifications that Freudian analysts have evolved over the years originated with classical technique and have a historical continuity with it. They were introduced as it became clear that classical technique didn't always work well enough for patients with severe problems of trust, of self-regulation, of self-reflexivity, and of symbolization. The classical method, when strictly enforced with these patients, sometimes resulted in losing the patient completely or producing a stalemate or a pseudoanalysis, where the patient goes through the motions of an analysis out of compliance or desperation, but without belief.

Working from the technical stance I described, these difficult patients often may and sometimes may not become amenable to strict classical technique. But at least they always know that the transference feelings they experienced in the treatment felt real to them and were acknowledged by me, and that the unconscious fantasies that emerged were their fantasies and not mine. For people who already have difficulty moving between levels of reality, nothing can be more important than learning to trust their own feelings in the heat of the analytic situation. If they can also learn to accept *my* feelings, then they have come a very long way toward resolving the sadomasochistic struggle over whose version of reality can be trusted. And the primacy of this struggle, between awareness and defense, between self and other, and between love and hate is, after all, an essential part of what we understand as the Freudian vision of life and of psychoanalysis.

REFERENCES

Bach, S. (1994). *The Language of Perversion and the Language of Love.* Northvale, NJ: Jason Aronson.

Ellman, S. (1991). *Freud's Technique Papers: A Contemporary Perspective.* Northvale, NJ: Jason Aronson.

Freud, S. (1915). Observations on transference love. *Standard Edition* 12:159–171.

Furman, R. and Furman, E. (1984). Intermittent de-cathexis—a type of parental dysfunction. *International Journal of Psycho-Analysis* 65(4):423–434.

Schore, A. (1994). *Affect Regulation and the Origins of the Self: The Neurobiology of Emotional Development.* Hillsdale, NJ: Erlbaum.

10

The "More Difficult" Patient and Differing Conceptualizations of Dynamics and Technique in Freudian and Relational Psychoanalysis

Richard Lasky

Mr. J., a graduate student, was referred to me by his department chairperson. This was not a self-motivated consultation: he was told by the department to either go into analysis or to leave the program. There is a certain kind of student that every teacher is familiar with and usually dreads—that is, the "sharpshooter," the student who challenges anything and everything, and who seems ready to take virtually any position as long as it is the opposite of the instructor's. There are many reasons why people behave in this way: people have authority problems; some do it for exhibitionistic reasons; some do it out of sadism, others in order to provoke an attack that will gratify masochistic needs; some people don't know any other way to develop an intimate relationship with someone else and, for them, a feeling of connection either does not exist or, if it does, it feels dead or empty without this intense, malignant quality. Most teachers have a student like this from time to time and have developed a number of strategies to try to keep such behavior under control, recognizing, however, that at best they will only be partly successful. It is a little bit like slapping at mosquitoes in the summertime—an irritating nuisance that comes with the territory but, certainly, nothing that one can't learn to live with.[1]

When Mr. J. began to suggest in classes that the instructor's opinions were not intellectual positions but, more likely, were motivated by neurotic conflict; when he felt free to speculate in class about what the nature of his instructor's conflicts might be; and when he actually began suggesting, again in class, to some of his instructors that they would benefit from a good analysis, the department chair became involved. Mr. J. was told to either work this out, himself, in an analysis or to do it, instead, somewhere else. Mr. J.'s chairperson said, when he made the referral, that he thought Mr. J. was quite shaken up by this, and he was guardedly optimistic about Mr. J.'s chances of analytically examining himself, even though this would be a treatment initiated under considerable coercion.

Mr. J. clearly had more than just a tendency toward action and he very much gave the impression, in our consultation visits, that his difficulties were more characterological than neurotic. He did seem to me to be in considerable distress and to be feeling under a great deal of pressure to gain some relief. Despite all of his acting out in school he had some resources that made considering an analysis for him a possibility; for example, he was very bright and very articulate, he had what looked at the time like a good defensive structure, and he appeared to have some capacity for self-reflection. On the downside, however, the extent of his capacity for sustained self-reflectiveness was not entirely clear, and I was not sure whether he was in conflict about having been made to see that he had some serious problems that needed working on or, on the other hand, whether what seemed like conflict was not merely frustration at having been foiled in getting what he wanted. One can't always tell ahead of time how these things will work out, so we decided to begin an analysis to see how it would go.

The typical neurotic patient comes to treatment with an overriding wish to resolve conflicts, and this wish is usually able to rise above an

---

1. My choice of metaphor is clearly in the language of countertransference, and I will return to this point shortly.

understandably intense ambivalence about the anxiety it will entail, and about the hidden gratifications that will have to be renounced. Certain character-disordered patients enter treatment for the express purpose of gratifying instinctual longings (sometimes whichever instinctual longings are paramount at the moment, and sometimes with long-range narcissistic goals in mind). Usually, they are consciously unaware of this or, at least, what they are aware of does not feel inappropriate or narcissistic to them. They no more walk into the analyst's consulting room knowing that they are seeking instinctual gratifications at the expense of conflict resolution than Mr. J. entered the classroom with the conscious thought, "I am not interested in any educational issues, all I want to do is to demolish the instructor." For such people, both their immediate behavior and their long-range intentions are so ego syntonic (as a result of compromised psychic structure, which is why we define them as character disordered) that they are truly unable to be adequately self-reflective about what they are doing, even when some residually reflective capacities are available to them in other areas. Beyond this, they are also actively motivated not to be reflective about much of what they want if the act of reflection itself runs the risk of bringing about real instinctual frustration and deprivation. And so, in such patients, both deficit and defense are at work in hindering reflective capacities and frustration tolerance when they are in conflict.

From the earliest moments of our work together, Mr. J. had very strong responses to my slightest interventions, particularly if they had any against-the-grain qualities. His reactions were pitted against my comments instead of being responsive to them and, initially, they took an innocent-seeming form, that is, of musing about why I chose to comment about one thing rather than another, or why I might have chosen this time rather than any other time to make my comments. His interest in these questions was entirely superficial and he was attempting to turn them against me by making me *his* patient rather than he remaining *mine*. These questions then progressed to teasing assertions about how unconsciously self-revealing my interventions were, and he clearly thought that I would find this as humiliating and narcissistically injurious as he did when I seemed to know something about him that he didn't know first. As he escalated this dynamic he felt compelled to list my flaws and then to question whether my psychopathology would permit me to be helpful to him. In time, Mr.

J. was genuinely convinced that I was infinitely more crazy than he was, or ever could be. This, in turn, progressed until we reached a point where Mr. J was explicitly in the same kind of rage with me that seemed to be implicitly fueling his behavior with his teachers. He was sufficiently open about his contempt for me by this time that he would now respond to any unwelcome intervention of mine by saying, "Fuck you, fat boy!" or "Eat shit, motherfucker!" or "That was the stupidest remark I ever heard! Where did you get your license to practice, you four-eyed retard, Macy's?" In his more benign moods he might only ask, "How can you be so off? Are we in the same room together, putz, or were you on the moon when I was talking?"

One might ask why, under these circumstances, I did not back away when I saw that he was getting out of hand? First, the definition of what is or is not getting out of hand is very easy to see with hindsight, but it can often be exceptionally hard to determine when you are in the middle of it. Second, one expects an intensification and a concentration of a patient's conflicts and defensive operations as the transference regression deepens. Third, for some patients who demonstrate this kind of exaggerated response to the analyst's interventions the very act of being able to put it into open and excessive action in the treatment brings it to their conscious attention, thus making it, for the first time, available for analysis. Fourth, we want to remember that there is a considerable difference between the analyst's intent when he makes an intervention and the received experience of it by the patient. And, finally, given what we know about the demand characteristics of the compulsion to repeat I think that even my best efforts to be nonconfrontational, to avoid unsettling Mr. J., and even active attempts to be as conciliatory as possible would likely have still been unsuccessful.

This discussion points to one of the most basic differences in how Freudian analysts and relational analysts look at transference. This chapter highlights a few of these differences. I don't particularly want to argue the rightness or wrongness of either position. It is not that I don't have an opinion about this—I think it's obvious that people identified with a particular school of thought believe its ideas have the most utility for them. Rather, I will articulate some of the ways they are different enough to have major consequences on how we then end up conceptualizing about and working with patients.

Freudians assume that the repetition compulsion determines the contents of a patient's transference. For Freudians the relationship with the analyst will only determine the particular *expressive shape* the transference comes to take in the analysis. The relational view suggests, instead, that the variables of each individual analyst's personality contributes not only to the shape the transference eventually takes but also creates the contents of the transference itself. This is a critical distinction in the two points of view and it explains why Freudians emphasize mainly displacement (and sometimes projection) in their definition of transference, and why some relational analysts view transference as a kind of *perception*. I will elaborate on this distinction shortly.

There are a number of ways one can understand Mr. J.'s behavior. First, as I have just mentioned, one can view it as a not unexpected analytic regression; a deepening of the transference that brings the conflict directly into the analytic setting. Next, one can view this dynamically, for example, from an oedipal perspective as revealed by his history. Mr. J.'s behavior replicated both the destructiveness and aggression he felt toward his father as well as the method he used throughout childhood—emotionally assaultive temper tantrums—to insert himself between his parents when he felt too left out. If one wished to view this from the vantage point of identification processes, one could see it as an identification with his mother who was prone to be quite accusatory in her dealings with others and who, when direct accusation was not available to her, would wound others under the guise of imparting helpful information. Along the lines of preoedipal pathology, particularly as it intersects with the pathological quality of his object relations, we would note that Mr. J.'s behavior and his language, both in school and in treatment, reflect the erotic analization of his inner world while, at the same time, making very clear both the aggressively tinged nature of his object relations as well as the sadomasochistic context in which the maintenance of object constancy felt most secure to him.

Rather than go into the specific details that I believe would support these various frames of reference, I will discuss a specific aspect of Mr. J.'s treatment to illustrate certain technical difficulties. We often find that some difficulties may be insurmountable even when we think we understand their dynamic operation in the patient quite well. The problem here was that, despite the many ways of looking at Mr. J.'s behavior I had at my disposal, a collaborative method of looking at them together seemed impossible. This was because Mr. J.'s intent in communicating with me was dominated by his need to use it mainly for discharge purposes. Speaking was, for Mr. J., more often than not, an automatic exercise in tension reduction (which is not to say that it didn't also have additional purposes, but those purposes were either subordinated to his need to reduce tension or simply unavailable for examination as long as interaction did not serve communicative purposes for Mr. J.). He ignored the content of what I said in favor of telling me to go fuck myself as a way of attempting to regulate dysphoric internal experience and he was, for the most part, satisfied if he achieved this result. He felt no real curiosity about what he said most of the time and no urge to go beyond it. This was not universally true of every utterance that ever passed his lips, nor was it true of every stage of his treatment, but it was most pronounced, early on, when my interventions served as a direct irritant to him (raising the stakes, one might say, beyond the level of tension that was tolerable to him).

What is Freudian about the way I have understood Mr. J., and what is Freudian about how I have understood the therapeutic (or, perhaps, not so therapeutic) interactions? The first Freudian concept I have used and, perhaps, the most obvious is my belief that Mr. J.'s interactions with me were designed to serve drive-discharge purposes more than they were intended for relational ends. This is not to say that they had no relational significance, but rather I am emphasizing how subordinated Mr. J.'s object-directed needs were to his need to reduce narcissistic (and other) tensions. It may be true that certain relational needs were gratified through drive discharge processes; however, the questions that were eventually raised in my mind about whether or not Mr. J. was analyzable were not centered on relational issues but on drive-discharge issues (that is, on the difficulties in structural, object-relational, and self-regulatory processes that may have been compromised as a consequence of these habitual drive-discharge patterns).

The question of how a feeling of trust can be developed with such a patient, the importance of how "ownership" of the treatment can be felt by certain kinds of narcissistically disturbed patients (of which Mr. J. was one example), the management of aggression with these patients (whether by acceptance, interpretation, or limit setting), how one might work toward building a working alliance with a patient like Mr. J., and, certainly, how one might help a patient like Mr. J. to develop more adequate symbolizing processes so as to gain some distance from sheer experience (which would then, most likely, have a strong influence on his ability to use human interactions for more sophisticated ends than simply the relief of unbearable tension states) are all questions that would probably occur to most analysts. However, I think they would occur with significantly different emphases in Freudian versus non-Freudian analysts.

There is a basic issue that separates Freudians from analysts of the various relational schools, a difference in conceptualization rather than one only of therapeutic tactics, that is of particular significance in both its theoretical and technical consequences. For Freudians Mr. J.'s behavior in analysis, in fact this kind of behavior as it may exist in any patient—behavior that is repeatedly acted out in many different settings and with many different people, behavior that repetitively enacts a particular, and often complex, fantasy constellation—is an important part of the patient's psychology that is not thought to be dependent on the actual behavior of the analyst. We think this is true even when, through accidents of circumstance, the analyst seems to provide reality confirmation for the patient's construction of him in either his behavior or personality style. Freudians think that others are used in symbolic ways according to the patient's inner needs. Freudians don't believe that they initiate either the need or the stereotypic manner in which they eventually become used. The reality attributes of analysts (except, sometimes, in countertransference dilemmas) either gratuitously coincide with the way the patient needs them to be, or their attributes are reworked in fantasy so as to seem to conform to the patient's inner needs. As I alluded to earlier, this reflects a concept of transference that is based on the displacement of complex fantasy constellations in the patient's mind. And because we think of this as stemming from the mind of the patient, Freudians find it quite unimaginable to define transference as a form of perception. Beyond this, we also think that transference is reflective of important intrapsychic processes that, however much they were nurtured in a relationship and however much the patient tries to foist that relationship onto us in the here and now, have become functionally autonomous parts of a person's psychology by the time we see them for treatment. Perhaps it is also useful to make a further distinction: Freudians do not equate the relationship with transference; relationships are manifest and their transferential significance is always partly, if not mostly, latent. Another way of putting this is to say that for Freudians, fantasy-dominated transference is not a current relationship that somehow manages to reflect the same kinds of issues that bothered the patient in the past; it is an illuminating, if sometimes frightening, demonstration of the many and highly inventive ways that we all, not just our patients, continually repeat and rework our understanding of reality so as to force it to conform to the nature of our inner needs, and, in the service of this, we use whatever props (including the people in our lives) come to hand. Freudians disagree with the relational idea that transference, and even psychic structure itself, cannot exist outside of a relational dyad. We dispute this assertion despite our full awareness of both the important influence of the original mother–infant tie on psychic development and the influence of the analyst's reality behavior on the treatment. For Freudians the bottom line is not the dyad without which there are no psychic processes; the bottom line is *intrapsychic* processes that then determine the subjective realities of the current circumstance or relationship.

Because of the distinctions we make between the transference and the relationship, we do not think that everything that happens between the analyst and the patient reflects a basic truth about the relationship. To use Mr. J.'s ideas as a case in point, we do not think, for example, that just because he says it there must be at least some grain of truth in his repetitive assertions that (if only I were honest enough to confront it in myself) I am a fat, four-eyed, retarded son-of-a-bitch, the kind of a putz who deserves to be told to eat shit and to go fuck himself, or that I probably bought my license to practice at the bargain basement of Macy's.

Despite the facts that I am fat, that I do wear glasses, that I do not always understand as much as I would wish to, and despite the fact that I sometimes get into destructive countertransference difficulties, none of this (individually or even taken together) is sufficient or even adequate to explain Mr. J.'s vehemence or his frankly assaultive exploitation of any of these facts. Some of the things he said about me can be recognized as patently absurd, whereas others are recognizably true. The use of things that were true about me, these "facts," were merely exploited by Mr. J. when he was in a state of conflict, and his conflicts existed well before he ever met me; his conflicts, not my personality or behavior, drove him, first, to perceive me in the way that he did and, then, to treat me in the way that he did.

To return to the countertransference language I commented on earlier, surely my fantasy of Mr. J. being like a mosquito that needed to be swatted could not have been lost on him, and surely when my countertransference was active it made the situation worse, not better. My choice of imagery and the wish expressed in it reflects the existence of a certain kind of transference–countertransference mutuality in the clearly sadomasochistic scenarios that developed between us, over time. However, even when one can point to the unmistakable presence of countertransference on my part, it does not necessarily follow that my countertransference was responsible for the kind of relationship Mr. J. needed to have with me; at times it may have made a bad situation worse, but it did not, in and of itself, create the bad situation to begin with.

I have heard it said, although I think it is a misrepresentation, that the Freudian emphasis on the patient's intrapsychic processes is a "one-person" psychology that leads us to disavow any responsibility for what happens in sessions. We have been criticized for attempting to be as objective, neutral, and abstinent in our dealings with patients as we can. We think of objectivity, neutrality, and abstinence as ideal conditions to strive toward that we well know we can never achieve in actuality and that reality circumstances would never actually permit. Our commitment to trying, nevertheless, to get as reasonably close to these conditions as reality *will* permit in no way suggests that we are unaware of how either our strengths or our deficiencies in this regard, or how the use we make of ourselves with our patients, helps to shape the course of an analysis. What we disagree about is whether either our lapses or the unique characteristics of our personalities are the factors that bring into action the specific contents and conflicts latently represented in our patient's transferences to us, which then surface in the analytic relationship that develops.

Another way of articulating this is to ask whether the characteristics and behavior of the analyst are treated as a foreground issue or as a background issue. In other words, if the analyst's characteristics and behavior are treated as a foreground issue (as in the relational models), then transference itself is a joint production of the analyst and the patient, and the problem that Freudians have with conceptualizing the transference in this way is that the concept of intrapsychic process is essentially jettisoned. When the characteristics and behavior of the analyst are treated as a background issue (as one finds in the Freudian model), intrapsychic processes are seen as superordinate and transference is seen as a compulsive kind of repetition, where the characteristics and behavior of the analyst (whatever they are) are being used—bent by unconscious processes—to give what are actually fantasy-dominated events the superficial appearance of perceived reality.

The purpose of putting reality aspects of the analyst to use in this way is mainly protective. Using a thin veneer of what looks like reality keeps the underlying fantasy aspects of the transference obscured, and its value, in terms of its defensive function, lies in its ability to keep anxiety, guilt, and other disturbing affects in check. Thus the patient's claim that he is responding to something rather than initiating it, and the subsequent claim that what he is responding to is a perception of us, is designed specifically to avoid a more accurate, but conflictual and perhaps even painful, quite different perception. That is, that he is continuously reworking what starts as a generally realistic view of the analyst, and of the analytic situation, in order to satisfy inner demands that require a suspension of how reality *can* be perceived in favor of how reality *must* be perceived. To put this more simply, and to bring us back full circle to Mr. J., Mr. J. needed to curse me out and treat me the way he did for reasons of his own, and not because I had somehow prompted it by doing something to him in the treatment that either caused it or, at least, deserved it. He not only chose the contents but he also chose the timing in ways designed to give the impression that his attacks had validity, that they were based on a perception of reality that he could convince himself he was entitled to respond to in these ways. Certainly Mr. J., as is true for all patients, was at times capable of a relatively realistic perception of me and of our relationship, although I think reality is always relative, for analysts as well as for patients. But this capacity all too often became partially compromised under the pressure of conflict and regression. The subsequent distortions are not just worthy of passing analytic interest, they are, in fact, the very stuff of analysis. For Freudians, this need to be able to find a justification to curse me out in a way that is seemingly based on reality, this compulsion to see me in a particular way and then to find presumably legitimate reasons to verbally assault me, does not (as it might for a social-constructivist or an intersubjectivist) raise a question of what I might have done to bring it about. The patient's constructions of us, that is, his very belief that he is justified in his views by a "reality" experience of (and with) us, is, for Freudians, the very thing that we think requires analysis rather than partial confirmation, which is what we think would happen were we to treat it as if it were based, even in part, on a purely veridical perception of us. Mr. J. did this with me; he did it with his teachers; he did it too many times and in too many ways for us to assume that he just had bad luck in finding teachers and an analyst. This is, of course, the very nature of a repetition compulsion. We regularly find ourselves in awe of the staggering power of intrapsychic processes as they interface with reality and of our remarkable ability to regularly bend reality in conformity to our inner needs as a common psychic event.

Despite all I have said about subjective, as contrasted with more realistic ways, of looking at what happens between patients and analysts, I am not suggesting that in this dyad the analyst has cornered the market on reality. I do think, however, that in any twosome where one member is actively suffering intense conflict, and is also highly regressed as well, the other partner may be able to be more objective about what is going on. That is never a guarantee of anything, of course, because we are always limited by the fact that we, too, process events through the lens of our own psyches. That is why, in the long run, all we can do is to suggest to our patients what we think might be going on, and eventually, as both partners chew on it and refine it together, it will either resonate with the patient's experiences and change some of the balances between the patient's conflicts and defenses, or it won't (in which case, we have to be free to reevaluate what we thought we knew).

It seems to me that looking at some of the problems raised in attempting to do analytic work with more disturbed patients gives us a particularly good vantage point for examining some of the basic assumptions that are unique to the analytic endeavor, Freudian or otherwise. This is because the exaggerated nature of both their needs and their experience of us helps us to see these phenomena, in sharp relief, as psychological rather than reality factors. With less troubled patients, the subtleties of their presentations often obscures more than it clarifies. Having to figure out the kinds of analytic conditions that are necessary before more profoundly disturbed patients can make use of what analysis traditionally has to offer, that is, structural growth brought about by insight, is a challenging task that has occupied the minds of Freudian analysts for some time now. We use a complex mix of interpretation with the supportive power of the analytic object relationship in the work we do with all of our patients. And, of course, with more disturbed patients the power of the relationship is often the deciding factor in what the patient is ultimately able to take in. There are some patients, however, who are unable to use any part of the relationship to their benefit and it is precisely in these types of cases that we can most effectively observe how intrapsychic processes can come to dominate and dictate the patient's experience of reality. These are also the very circumstances in which we are most vulnerable to extreme countertransference reactions and enactments, which then also throw our own relation to reality into greatest question. Just as is the case for our patients, it is not the reality of our patient's behavior but rather what it triggers off in us that dictates our compromises with reality at these times.

11

Deficit and Conflict:
An Attempt at Integration[1]

Andrew B. Druck

The interplay of deficit and conflict in our clinical work can only be considered in the context of three somewhat controversial assumptions. The first assumption is that there *is* such a thing as structural or developmental deficit. I define the concept broadly, to refer to compromised ego or superego capacities that transcend the more limited effects of neurotic symptoms. I use the term *deficit* in its most global sense. I will not discuss different concepts of deficit or differences between concepts of deficit, ego weakness, developmental arrest, and other such terms. I am here condensing what Pine (1990, 1994) has termed "deficit," which refers to "an insufficiency of appropriate input from the surround—ordinarily from the primary caretakers" (Pine 1994, p. 223) and "defect," which is one

---

1. This paper is dedicated to the memory of Dr. Fred Wolkenfeld, who died suddenly and prematurely in 1995. Dr. Wolkenfeld was an outstanding analyst, superb teacher, and one of New York University's most popular supervisors. He brought together a clear and brilliant mind, dedication to his patients and supervisees, enthusiasm for life, and a warm and generous heart. He is missed by colleagues, supervisees, and patients.

of several possible results of a deficit. For Pine, a defect, which may be subtle, pertains to some aspect of psychic structure that "is not fully serviceable for the patient" (1994, p. 231). One advantage of Pine's valuable distinction between deficit and defect is his elaboration of other consequences of insufficient parental input, including difficulties in adequate internalization leading to certain kinds of enacted internalized object relationships, and the development of what Pine terms "raw wounds" which are "ongoing painful subjective states of self" (Pine 1994, p. 224). My concern here is with both deficits and defects, with emphasis on what Pine terms "defects." I prefer to use the general term *deficit* instead of Pine's term *defect* because, in my mind and I believe in the mind of many readers, defect refers to structural difficulty due to a physiological given, such as mental retardation, while deficit refers to an aspect of mind that is more changeable. In other words, I believe that Pine and I address essentially similar clinical phenomena and understand them along similar lines, but use different terms. Pine distinguishes between the process of environmental stimulation and its differing results, while I am mostly concerned with the result, within which I find different gradations.

In clinical work, considerations of deficit become relevant as we evaluate a patient's capacity to contain anxiety or depression, to tolerate separation from the analyst, to develop an analyzable transference regression, and to feel relatively secure and real within the usual analytic situation. In broader terms, developmental deficit is often a major factor when the patient has difficulty experiencing himself as psychologically separate from the analyst.

Structural impairments can, and must, be demonstrated clinically, as Pine (1974b) has noted. The diagnostic decision that a clinical phenomenon is partially or largely the result of a deficit is a difficult one, and may take a good deal of time. We evaluate a patient's manifest verbal descriptions and his associations to what he has said. We also observe indications of structural difficulty. A patient who speaks of feeling alone and fragmented during his therapist's vacation is different from one who regresses structurally during these vacation periods and engages in active, frantic, panicked, and sometimes self-destructive attempts to reestablish structural equilibrium (Adler 1985).

Evaluation of structural level is essential as we deal with patients who are not responsive to purely conflict-based interventions. It is also a concept that fits our diagnostic system. Once one observes differences between levels of ego and superego structure and between levels of object relations capacity, then one is faced with the question of what makes the difference. If conflict is ubiquitous, then it alone cannot be a differential factor in making a diagnosis. While one may argue that differences in types of conflict or in patterns of conflict may account for differences in diagnosis, these factors alone seem to explain differences within a given structural level (for example, between hysterical and obsessional patients within the neurotic level of structure) better than differences that cross structural levels (between, for example, a neurotic hysterical patient and a schizophrenic patient). One could explain differences between levels of structure by focusing on the degree to which conflict affects usually autonomous areas of ego and superego functioning, but this explanation alone seems a bit stretched. At a certain point, magnitude of quantity and degree leads to changes in quality and kind. Thus if ego and superego are severely influenced by conflict, at a certain point their capacity to function optimally will be changed and these changes will then have to be taken into account in understanding psychopathology. A more comprehensive diagnostic system, one that helps us understand differences within and also between structural levels, requires focus on both dynamic and structural considerations. Kernberg (1976) has proposed such a diagnostic system.

Structural levels are a function of development. Such development is based on constitutional variables and on a child's early object relations, as a host of analysts have described, including Jacobson (1964), Mahler and colleagues (1975), and Loewald (1980a,b,c). In the concept of neurosis, we assume structural achievement within which conflict is embedded; there are developed structures for structural conflict. Thus we speak of a neurotic level of functioning, as opposed to a lower structural level of functioning. I am here considering the developmental strengths and achievements of childhood that make possible neurosis as opposed to borderline or psychosis, in addition to the conflicts of childhood that persist as fixations and form the nucleus of neurotic difficulty in adulthood. It is this kind of structural development that Freud assumed in his discussion of fixation and regression. *Thus adequate development of psychological structure becomes the defining trait of neurosis; it is not conflict, which can be found at all levels of development.*

The second assumption is that deficits are caused in a number of ways. Whether varying structural levels are caused by severe regression resulting from oedipal-level conflict (Arlow and Brenner 1974), too early, intense, and unassimilable conflict that is inherently ego-weakening (Kernberg 1975), early traumatic situations, inadequate parenting (Stolorow and Lachmann 1980), or all these (and other) factors in combination (Buie and Adler 1973), the clinical result is that global structural level or, in other instances, a particular ego and/or superego capacity is compromised. While most analysts who accept the notion of deficit believe that something has gone wrong developmentally, acknowledgment of deficit does not mean that we must reject modern conflict theory or that we must subscribe to theories of pathogenesis that focus almost exclusively on traumatic early development (Arlow 1986, Gill 1994). One may fully believe in conflict theory and acknowledge the interplay of conflict and early developmental failure in the etiology of deficit (see, for example, Grossman [1986, 1991] and Steingart [1995]). The issue remains how one deals with a situation in treatment where the patient is unable to do the analytic work, whatever the origin of this difficulty.

For example, imagine a fire in your stove, then a fire in your kitchen, then a fire on your block, then a fire in your neighborhood. In all these fires, the principles of combustion remain basically the same, as do principles of firefighting. However, whatever the cause of the fire, its growing magnitude and intensity affects both the process of combustion— the fire will spread more rapidly and its heat will burn objects with higher kindling points—and the firefighter's entire approach to controlling and extinguishing that particular fire. At a certain magnitude of conflict, its effects become virtually indistinguishable from developmental deficit.

The third assumption is that recognition of deficit as one variable in the mix of pathogenic variables does not mean that we must abandon our basic psychoanalytic stance. Some analysts mistakenly believe that deficit is an all-or-none proposition (conflict *or* deficit) and that diagnosis of deficit means there is a developmental hole in the patient that must be filled by the analyst in a futile, doomed, and ultimately misdirected attempt at substitute parenting rather than analysis (Arlow 1986). These analysts assume that work with deficit focuses on the patient–analyst experience as a major mutative factor, and does so at the expense of analyzing unconscious conflict.

I believe that these analysts are mistaken. Consideration of deficit *expands* our understanding of patients and *deepens*, rather than limits, an analysis. As one small example, our understanding of fluctuating part-object transferences and of primitive defenses such as projective identification—both predominantly seen in patients with deficits—has greatly added to our analytic understanding and analytic capacity. Conflict theorists fear that analyses may become compromised if we focus too much on deficit and too little on analysis of intrapsychic conflict. This is an unnecessary choice. It also disregards a second danger, that analyses may become too "as if" in nature, superficial, or stalemated if we do not appropriately address patient difficulties that fall outside a verbal, conflict-oriented paradigm.

With regard to the objection that our traditional psychoanalytic posture—relying on interpretation of unconscious conflict—is threatened by consideration of deficit, many analysts have shown that the classical analytic stance is far more complex, varied, and multidimensional than has been thought (for example, Druck 1994, Grunes 1984, Lasky 1993, Pine 1985, 1988, 1990, Stone 1961). Several analysts have demonstrated how consideration of developmental deficits can add to psychoanalytic understanding and precision of clinical intervention. Pine (1976, 1984) discusses how the analyst can more sensitively interpret in situations where the patient's deficits would otherwise make it difficult for him to hear the interpretation. Others (Kernberg 1975, for example) have shown how early attachment needs may defensively be expressed as sexual in nature and how the analyst must consider the conflating of wishes from different developmental levels in making his interventions. Blanck and Blanck (1979) have discussed the manner in which needs for separation and boundary maintenance may be expressed aggressively. Kernberg (1984) has demonstrated how primitive defenses may function in psychotic patients to establish a boundary, while in borderline patients the same defenses are used to protect the individual from too threatening aggressive self and object representations. Buie and Adler (1973) have shown how conflicts around loss of self, envy, and other factors interfere with a patient's desire to achieve a close enough relationship to his analyst so that deficits in internal holding are minimized and ameliorated.

In each of these situations—and I could cite dozens—analysts from different Freudian frameworks have demonstrated how they integrate understanding of different kinds of deficits into their work in a manner that enhances their understanding of the patient. Whether they discuss the impact of different deficits on how the patient *hears* and *uses* analytic interventions or how early needs and early wishes become combined, expressed, and defended against in different mixtures and combinations, these analysts are all considering the interplay of preoedipal and oedipal wishes, fears, trauma, reality of life experience, fantasy transformations of that same life experience, defenses against all of these factors, ego and superego difficulties, and attempts at adaptation to these difficulties, with all of these shaped by each other. These analysts differ in the degree to which they enlarge their conception of the psychoanalytic situation, but all emphasize, to one extent or another, the differing degrees of holding, support, abstinence, and confrontation that are inherent in the traditional analytic stance. It has been demonstrated time and again that analytic experience and insight work in tandem rather than in opposition.

Even interpretation itself, long considered the paradigmatic mutative element in classical psychoanalysis, is not a simple act. It is sometimes asserted that interpretation of transference is the defining therapeutic agent in psychoanalysis while the positive and uninterpreted patient–analyst experience is the main factor in psychotherapy of patients with deficits. Tarachow (1962) used just this criterion to differentiate between psychoanalysis and psychotherapy, but as I have discussed elsewhere (Druck 1989), even Tarachow vacillates on this point. However, we now realize how closely interpretation and object relationship are intertwined. Interpretations are extremely complex units of behavior. Tarachow (1963) discussed how interpretations are simultaneously gratifying (in terms of knowledge to the patient about his internal life and evidence that the analyst understands him) and depriving (of the patient's unconscious transference wish towards the analyst).

There are additional aspects to interpretations, all of which may work simultaneously: Interpretation of transference fears may make it possible for patients to benefit from certain potentially developmentally facilitating experiences inherent in the psychoanalytic situation, experiences which, for dynamic reasons, the patient may reject (Adler 1985, Buie and Adler 1973). Interpretation may also function as a "marker" of experience between patient and analyst (Grunes 1984) or help the patient move from an action-oriented, presymbolic level to a more symbolic mode of communication (Freedman 1985). Here insight helps the patient synthesize and then reflect upon an interaction between himself and the analyst, be it a form of expression through action or a developmentally necessary experience that had its own useful effect. An interpretation may help a patient maintain structural equilibrium in the face of threats to it (Stolorow and Lachmann 1980). Finally, timing and level of interpretation have long been ways through which the analyst influences pace and depth of analytic regression.

It is simply impossible to consider the impact of an interpretation on a patient's intrapsychic balance apart from simultaneous consideration of the interpretation's context in the analyst–patient relationship. I am not referring here to the patient's transference *distortion* of an interpretation (Kernberg 1975, 1976); I am, however, emphasizing the role of interpretation as an aspect of the underlying therapeutic relationship. Interpretation rests on the underlying therapeutic object relationship the way a boat floats in the ocean. An interpretation can only go with the underlying tide of the object relationship, in its complexly intertwined transference and working alliance combination. In fact, in periods of projective identification, the analyst may not even be able to internally *conceive* of certain interpretations—never mind *verbalize* them to the patient. It is only after the transference has shifted that certain interpretations become conceivable and interpretable to both patient and analyst.

While we think we are successfully responding to a presumed deficit through interpretation of conflict (and therefore confirming a belief that it can and should be treated as a symptom due primarily to intrapsychic conflict), we may *also* be helping a patient stabilize at a higher level of ego development through an object relationship established via the medium of interpretation.[2] In other words, the interpretation, which clarifies to the patient an aspect of unconscious conflict and defense, may *simultaneously* function as a vehicle of object connection; the music may matter as much as the specific words. Interpretation may help a patient establish an ego boundary, feel affirmed, or feel safe from superego pressure. What we think works may not be the most important factor in the mix of what actually does work or produces the most of many mutative effects. Wallerstein (1986) obtained just this finding in his analysis of the Menninger research project.

Instead of contrasting interventions in terms of their degree of support or insight, in a manner that reinforces the alleged dichotomy between conflict or deficit, we could more profitably think of interventions as *stabilizing* or *destabilizing*, both within the patient's intrapsychic structure

---

2. Parenthetically, the interpretation may miss deeper issues, implicitly collude in sealing off more anxiety-producing fears, and encourage a "false" analysis; Balint (1968) is one of many analysts who have made this point.

and within the patient–analyst object relationship. We may have a rough idea of whether an intervention will be more or less one or the other but we could be wrong, since it will depend on so many variables. Whether the same intervention is stabilizing or destabilizing will depend not only on the patient's structural level but also on the therapeutic object relationship at that particular moment. It will also depend on the kind of environment within which the patient feels most safe. A confrontation will be stabilizing to one patient and destabilizing to another not necessarily because of differences in their structural level but because of the kind of environment within which they feel most safe. I will discuss this issue later.

With these three assumptions in mind, we can consider certain characteristics of deficit and its interaction with conflict. This topic has been approached in different ways. Some analysts have shown how preoedipal difficulties and their consequent structural deficits affect later oedipal conflict (Kernberg 1975). Others have described how some deficits bring on their own particular conflicts (Eagle 1984, Pine 1990, 1994). Yet others have discussed how specific deficits affect a patient's capacity to work in psychoanalysis (Bach 1983, 1994, Freedman 1985, Pine 1985, 1990). I will focus on the interplay of conflict and overall structural level. Because of space limitations, I will be schematic in my presentation.

TO WHAT EXTENT IS A DEFICIT CONSTANT?

Just as defenses fluctuate with the ebb and flow of anxiety, so too can we expect level of structural organization to vary (Loewald 1980d). There are alternations—sometimes major—between levels of functioning in patients with deficits. These alternations consist of shifts in particular forms of structural capacity and function, along with concomitant shifts in self and object representations. We can observe such variations most vividly in a patient's part-object transference, both upward (to a more whole object transference) and downward (to more paranoid or merged states). Deficit is a *process* variable rather than a static concept. A deficit may be understood as reflecting greater potential for ego or superego regression in response to internal or external stress. Further, just as we expect earlier wishes, fantasies, and conflicts to emerge with transference regression, we might also expect to see some evidence of earlier developmental stages of structural development as an analysis deepens.

A deficit may be potentiated or lessened in different conditions. There are times and environments within which a deficit presents more strongly, along with other times and environments within which the deficit is muted and the patient functions at a higher structural level. We might observe varying manifestations of deficit at certain *times* of conflict and in certain *areas* of conflict. (This is also true for defects, where there is something more demonstrably wrong or "broken" in someone. A person's actual, measurable, "real" learning disability, in itself and in the conflicts aroused by the person's experience of and meaning attributed to it, will be potentiated more on a school examination than on the baseball field.) As such, deficits (and even, in some cases, defects, depending on the degree to which they affect the patient's capacity to self-reflect) become amenable to psychoanalytic inquiry. One can begin to ask how certain internal conflicts and environmental disruptions, in combination with each other, affect the deficit process (the intensity of its disruptive effects, for example).

Some analysts believe that a working alliance reflects achievement of a particular kind of ego-supporting part-object transference (Adler 1980). The borderline or narcissistic patient will do his best analytic (i.e., self-reflective, insight-oriented) work when the structurally holding aspect of transference is present. Structural support, which may be in the forefront or background of the transference, can be disrupted by the analyst's premature interpretation or confrontation, or by a patient's conflicts that lead him to believe that his own aggression or envy has killed the analyst or will cause the analyst to retaliate against him at any moment. When the holding is disrupted, for whatever reason, one often sees structural regression, expressed in many forms, including overwhelming anxiety or depression, failure of major ego functions, dangerous acting out, or a psychotic paranoid transference. The regression is usually reversible once the structurally holding aspect of the transference is reestablished. This illustrates how a deficit's effect is variable, depending on the analytic environment. The patient's dynamic conflicts, his structural capability, and the analytic relationship are linked in an ongoing proces.

We see here clinical illustration of a basic proposition: that the object relationship in psychoanalysis, analogous to the parental relationship, is crucial in its structure-promoting properties. The analyst, implicitly or explicitly, to a greater or a lesser extent, as part of his usual and customary role, supports specific ego and superego functions as well as the patient's capacity for overall ego and superego development. This is not a Freudian theory of object relations. It is, rather, a theory of how object relations are crucial in the development of psychic structure (Jacobson 1964, Loewald 1980a,b,c, Mahler et al. 1975). Experiences of loving nurturance, as well as of limit setting, are necessary to provide an environment within which ego and superego functions can develop optimally. These object relationships become internalized and depersonified as structural functions (Jacobson 1964, Kernberg 1975, Loewald 1980a,b,c). To the extent that these relationships have been successful in this regard, the patient functions at a higher structural level (neurotic). To the extent that they have not, then the patient (conflictually) seeks, in his daily life and with the analyst, relationships to meet the structural deficit. Patients with deficits seek relationships for both drive and fantasy-based motives (the repetition compulsion) as well as for adaptive and structurally based motives. These are inevitably intertwined and can only be artificially separated for the purpose of making a particular point in discussion. However, to the extent that patients seek structural aid from their environment, their level of function is necessarily more fluid and variable.

I stated above that interventions may be more or less stabilizing depending on the analytic environment. Shifts in structural level are quite dependent on the particular analyst–patient pair. Certain analysts work better with certain kinds of regressions or enactments than others, and a particular transference-countertransference constellation can lead to analytic impasses that would not necessarily exist with other pairings (Kantrowitz 1993a,b). Thus the analyst's own character is of fundamental importance. Yet I believe that the matter may be more complex, and include broader expressions of the analyst's character, including his ideas about an optimal treatment approach as it intersects with the patient's particular conflict-deficit configuration.

Blatt and Blass (1992) have written that relatedness and self-definition are two intertwined aspects of personality functioning. They believe that individuals who emphasize one aspect have different personality styles than individuals who emphasize the other. They use the terms *anaclitic* to describe people who emphasize relatedness and *introjective* for those who emphasize self-definition. Blatt (1974) discusses how introjective depressives differ from anaclitic depressives. Blatt (1992) further presents re-analysis of the Menninger research study and concludes that these two personality types respond differently to psychoanalysis and psychotherapy because of the interaction between degree of patient–analyst contact in the differing therapeutic modalities and the particular conflict-defense configurations of these two patient types:

> The data of the present study indicate a significant patient-by-treatment interaction in which the congruence between the patient's character style and important aspects of the therapeutic situation determine the efficacy of treatment outcome. . . . These results suggest that we must be aware that the therapeutic context presents at least two major dimensions to patients—a therapeutic relationship and the possibility of insight and understanding. . . . Though these two dimensions are intertwined in the therapeutic process, some patients seem to value and be more responsive to the quality of the therapeutic relationship, while other patients seem to value and be more responsive to the interpretive activity of the therapist and the process of therapeutic insight. While most patients undoubtedly gain from both of these therapeutic dimensions, the results of the present study suggest that different types of patients may be more responsive to one or the other of these dimensions of the therapeutic process. [Blatt 1992, pp. 715–716]

Blatt and Blass (1992) discuss how other psychoanalysts have made similar distinctions in patients. They include Balint's (1968) distinction between ocnophiles, who seek object connection in order to feel safe, and philobats, who feel safer when there is more space between themselves and their analyst. I would suggest that these kinds of patients may differ in structural level as well as in major dynamic conflict, predominant style of defense, and the like. For patients with some kinds of conflict-deficit configurations (Balint's ocnophiles, for example), who seek object connection in order to feel safe, certain treatment approaches are more structurally holding, while for patients with other kinds of conflict-deficit configurations (Balint's philobats, who feel safer when there is more space between themselves and their analyst), those *same* analysts doing the *same* kind of treatment may sometimes contribute to further structural disorganization.

So, paradoxically, a Kernbergian environment, with its emphasis on confrontation, is in some way supportive and safe for a philobat, while the same environment is highly dangerous for an ocnophile. In a similar way, an ocnophile will easily feel understood and held by a Kohutian, while a philobat may experience the very same Kohutian as a wimp, who doesn't understand the depth of his aggression and paranoia and who pushes too quickly for what is felt to be dangerous object connection.

This hypothesis helps us understand why analysts with diametrically opposite treatment approaches—Kernberg (1975) and Kohut (1971), for example—all report success. These findings pose a real question about what makes a difference in treatment, and I believe that its answer will be found only if we add structural considerations to dynamic ones. The different analytic environments established by Kernberg and Kohut may have a different effect depending on what kind of patient they are seeing. In other words, I think Kernberg and Kohut are both successful because they treat different kinds of patients; ocnophiles thrive in a Kohutian environment and may leave a Kernbergian setting, while philobats may feel more held and understood by a Kernbergian-oriented therapist and more vulnerable with a Kohutian. Thus I am suggesting that the entire analytic "atmosphere" or ambiance established by a particular analyst–patient pair—an ambiance that includes the analyst's character and his ideas about how to conduct treatment—affects the ways in which a deficit becomes manifest and whether analysis of that aspect of the patient is possible (Druck 1995).

These remarks apply mostly to the opening phase of treatment, and refer to the ease with which different patients will become enaged in treatment in different kinds of analytic settings. Ocnophiles and philobats express different aspects of the same kind of conflict and, in a good analysis, all aspects should emerge and be analyzed.

THE KINDS OF DEFICITS LEAD TO DIFFERENT ISSUES
IN PSYCHOANALYSIS

Different deficits lead to different kinds of difficulties in a given treatment. For example, certain ego deficits, such as annihilation anxiety under stress, difficulty with libidinal object constancy, or difficulties in stable self-esteem regulation, often lead to movement toward the analyst, because the analyst is used for structural support. Patients with these kinds of difficulties may be expected, all other factors being equal, to begin treatment, and present in a more pronounced way in an analytic regression, with conflicted wishes for closeness and affirmation from the analyst.

Wishes toward the analyst will almost always be an amalgam of what the analyst regards as legitimate needs for structural support and transference wishes that need analysis. Because these variables are so entangled, it is difficult for the analyst to find an appropriate balance of gratification and abstinence so that the proper analytic climate may be established and maintained. Further, it will be difficult for the patient to find a way to feel comfortable with what he wants from the analyst and yet self-reflective about those same needs. Both analyst and patient will struggle to find a way to meet and still analyze conscious and unconscious wishes that are experienced as both legitimate and illegitimate by both parties. This is why it often takes a great deal of time for the patient and analyst to find a comfortable way of working together, and why much of the treatment, especially at the beginning, will be marked by differing periods of trust and then misunderstanding leading to emotional storms (Bach 1994, Ellman 1991).

Superego deficits present different kinds of problems. One may enumerate at least three related types of superego deficits. Modell (1965) has written of one form, where the patient cannot experience signal guilt. In the same way that primary, or panic, anxiety can be catastrophic and secondary, or signal, anxiety is adaptive, primary guilt differs from secondary guilt. Modell states, "Primary guilt is diffuse, pervasive, and, at its worst, can interfere with all personality functioning. Secondary guilt tends to be circumscribed and limited" (p. 329).

A second form of superego deficit has been described extensively by Kohut (1971), Bach (1983, 1994), and many others. Here patients have great difficulty in self-esteem regulation and become quite sensitive to narcissistic slights. They seek from the therapist a certain form of transference that will allow them to achieve and maintain adequate self-esteem regulation, and to integrate what Bach (1994) calls "objective awareness" and "subjective self-awareness." From a broader perspective, they seek an analytic environment within which they can find and consolidate what feels to them to be a real and authentic sense of self and object.

Finally, in contrast to the vulnerable clinging narcissistic patient, and often in defense against that very vulnerability, is the superego problem presented by the grandiose narcissist, described by Kernberg (1992) as the malignant narcissist, and by many modern Kleinians, including Betty Joseph (1982):

> I get the impression from the difficulty these patients experience in waiting and being aware of gaps and being aware of even the simplest type of guilt that such potentially depressive experiences have been felt by them in infancy as terrible pain that goes over into torment, and that they have tried to obviate this by taking over the torment, the inflicting of mental pain, onto themselves and building it into a world of perverse excitements, and this necessarily militates against any real progress towards the depressive position. [p. 138]

In the first two forms of superego deficit, the technical difficulties are similar to the difficulties encountered when working with patients with most ego deficits. However, in this last form of superego difficulty, one universally seen as the most intractable, we see an amalgam of conflict and deficit in the most problematic combination. Lear (1996) evocatively captures the fluid and dynamic situation involved here.

> The effect [of parental aggression] has been so fundamentally devastating that the child's psyche is not merely disorganiz*ed* but disorgani*zing*. It cannot grow in response to normal nurturing, for in its disorganized state, it tends to disorganize its own experience. This psychological state is destructive: it tears asunder what would normally be organizing worldly experiences, while remaining actively disorganized itself." [p. 696, his italics]

One finds narcissistic pleasure in not needing others and in defeating them, which defends against and adapts to a superego deficit, the deficit being the lack of integration of experienced, and what has defensively become idealized, self and object representations (Schafer 1967) or, as Kernberg (1975) thinks of it, a defensive fusion of ideal self, ideal object, and actual self images. Difficulties of the grandiose self rather than the fragile vulnerable self lead to basic mistrust of the analyst, intense conscious and unconscious wishes to "win" by defeating the therapist, a "perverse" and "mechanistic" (Bach 1994) relationship with the analyst, and the most difficult stalemates in treatment.

Thus, the interaction of different kinds of deficits and conflicts, as they combine in different character constellations, lead to different technical problems and differing prognoses. This, then, is another way in which conflict and deficit interact: in the kinds of characters that are developed, character organizations that express and/or defend against deficits that are feared to be overwhelming as well as unconscious fantasies organized around sexual and aggressive wishes.

TYPOLOGY OF CONFLICT/DEFICIT INTERACTION

These considerations lead to a rough typology that can be constructed about the role of deficit in treatment. While it should be clear that I am making gross and artificial distinctions, and that deficits and conflicts are many-faceted, layered, and interconnected, it is hoped that these distinctions will clarify certain issues.

In the first case, the deficit itself is the presenting problem for the treatment. This may occur, for example, when the patient presents with problems in self-esteem regulation (Kohut 1971), problems integrating objective awareness and subjective self-awareness (Bach 1994), problems with libidinal object constancy (Pine 1974a), problems with annihilation anxiety (Hurvich 1989, 1991), and other such difficulties. The deficits may be the main reason for presenting problems such as eating disorders, phobias, and obsessional difficulties, to name just a few. Here treatment revolves around ways in which the deficit is pervasive and is expressed in various areas of function. Major conflicts are tied to this overarching deficit. Buie and Adler (1973), for example, have explored the way in which, for patients with deficits in adequate holding introjects, unconscious conflicts centered around the process and meaning of internalization interfere with their attempt to establish and maintain a needed holding introject and to internalize the analyst. While these patients present conflict from all psychosexual levels, their major conflicts tend to center on threatened loss of self-object boundaries and on opposing positive and negative self and object representations. Such conflicts may be expressed as oedipal conflicts related to anxiety over sexual and aggressive wishes, but these are often vehicles through which more primitive anxieties appear. Furthermore, certain aggressive wishes or actions may enter the analysis so that the patient can create a boundary between himself and his analyst when he feels that his autonomy is threatened. With these patients, the analyst is concerned with containing projected aspects of the patient as well as analyzing conflict pertaining to these deficits, while simultaneously meeting the patient's structural needs in a way that does not compromise the analytic situation.

In the second case, the deficit is not necessarily the presenting problem, but it interferes with analyzing the presenting problem. Here the deficits might be problems with symbolization leading to gross reliance on enactments (Freedman 1985), emotional flooding (Volkan 1976), or problems with impulse control, along with, perhaps, the above deficits. The conflicts emerge from all levels of psychic development and may not be as directly tied to the deficits as they are in the first case. In this second type, I am speaking more of generalized difficulties in ego and superego functioning rather than central deficits that become major organizers of the analytic work. Work on deficits in this situation raises issues similar to those discussed by Pine, in his paper on the interpretive moment (1984) and in his papers on deficit and defect (1990, 1994).

The third case includes certain superego difficulties discussed by Joseph (1982), Kernberg (1992), Modell (1965), and others, where it is hard to differentiate deficit from severe early conflict around aggression and envy. Here is a situation where combinations of severe early conflict and developmental failure, in early interaction, combine to corrupt the foundation of a psychic structure. One can readily hypothesize a complex amalgam of conflict that is tied to a deficit while simultaneously defending against it. For example, Bach (1994) writes:

> It is these *experiences of omnipotence* in the phase of absolute dependence that constitute part of the foundation on which trust in oneself and in the world is built. Indeed, it is when these *experiences of omnipotence* are lacking and the object's failures impinge on the child that a reactive *defensive omnipotence* arises to deny and overcompensate for feelings of annihilation and death of the self. [p. 172, his italics]

The complexity of this situation leads some analysts to focus on the role of early conflict (Joseph 1982, Kernberg 1992) while others focus on early deficit (Bach 1994, Kohut 1971). The therapeutic difficulty here is that the patient fears and mistrusts the analyst in a way that makes taking in his interpretations equivalent to submission, castration, and loss of boundaries (Kernberg 1992). It becomes difficult for the analyst to become part of the patient's internal world in a way where he can be trusted as an object of internalization and structural growth rather than a foreign object seen as intruding on the patient's autonomy.

CASE ILLUSTRATION OF WORK WITH DEFICIT AND CONFLICT

Mr. B., a man with a history of severe anxiety and depression, associated with suicidal ideation and two sudden suicide attempts, was in his third year of a four-times weekly analysis with a woman analyst. His life was chaotic; he would engage in many short-term relationships, move from job to job, and endure severe levels of anxiety and depression, often dealing with them through action. He had been in many therapies, none successful. After an extended consultation, and consideration of the risks, it was decided that he try psychoanalysis.

In Mr. B.'s first year, he would often rise from the couch during sessions or come late and leave early. His analyst understood these actions as measures through which Mr. B. concretely regulated his anxiety in the session. By actively creating actual space, he protected himself from what he experienced to be passive acceptance of intrusion, by his inner feelings as he regressed, and by the analyst. In the latter case, he projected his wishes for merger onto her and then had to defend himself from these wishes, which he now experienced as coming from her. The analyst accepted these enactments and, over time, helped Mr. B. become interested in them, so that, by year's end, he was able to understand them and settle in. He stayed through sessions, his mood became more stable in and out of the analysis, and his behavior on the job and in his relationship became more steady.

As year three began, Mr. B. became more aware of liking the analyst in a way that he could not quite verbalize. However, he felt that he needed her more than he wanted to. He felt he depended on her too much. When the analyst tried to address these transference fears, Mr. B.'s fears became heightened. He grew visibly uncomfortable and eventually accused his analyst of wanting to seduce him into depending on her and perhaps even more; he wasn't sure whether or not she had more nefarious motives. Mr. B. abruptly quit treatment, but continued to phone the analyst daily. After two weeks of this, he agreed with his analyst's suggestion that he come in to discuss the situation.

Mr. B. said that, when he quit, he felt liberated from what he saw as her ego and superego control. He now (retrospectively) felt her attempts at understanding his wishes to be attempts at controlling his behavior, and expressed great anger at her constraining him. He responded to his new freedom by acting, in many areas of his life, as he felt he had been prohibited from action. He also felt angry that he had been seduced into what he now felt was an overly dependent transference relationship. He blamed his therapist for this relationship and was determined not to "be a sucker" again. He would not associate to this image. He agreed to return but only on a once-weekly basis.

Mr. B. began to test what he saw as his independent wings. As he began to act (for example, suddenly proposing to his girlfriend and telling off his boss), he announced his actions rather defiantly to his therapist, simultaneously (and unconsciously) asking her to intervene while overtly defying her and praising his newfound assertive capacity. As he acted—at first, in many ways, appropriately—there developed more and more an edge of desperation and possible poor judgment. Mr. B. began to describe feeling more driven than assertive; he seemed to feel rushed, taking action to counteract an internal fear of being taken over by others and becoming dominated or totally lost and abandoned.

The therapist initially did not address any of this. She felt that to address the actions would be premature and would seem to the patient to be again dominating him and questioning his capacity to act. She did not comment on the Mr. B.'s assertions that she had inappropriately created a dependent transference. She believed that while Mr. B.'s manifest complaints reflected his desire for independence and autonomy, his daily phone calls after he "quit" expressed the more unconscious side of his ambivalence: his feeling fragile, lost, unanchored, and extremely vulnerable without her, along with his projecting his wishes for connection and merger onto his therapist so that, for example, it was the therapist who was responsible for the content and intensity of his transference. He needed the presence of a therapist to feel anchored, but to admit such a need was unacceptable. Still, she felt that, at this point, Mr. B. needed to control the analytic space. In his current state, analogous to a panicked psychotic transference, Mr. B. had nothing that he, himself, wanted to understand about himself that would require interpretation from her. Thus there was no working alliance. She could only address actions that were ego syntonic. To attempt this would actually enact Mr. B.'s fear, which was of being impinged upon and thus transferentially controlled.

As Mr. B. began to complain more of feeling controlled by internal forces than controlling them, as he began to call his therapist anxiously between sessions, as he began to concoct wilder solutions to deal with what he saw as threats from others, as he provoked fight after fight with his fiancée and endangered their relationship, as his work situation became more tenuous, and as he began to complain of feeling less and less safe in his own home, the analyst felt that now Mr. B. himself was troubled by what was happening to him. At this point, there was more potential for a working alliance; Mr. B. more consciously wanted assistance from an analyst whom he saw as potentially helpful rather than as impinging or controlling.

The analyst understood the analytic problem as regression in response to unconsciously sexualized dependence needs in the transference. These needs were defended against by projection and action. Unfortunately, the patient's deficits made this difficult to analyze directly. The deficits included a propensity for annihilation anxiety leading to concrete action rather than a more developed capacity for signal anxiety and symbolization. This ego weakness made for defenses that were not only ineffective at modulating anxiety but led to self-object confusion, so that it became unclear to Mr. B. just *who* wanted *what* from *whom* in the analytic situation. Once boundaries became blurred, Mr. B. became even more anxious and redoubled his efforts at reassuring himself of his separate identity, primarily through leaving. However, Mr. B. also needed to feel connected with his analyst in order to feel internally stable. It was only after he had established a feeling of psychic connection with his analyst that he had become able to tolerate anxiety and depression and then work better, within the analysis and outside. Now that Mr. B. had "terminated" treatment, he was faced with regaining that connection in the face of his transference fears. Now that he had established that he was separate from his analyst, he had to re-find her, but on his own terms. He could only do this through phone calls, from his own created and separate space.

Commenting on his transference anxiety directly only made the problem worse, because it implicitly pulled the patient into an object relationship that he feared too much to analyze. The analyst chose to speak to Mr. B. of his difficulty staying in a balanced position with her that let him feel not too close but not too far. She then spoke of his fears that made achievement of that position difficult: that he would lose his autonomy if he got too close and of his panic if he felt too alone. For this patient, this was the most important work; it was insight into what he was most conflicted about: the interplay of his wishes and his ego capacities to modulate the wishes so they felt less imperative, concrete, and consequential.

Conflict over unconscious sexual wishes toward his analyst remained crucial for Mr. B., but for him the stakes were higher because conflict brought about not only a fantasied danger situation but also ego weakness, ineffective solutions to the conflict that exacerbated the weakness, and threat of loss of structural integrity. One way to begin to address the mix of these kinds of issues was to stress the adaptive side—what the patient was trying to accomplish (to find a safe place) rather than solely what he wanted to avoid. It was only after this conflict had been addressed that the analyst began to address the patient's unconscious sexualized dependent wishes. Here, too, she focused not on the wishes themselves but on how these wishes made the patient feel invaded, not the master of his own mind, and confused. She spoke too of how his solutions to these feelings created greater problems. Thus Mr. B.'s defenses were addressed not only as a means of showing him how his mind worked (although it certainly did this) and not only to make clearer Mr. B.'s unconscious transference wishes (which it also did), but in order to help him gain control over his panic in the transference. The analyst's goal was using insight to help him gain increased ego functioning first, with fuller elaboration of the unconscious drive derivatives second.

Is this just analytic tact? Of course it is, but it stems from appreciation of the holding and sustaining function in the therapeutic object relationship. The thrust of the analyst's interventions was first to stabilize the patient's ego functions through helping him maintain optimal connection in the treatment, and then, within that context, to explore intrapsychic conflict. The working alliance was monitored constantly through observation of the patient's level of ego and superego functioning, particularly as it affected the patient's capacity to do analytic work. The therapist did not lead with interpretation of defense against drive derivatives. Instead, she led with patient difficulties in feeling safe within the analytic relationship. Both conflict and deficit were the subject of analytic attention without any major modification of the traditional psychoanalytic posture.

IS THIS TRADITIONAL SUPPORTIVE PSYCHOTHERAPY?

Initial formulations of supportive therapy were limited in ambition and scope (Wallerstein 1989). The therapist sought to strengthen certain defenses in a fragile structure and perhaps allow for certain limited forms of insight, with major focus on the therapist's influence as an auxiliary ego or superego as an agent of change. Over the years, the entire context of our assumptions about supportive therapy changed. The goals became much more ambitious as we began to understand more clearly the analyst's role in helping structure develop and as we began to enlarge our conception of what was wrong with the patient. It was demonstrated that the combination of interpreting conflict with attention to a patient's structural difficulties could lead to major structural change, a traditional goal of psychoanalysis.

Differences between traditional supportive psychotherapy, which is indicated for certain patients, and psychoanalysis or intensive psychoanalytic therapy with patients who have major ego or superego deficits may be summarized as follows: Traditional supportive psychotherapy supports defenses in order to strengthen overall repression. Support in working analytically with a patient who has a developmental deficit facilitates the patient's ego and superego capacity to analyze and regress further, in the service of exploration and reflection. Supportive psychotherapy has limited goals and its employment precludes full transference regression and analysis. The more intensive treatment has ambitious goals and relies on full transference regression and analysis. The former aids repression while the latter attempts to analyze conflict and unconscious fantasy as fully as possible, with due concern and regard for developmental difficulties that make such analysis more complex. Thus despite superficial resemblances between these two modalities, there is a world of difference.

ARE CONFLICT AND DEFICIT IN OPPOSITION?

Advocates of conflict-based pathology and advocates of developmental deficit-based pathology often write as if these two are in opposition and lead to drastically different psychoanalytic stances. However, there is no conceptual reason why these aspects of mental life should not be seen as interwoven, with different elements contributing different degrees of influence to given aspects of mental life, in different people, and in different transferential situations within the evolution of an analysis.

Brenner (1994) and other analysts write that elements of the mind are linked together in a constantly changing interconnected interplay of wish, unpleasurable affect, defense, and self-punishment. I agree with these analysts, but believe we must add to these elements at least one additional factor: the mind's capacity to tolerate and contain this mix of conflict and defense. One's level of ego and superego structure will greatly influence the intensity, the form, and even the very nature of all of Brenner's components—wish, anxiety or depressive affect, defense, and self-punishment. Each of these will be experienced in more primitive, intense ways in patients with lower structural levels. The patient's capacity to analyze conflict will also be greatly affected. He will express himself in more concrete, action-oriented ways, and will have difficulty feeling safe and owning his analysis. In this kind of situation, transference-oriented interpretations will be "above" his structural level and lead to reactions that complicate the treatment. Thus structural level is a central factor in diagnosing, understanding, and working with patients, and its varying effects must be theoretically considered. I have tried, in a highly schematic way, to outline directions in which such considerations can lead.

ACKNOWLEDGMENTS

I would like to thank Drs. Marvin Hurvich, Richard Lasky, and Joyce Slochower for their comments on an earlier draft of this chapter.

REFERENCES

Adler, G. (1980). Transference, real relationship and alliance. *International Journal of Psycho-Analysis* 61:547–558.
——— (1985). *Borderline Psychopathology and Its Treatment.* New York: Jason Aronson.
Arlow, J. A. (1986). The relation of theories of pathogenesis to therapy. In *Psychoanalysis. The Science of Mental Conflict. Essays in Honor of Charles Brenner,* ed. A. D. Richards and M. S. Willick, pp. 49–63. Hillsdale, NJ: Analytic Press.
Arlow, J. A., and Brenner, C. (1964). *Psychoanalytic Concepts and the Structural Theory.* New York: International Universities Press.

Bach, S. (1983). *Narcissistic States and the Therapeutic Process.* New York: Jason Aronson.

—— (1994). *The Language of Perversions and the Language of Love.* Northvale, NJ: Jason Aronson.

Balint, M. (1968). *The Basic Fault.* New York: Brunner-Mazel.

Blanck, G., and Blanck, B. (1974). *Ego Psychology: Theory and Practice.* New York: Columbia University Press.

—— (1979). *Ego Psychology II.* New York: Columbia University Press.

Blatt, S. J. (1974). Levels of object representation in anaclitic and introjective depression. *Psychoanalytic Study of the Child* 29:107–157. New Haven, CT: Yale University Press.

—— (1992). The differential effect of psychotherapy and psychoanalysis: the Menninger psychotherapy research project revisited. *Journal of the American Psychoanalytic Association* 40:691–724.

Blatt, S. J., and Blass, R. B. (1992). Relatedness and self-definition: two primary dimensions in personality development, psychopathology, and psychotherapy. In *Psychoanalysis and Psychology: An APA Centennial Volume,* ed. J. Barron, M. Eagle, and D. Wolitsky, pp. 399–428. Washington, DC: American Psychological Association.

Brenner, C. (1994). The mind as conflict and compromise formation. *Journal of Clinical Psychoanalysis* 3:473–488.

Buie, D. H., and Adler, G. (1973). Definitive treatment of the borderline personality. *International Journal of Psychoanalytic Psychotherapy,* vol. 9, 1982–1983, ed. R. Langs, pp. 51–87. New York: Jason Aronson.

Druck, A. B. (1989). *Four Therapeutic Approaches to the Borderline Patient: Principles and Techniques of the Basic Dynamic Stances.* Northvale, NJ: Jason Aronson.

—— (1994). Multiple models and the psychoanalytic stance. *Psychoanalytic Inquiry* 14(2):243–260.

—— (1995). *Paradigmatic borderline patients.* Unpublished manuscript.

Eagle, M. (1984). *Recent Developments in Psychoanalysis.* New York: McGraw-Hill.

Ellman, S. (1991). *Freud's Technique Papers.* Northvale, NJ: Jason Aronson.

Freedman, N. (1985). The concept of transformation in psychoanalysis. *Psychoanalytic Psychology* 2:317–339.

Gill, M. (1994). Conflict and deficit. *Psychoanalytic Quarterly* 63:756–778.

Grossman, W. I. (1986). Notes on masochism: a discussion of the history and development of a psychoanalytic concept. *Psychoanalytic Quarterly* 55:379–413.

—— (1991). Pain, aggression, fantasy, and concepts of sadomasochism. In *Essential Papers on Masochism,* ed. M. Hanly, pp. 125–150. New York: New York University Press, 1995.

Grunes, M. (1984). The therapeutic object relationship. *Psychoanalytic Review* 71:123–143.

Hurvich, M. (1989). Traumatic moment, basic dangers, and annihilation anxiety. *Psychoanalytic Psychology* 6(3):309–323.

—— (1991). Annihilation anxiety: an introduction. In *Psychoanalytic Reflections* on Currrent Issues, ed. H. B. Siegel et al., pp. 135–154. New York: New York University Press.

Jacobson, E. (1964). *The Self and the Object World.* New York: International Universities Press.

Joseph, B. (1982). Addiction to near-death. In *Psychic Equilibrium and Psychic Change,* ed. M. Feldman and E. B. Spillius, pp. 127–138. London and New York: Routledge.

Kantrowitz, J. L. (1993a). The uniqueness of the patient-analyst pair: approaches for elucidating the analyst's role. *International Journal of Psycho-Analysis* 74:893–904.

——— (1993b). Impasses in psychoanalysis: overcoming resistance in situations of stalemate. *Journal of the American Psychoanalytic Association* 41:1021–1050.

Kernberg. O. F. (1975). *Borderline Conditions and Pathological Narcissism.* New York: Jason Aronson.

——— (1976). *Object Relations Theory and Clinical Psychoanalysis.* New York: Jason Aronson.

——— (1984). *Severe Personality Disorders.* New Haven, CT: Yale University Press.

——— (1992). *Aggression in Personality Disorders and Perversions.* New Haven, CT: Yale University Press.

Kohut, H. (1971). *The Analysis of the Self.* New York: International Universities Press.

Lasky, R. (1993). *Dynamics of Development and the Therapeutic Process.* Northvale, NJ: Jason Aronson.

Lear, J. (1996). The introduction of eros. *Journal of the American Psychoanalytic Association* 44:673–698.

Loewald, H. (1980a). Ego and reality. In *Papers on Psychoanalysis,* pp. 3–20. New Haven, CT: Yale University Press.

——— (1980b). On Internalization. In *Papers on Psychoanalysis,* pp. 69–86. New Haven, CT: Yale University Press.

——— (1980c). Instinct theory, object relations, and psychic structure formation. In *Papers on Psychoanalysis,* pp. 207–218. New Haven, CT: Yale University Press.

——— (1980d). On the therapeutic action of psychoanalysis. In *Papers on Psychoanalysis,* pp. 221–256. New Haven, CT: Yale University Press.

Mahler, M., Pine, F., and Bergman, A. (1975). *The Psychological Birth of the Human Infant.* New York: Basic Books.

Modell, A. (1965). On having the right to a life: an aspect of the superego's development. *International Journal of Psycho-Analysis* 46:323–331.

Pine, F. (1974a). Libidinal object constancy. In *Psychoanalysis and Contemporary Science,* vol. 3, pp. 307–313. New York: International Universities Press.

——— (1974b). Pathology of the separation-individuation process as manifested in later clinical work. *International Journal of Psycho-Analysis* 60:225–242.

——— (1976). On therapeutic change: perspectives from a parent–child model. In *Psychoanalysis and Contemporary Science,* vol. 5, pp. 537–569. New York: International Universities Press.

—— (1984). The interpretive moment: variations on classical themes. *Bulletin of the Menninger Clinic* 48:54–71.

—— (1985). *Developmental Theory and Clinical Process.* New Haven, CT: Yale University Press.

—— (1988). The four psychologies of psychoanalysis and their place in clinical work. *Journal of the American Psychoanalytic Association* 36:571–596.

—— (1990). *Drive, Ego, Object, and Self.* New York: Basic Books.

—— (1994). Some impressions regarding conflict, defect, and deficit. *Psychoanalytic Study of the Child* 49:222–240. New Haven, CT: Yale University Press.

Schafer, R. (1967). Ideals, the ego ideal, and the ideal self. In *Motives and Thought: Psychoanalytic Essays in Memory of David Rapaport. Psychological Issues,* ed. R. R. Holt, pp. 131–174. Monograph 18/19. New York: International Universities Press.

Steingart, I. (1995). *A Thing Apart: Love and Reality in the Therapeutic Relationship.* Northvale, NJ: Jason Aronson.

Stolorow, R. D., and Lachmann, F. M. (1980). *Psychoanalysis of Developmental Arrests.* New York: International Universities Press.

Stone, L. (1961). *The Psychoanalytic Situation.* New York: International Universities Press.

Tarachow, S. (1962). Interpretation and reality in psychotherapy. *International Journal of Psycho-Analysis* 43:377–387.

—— (1963). *An Introduction to Psychotherapy.* New York: International Universities Press.

Volkan, V. D. (1976). *Primitive Internalized Object Relations.* New York: International Universities Press.

Wallerstein, R. (1986). *Forty-two Lives in Treatment.* New York: Guilford.

—— (1989). Psychoanalysis and psychotherapy: an historical perspective. *International Journal of Psycho-Analysis* 70:563–591.

PART V

WHAT IS UNIQUE
ABOUT FREUDIAN TECHNIQUE?
SUMMARY AND CONCLUSIONS

12

The Unique Contribution of the Contemporary Freudian Position

Steven J. Ellman

One may conceive of the present state of psychoanalysis as involving several sets of dialectics crashing against each other and battling over the fate of psychoanalytic treatment and theory. However, as opposed to Hegel and Marx's view of the dialectic where thesis and antithesis are sibylline faces etched on the granite of historical determinism, my views are engraved by the events of the past seventy years. During this time countries that represented either communism or capitalism have fought for control of the planet, usually without serious consideration of the worker or the society that either system was intended to benefit. The dialectic masked a battle that turned out to be about power rather than about historical or economic ideas for the good of the worker. In psychoanalysis we are in a much less extreme way heading toward a similar fate. For instance, in debating whether analysis is a one- or two-person field we are forgetting about the patient and the patient's experience of the analytic situation. In addition, in this warring dialectical struggle we are losing Freud's vision of the analytic process. The hope is that we can aspire to a different idea of the dialectic, that is, the way one often views Mozart's dialectical ability to attain and retain while at the same time going beyond established standards. Mozart's genius was to simultaneously remind us and surprise us, and I hope we can partake in a minuscule portion of this unrivaled creator's ability to concurrently retain and create. In this chapter I restate Freud's vision in contemporary terms and try to show how postmodern Freudianism is not an oxymoron.

Although there are many divergent themes among analysts who describe themselves as contemporary Freudians,[1] there are certain essential concepts that I believe are common to the present group of New York University Freudian analysts. There is a common ground that these analysts inhabit that guides their clinical interventions and is directly related to their shared theoretical assumptions. As I attempt to delineate this common ground I will try to look at some of the similarities and differences between this Freudian group and other theoretical positions. I will also look at some differences among the NYU Freudians. Perhaps surprisingly I will try to look at the differences between the NYU Freudian group and what in the United States has been called classical analysis. In Chapter 13 Martin Bergmann states that classical analysis ended in this country after World War II. This is one view, but Lipton (1977, 1979) has shown that the term *classical* came into being after the war and was certainly used at New York Psychoanalytic Institute in the 1970s and 1980s. I would say that what Richards and Lynch (Chapter 1) call structural analysts would have previously been labeled classical analysts. Late in the chapter I use the term *structural analysis.*

Some of the analysts in the NYU group identify themselves as Freudian analysts but not as classical analysts. I will try to show how this group's position diverges from a number of propositions put forth by classical analysts in the United States. I will also attempt to show that while the classical analysts at NYU have been influenced by many analysts associated with the classical position, the way they have internalized this position is unique to the NYU Freudians. Moreover, at the end of the chapter I will look at the common ground occupied by all or at least most of us. In

---

1. I am going to take as my sample of Freudian analysts those analysts who have written chapters in the present volume. This of course is a biased sample that has not been randomly selected. At the end of the chapter I will say a few words about the bias inherent in this group of analysts.

attempting to delineate this common ground I will specify the group's boundaries by referring to other positions and depicting points of convergence and divergence with these theoretical orientations. The groups that I will refer to in this depiction are the Kleinians (from London), some relational analysts, and self psychologists. After an introductory definition I will give a brief historical overview of the Freudian position and then begin the discussion of comparative positions. I will also follow Martin Bergmann's advice (Chapter 13) and try to understand some of the reasons for the theoretical plurality that is being experienced in contemporary psychoanalysis.

PRECURSOR TO A DEFINITION

We begin this comparison by looking at some of the assumptions that O'Shaughnessy (1997) (a London Kleinian) maintains are common to all analysts: "The recognition of an unconscious, of the ego's need for defenses against intense anxieties, the assumption of the past in the transference situation with the analyst, symbolism, and so on are common assumptions of analysts across theoretical perspectives" (p. 34). Here the criteria that O'Shaughnessy has assembled are ones that self psychologists and relational analysts have essential disagreements with, while Freudian analysts agree with the list but disagree in important ways about how this list is realized and treated in the clinical situation. Thus while I believe there are important conceptual agreements between Freudians and the Kleinians, there are important clinical differences between these two groups. In this chapter I attempt to portray the disparities between the groups. I think Schafer's (1997) term *Freudian Kleinians* aptly captures the common theoretical ground these two groups occupy.

THE INEVITABLE FREUD

Freud in beginning his development of psychotherapeutic procedures was immediately drawn to the symbolizing functions of the mind. In one of his early publications with Breuer (Breuer and Freud 1895) he calls our attention to the parallel of the symbolic aspect of symptom formation and the symbolism that "normal people" form during dreaming. In describing the formation of symptoms, he states,

The connection is often so clear that it is quite evident how it was that the precipitating event produced this particular phenomenon rather than any other. . . . In other cases the connection is not so simple. It consists only in what might be called a "symbolic" relation between the precipitating cause and the pathological phenomenon—a relation such as healthy people form in dreams. [pp. 3–4]

In this same publication Freud tries to understand the experience of shame and the relationship of shame to an individual's defensive struggle with experiences that affect one's evaluations of the ego or self. These tendencies of Freud's that are present in every period of his career were overshadowed in the United States[2] by his proclivities toward mechanistic and authoritarian pronouncements. Thus in the same volume that demonstrates Freud's sensitivity to meaning and the experience of shame in normal and pathological outcomes, he and Breuer put forth several mechanistic concepts. The mechanistic protrayal of abreactions in the cathartic method are subtly included in Freud's statements in his elucidation of the pathogenic memory model. At one and the same time, in Chapter 4 of "Studies on Hysteria" (Breuer and Freud 1895) Freud goes beyond Breuer's methods of treatment while accepting some of Breuer's neurophysiological assumptions and mechanistic concepts. Breuer's neurophysiological assumptions are quite interesting and represent some of the better conceptual thinking of his time. It is the way that Freud applies these concepts in a mechanistic way that is the tension between his psychological or experiential side and his mechanistic side. Thus we can see several types of tensions in Freud's early writings and in his actual practice as a clinician (Ellman 1991).

If we are to briefly leave aside the contradictions in Freud's pronouncements, we can sum up his ideas about analytic technique by saying that first the patient must become attached to the analyst (Ellman 1991) and then the analyst is in a position to analyze the patient's transference reactions. If this is done appropriately, then the analyst is in a condition to understand the psychic reality of the patient in genetic (developmental), dynamic, and topographic (later structural) and economic (his energic

---

2. If is my view that each country and indeed groups within countries have characteristic readings of Freud. These "readings" sharply influence the debates in psychoanalysis within a given country.

assumptions) terms. Freud advises us that the transference is the main vehicle of the treatment and that we must set up appropriate conditions for the transference to unfold in the analytic situation. This simplification of Freud's views is contradicted by the fact that in his actual practice transference was never the central focus of his technique. Even in his writings he oscillated between advocating allowing the transference to unfold and his later statements in "Beyond the Pleasure Principle" (1920), "Remarks on Theory and Practice of Dream Interpretation" (1923a), and "Analysis Terminable and Interminable" (1937b) where the transference plays a less important role (Ellman 1991).

Interestingly, the body of work that numerous contemporary Freudians refer to as signaling a change in technique (Freud 1920, 1923a, 1926) involves essays that Freud never integrated into his clinical approach to psychoanalysis. It is the structural theory in many Freudians' view that changes psychoanalytic technique from a "depth psychology" to a method that values the "restoration of the ego to its integrity" (A. Freud 1936, p. 4). It is only in contemporary times, however, that writers like Busch (1995) and Gray (1973, 1982, 1992) have systematically spelled out the implications of a psychoanalytic technique that is solidly wedded to the structural theory. While Arlow and Brenner (1964) attempted this task much earlier, the implications of their interpretation of the structural theory still resonated strongly with some of Freud's earlier concepts. Subsequently, Arlow (1969, 1979, 1985, 1990) and Stone (1967) took yet another approach to spelling out the implications of the structural model. Recently Brenner (1996) has cast out many of the concepts of the structural model in a radical streamlining of his theory of psychoanalytic technique.

This brief review is intended to show that not only can we see several types of tension in Freud's writings and in his actual practice as a clinician, but these tensions persist even among Freudians who adhere to the structural model. In addition there are other tensions between contemporary Freudians who downplay parts of the structural model and attempt to integrate aspects of other psychoanalytic theories into their approach. This latter group is significantly represented in the NYU Freudians as *self and object Freudians*, a term used to show the relationship to Jacobson's *Self and the Object World* (1964), which I think begins a Freudian object relations position in the United States. It was continued in the United States by Loewald (1980) and in Britain by Winnicott and many others who I think are close in spirit to the American object relations theorists.

That these tensions exist is not surprising since we can note briefly that Freud on the one hand is the writer who states that psychoanalysis is after all a treatment of love while on the other hand and during the same era Freud characterizes the analyst as similar to the surgeon in his detached attitude (Ellman 1991). He is a writer who inveighs against early interpretation, since this type of intervention would be crude at best and often seen as cruel by many analysands. In discussing early interpretations he says, "Such conduct brings both the man and the treatment into discredit and arouses the most violent opposition, whether the interpretations be correct or not" (Ellman 1991, p. 187). Despite these wise words Freud in most of his recorded treatments interprets early and with considerable depth and force. These seemingly discrepant attitudes may be brought under a coherent conceptual rubric but have not been in the main reconciled in the classical tradition, and certainly not in Freud's writings. The discordant notes that I have highlighted are intensified if one believes as I do (Bergmann and Ellman 1985, Carsky and Ellman 1985, Ellman 1992, 1997a) that Freud developed four fairly distinct theoretical perspectives that he never integrated or systematized. Thus Freud not only had several areas of tension in his ideas about psychoanalytic technique, but his general theory of psychological development shifted considerably over the decades. In a future publication I hope to show that most of the major contemporary theoretical positions derive from different aspects of Freud's writings.

SOME UNIFYING THEMES

I have briefly outlined the inherent tension in Freud's writings. Now I will attempt to show how the NYU Freudians have built on the scaffolding that Freud originally erected. One crucial aspect of convergence is the group's interest in the surface of the mind. In Freud's papers that outlined the structural theory (1920, 1923b, 1926) he began to look at the mind as having properties that regulate both endogenous and exogenous stimulation. Through the concept of the stimulus barrier he maintained that the infant is able to protect itself from intense external stimulation, that if perceived in unmodulated form would be traumatic. In a similar fashion he began to recognize that defenses that he had previously conceptualized as being "acts of will" at times operated in a more automatic manner and are outside the patient's awareness, or are unconscious.[3] Exhorting patients to put aside their inhibitions or to try harder to remember is a futile task at best if one seriously takes the assumptions of the structural model into account. One may conceive of defense as an act of will, but patients are consciously unaware of their defensive efforts. It is also true that the structural model for the first time allowed Freud to conceive of unconscious processes as having an adaptive function, adaptive in the sense that unconscious defensive operations allow the individual to ward off anxiety that might otherwise be traumatic or might interfere with ongoing relations with reality. It was Hartmann (1939) who further delineated the implications of the adaptive position in psychoanalysis.

In a similar fashion the structural model allowed Freud to ease a dichotomy that was established in the topographic model, in which tension was postulated to exist between the unconscious and conscious systems and in a parallel fashion between primary and secondary process. The unconscious was thought to operate solely in terms of primary process (irrational) thought, while the conscious system if operating optimally was a rational system operating according to the principles of the secondary process. This dichotomy led early analysts to search for and interpret the primary process to allow the conscious system to become aware of and gain control of the unconscious system. Although Freud never realized the clinical benefits of his new conceptualizations, some contemporary analysts have begun to recognize the possibilities that the structural hypotheses begins to unlock.[4] Thought now could be viewed not as either primary or secondary process but as complicated amalgams of both processes. The ego (or the person) might also be seen as having capabilities that are not

---

3. To maintain that Freud thought defenses were acts of will is at best an oversimplified position and at worst totally inaccurate. Freud early in his career thought that defenses were conscious and he could combat defensive maneuvers of the patient by exhorting the patient toward greater efforts. Hence the pressure technique was invented to literally and concretely exhort the patient to try harder to remember. By the time Freud wrote the technique papers, he had already conceived of defense as involving unconscious processes (Freud 1915a,b), but this conceptualization was logically incompatible with what is today called the topographic model. Thus it was not until Freud wrote the structural theory papers that he reconciled his growing appreciation of defense as an unconscious process with the theoretical structure that he was putting forth.

4. While I believe the structural model has pointed out several of the deficiences of Freud's earlier ideas, from my standpoint it is not an adequate theory or even a particularly good theoretical metaphor.

captured by either concept (primary or secondary process). For clinical purposes the important aspect of this new conceptualization is that the analyst's focus is now on the patient's experience. The topology of the surface of the mind is now the appropriate place to begin the psychoanalytic exploration. This topology is often complicated with splits and fissures that Freud hinted at but certainly did not fully envision.We might reiterate as an historical note that the clinical implications of the structural model were never realized by Freud in either his writings about psychoanalytic technique or in his actual practice of psychoanalysis. Some analysts need to see Freud as moving toward contemporary technique in terms of his concepts of treatment as well as his actual practice. In fact, just the opposite was the case; although Freud's theoretical writings open up a new avenue of thought in terms of psychoanalytic treatment, both his actual practice as well as his limited writings on technique tended to return to his earlier conceptualizations (Ellman 1991).

BEGINNING THE TREATMENT

Although Freud has suggested that early interpretation is rude at best, his ideas about trial analyses are essentially designed to see how a patient responds to interpretation. Thus for Freud and for many analysts after him the question of analyzability centered on the patient's receptivity to interpretive efforts. Aspects of both the classical and Kleinian tradition see the patient's receptivity as an important prognostic factor for, as well as eventually a result of, analytic treatment. Winnicott (1965), Balint (1968), and, later in the United States, Kohut (1968, 1971) raised the question of the analysis of analysands who cannot tolerate interpretive efforts. This in many ways is a central question that members of the NYU group have confronted and in part distinguishes some of their positions from Kleinian and classical positions.

Perhaps there is no place where some members of the group have utilized divergent concepts as we have in terms of conceptualizing the beginning of the treatment. Here clearly Winnicott's ideas have had a profound effect on focusing the analyst on the patient's subjective states and vulnerabilities. This may seem like a strange statement, for it should be a given in psychoanalysis that the analyst's focus is on the patient's pain, suffering, and vulnerabilities. This may seem even more obvious when one realizes that these states that reflect psychic conflict are particulary the states that make it difficult for patients to participate in the analytic process. Certainly at the time he was writing, Winnicott was not stating the obvious and he and authors such as Balint were helping open the portals of analysis to a wider group of patients then Freud envisioned.[5]

Winnicott and Balint were clearly stating a different way of entering the patient's world than had been put forth by classical analysts in the United States. They did not, however, offer systematic ideas about psychoanalytic technique nor did they talk the diagnostic language of Freudian psychoanalysis. In the United States it was Stone (1961), Zetzel (1966), and most powerfully Kohut (1971) who began in Stone's language to widen the scope of psychoanalytic treatment. In this context I will focus on Kohut's contributions and from a certain point of view will look at what may be regarded as limitations or at least differences from the Freudian perspective.

It was Kohut who first pointed out the logical difficulties with some of Freud's views on narcissism. Freud (1916/1917) in effect posited that individuals with narcissistic disorders do not have enough object libido to form a transference relationship. Kohut in a succinct manner both implicitly and explicitly maintained that narcissism is not the opposite of object relations (as Freud had implied), but rather narcissism interfered with the capacity for object love. In Kohut's view it was not that narcissistic patients could not form transference relationships, but rather that the transferences would be (not surprisingly) narcissistic in character (idealizing or mirroring [Kohut 1971, 1977]). He also presented clinical illustrations about the difficulties in establishing consistent interpretable transference

---

5. In some ways this is an anachronistic and misleading statement. Freud early in his career in his paper "On Psychotherapy" (1905b) attempted to set a fairly narrow window for the type of patients that could be treated by his new method. By the end of his career he acknowledged his difficulties in treating certain types of patients and suggested in the constructions paper (1937a) that a good deal could be learned from the treatment of psychotic patients. In between these distant dates Freud states in the introductory lectures (1916/1917) that insofar as narcissistic factors enter the treatment, the possibilities for success are dimmed. Here he is reaffirming his earlier narrow range of analyzability. However, in his actual practice Freud saw a wide range of patients and rarely seemed to understand or be concerned with the patient's diagnostic status. Thus we see a typically contradictory picture in Freud's statements and practice. What I have previously concluded is that Freud was willing to undertake a patient if there was a positive transference and the patient was bright and verbal (Ellman 1991).

states in narcissistic patients. It is his work in establishing the conditions for a transference relationship to flourish that has established Kohut's influence on some members of this Freudian group. The conceptualization of analytic trust could not have been arrived at in the same way without Kohut's ideas concerning the importance of mirroring in the early treatment situation. Kohut's sensitivity to narcissistic patients' aversion to early interpretation suggested that interpretive efforts were not the best way to initially begin a therapeutic relationship.

Bach's (1985, 1994) emphasis on the unification of states and Grunes's (1984) concept of the therapeutic object relationship are two of the concepts that are directly related to the establishment of interpretable transference states. All of the NYU Freudians conceive of transference as a ubiquitous occurrence but the question of when the patient is able to tolerate transference interpretations is yet another one that Winnicott, Kohut, Bach, Steingart, and Grunes have all addressed. In this conceptualization some patients need what Winnicott (1962) has called "holding." I have defined holding (in the analytic situation) as a type of reflecting or mirroring that involves the interpenetration of states, and the communication of this interpenetration. This interpenetration may be accomplished in a number of nonverbal ways or verbally by mirroring or through synthetic comments that show the patient similarities across states. Some analysts are able to listen in a manner that demonstrates that they are with the patient and experiencing their states. They do this by a nod or a movement or a subvocalized affirmation or reflection. Holding developmentally has a physical meaning that I am assuming is symbolically awakened in this therapeutic version of holding.

In the beginning phase of treatment or of a new transference cycle, the analyst is usually called upon to contain aspects of the patient's destructive tendencies (Bion 1962, 1967). Unless this can be done effectively, it is difficult to have interpretable transference states. Thus in this formulation holding and containment are frequently necessary preconditions that allow the patient to develop the analytic trust necessary to tolerate and utilize transference interpretations later in the treatment.

This formulation is in part a response to modern structural theory (previously referred to as classical theory) and an attempt to clarify the controversies surrounding the issue of therapeutic alliance that Richards and Lynch highlight in Chapter 1. They state,

Elizabeth Zetzel and Ralph Greenson saw it as redressing the inadequate attention to the real relationship that typified the reigning ego-psychological approach. Their position was opposed by Brenner, who considered the concept superfluous and even countertherapeutic, and by Martin Stein, whose paper "The Unobjectionable Part of the Transference" offers the clearest statement of the way in which positive transference can be enlisted by patient and analyst together in the service of resistance. [this volume, p. 16]

Brenner (1976, 1979, 1982) in criticizing this concept considered the therapeutic alliance as a form of positive transference. If this is the case, then clearly, as Stein (and Brenner) maintained, the transference should be analyzed. Although Brenner's logic was impeccable, his criticism did not address issues that the concept attempted to remedy. Thus, although Brenner won the debate that he engaged in with Stone, Greenson, and Zetzel, it simply meant to some of the NYU Freudians that other concepts were needed to describe the therapeutic object relationship. Interestingly, Loewald is not featured in the review of what Richards and Lynch call contemporary structural theory. However, for many of the NYU Freudians, he is the conceptual lynchpin that allows them to utilize some of Kohut's ideas on technique while staying within the Freudian conceptual framework that Loewald established. In this volume Grunes (Chapter 6) has emphasized the importance of Loewald's contributions. Using his and Winnicott's concepts, one can begin the treatment in the manner that Bach (1985) and I have described and still attempt to allow the transference to unfold. I have tried to demonstrate that the concept of analytic trust does not depend on transference phenomena and therefore is not subject to the criticisms that Brenner and Stein (1981) have leveled at the therapeutic alliance. Rather analytic trust is built on the extent to which the analyst can interpenetrate the patient's world. To the extent that the analyst can accomplish this task the analysand can experience being understood in a manner that is influenced by, but not dependent on, their transference reactions. At times this trust allows previously uninterpretable transference to enter the analytic field.

We can delineate three types of contemporary Freudians; the contemporary structuralists (derived from the classical position), Freudians who are influenced by and incorporate self psychological and object relations perspectives (self and object Freudians),[6] and ego psychological analysts such as Paul Gray (1994) and Fred Busch (1995). Gray and Busch emphasize the role of defense interpretation in order to free up ego capacities and allow the patient greater possibilities for self-discovery. Gray and Busch rarely interpret unconscious or transference manifestations at any stage in the treatment. Rather, it is their position that throughout the analysis the appropriate role for the analyst is to interpret defensive maneuvers as they appear in the patient's consciousness. This allows the patients to experience the analysis as a "conscious and voluntary co-partnership with the analyst" (Busch 1995, p. 15). The co-partnership that the ego psychologists strive for is not considered to be a result of a positive or unobjectionable transference. It is a consequence of the work of the analysis and in this formulation occurs as a result of the uncovering of defensive processes, which leads to increased self-knowledge and gradually enhanced ego capacities. I would interpret the results of their work as the development of analytic trust; it progressively becomes apparent to the analysand that the analyst is facilitating a process that results in a new type of understanding.[7] Two of the three perspectives emphasize either a partnership with the analyst or some type of therapeutic relationship as important to the analytic process. The contemporary structural position does not admit any concept of therapeutic object relationship into their theoretical stance. I have stressed the importance of analytic trust in the beginning phase of the treatment, but it is my view that the same type of questions arise in different phases of the treatment. Thus it is not simply the beginning phase of treatment where one finds disagreements in the Freudian position. One can see the divergent positions in terms of the importance of the therapeutic relationship throughout the analytic process.

Where are the agreements in the Freudian positions that I have outlined? All of the Freudians start from the surface of the mind. Thus whatever the Freudian position, interventions are based on at least

---

6. I choose this term in remembrance of Edith Jacobson's volume *The Self and the Object World*. In my view she is the primary object relations theorist in the United States. She is one of the first to meaningfully relate Freudian thought to object relations theory.

7. From my perspective it would be difficult to adhere to the ego psychological position with more difficult patients, but this is something that we should consider an empirical question.

derivatives or elements of fantasy that reach consciousness. Freud's initial onion skin metaphor (1895) has retained some currency in that not only do all Freudians start from the surface of the mind, but all share in what Bergmann (Chapter 13) calls "the gratitude for Freud's opening the way to us for the understanding of the unconscious" (this volume, p. 294). Thus the concept of the unconscious is crucial to all Freudians. The prescribed pathways to the unconscious vary a good deal, however, and we can now see a different coalescence between the three Freudian groups. Although the self and object Freudians start with the meeting of an interpenetration of subjectivities, this is done so that one can be in a position to interpret the transference. The contemporary structuralists are virtually always in a position to interpret transference, while the ego-psychological analysts do not see transference analysis as a prime function of the analytic task. Here we can see that the self and object Freudians join the structuralists in the placing of transference as a central task in psychoanalysis. Brenner's pivotal concept (compromise formation) is one that is derived from and an important extension of Freudian thought. Thus most Freudians accept the concept of compromise formation and agree that it is hard to imagine a mental event that is not a product of compromise formation. How this concept guides clinical interventions is a topic to be dealt with in the transference section. If we summarize the positions we can say that the ego-psychological analysts and the self and object Freudians have some points of agreement in beginning the treatment and in the importance of the therapeutic relationship. The self and object Freudians and the structuralists share the view that the understanding of the transference is the pivotal goal of an analysis, and the prime way to make the products of unconscious fantasy real in the analytic situation.

If we were to transpose these rough distinctions to the British shore, we might say that the self and obect Freudians are Freudians who in terms of technique have utilized and extended a good deal of Winnicott's and Balint's ideas. On the other side there is stronger similarity between the structuralists and the Kleinian positions in terms of the importance of transference analysis and the central, ubiquitous role of interpretation. This leaves out the content of the interpretations and how transference is conceptualized (see Transference and Enactments, below). In returning to the United States we can see that in the beginning of the treatment self and object Freudians may seem similar to various self psychologists, and intersubjectivity and relational analysts. The difference is that self and object Freudians see entering the patient's world as the beginning of the analysis, not the sole transmutative element of the analysis. To make one last comparison, we can say that the role of observing ego (see Richards and Lynch, Chapter 1, and Grand, Chapter 5) that Sterba (1934) highlighted is an important aspect of treatment in both the ego-psychological and the self and object Freudians position. It is relatively unimportant to the structuralists and the Kleinians.

SOME TECHNIQUE QUESTIONS THAT RELATE TO PHILOSOPHIC ORIENTATION

In the critique of Freudian psychoanalysis put forth by intersubjectivity and relational analysts (Hoffman 1983, 1992), the analyst is portrayed as believing that he is an objective decoder of the patient's experience. The decoding occurs when the analyst interprets. In addition, the analyst believes that his view of reality is superior to the patient's. Transference in this portrayal is created by the analysand with the neutral analyst seen as a recipient of the transference. This critique is quite relevant to the classical tradition of the United States and to Brenner's contemporary structuralist position. The analyst in this tradition is pictured as a neutral observer who does not appreciably affect the analytic field. On the other hand, an intersubjectivity-relational position in its strong form maintains that the analytic field is a joint construction between analyst and analysand. This position also maintains that transfiguration occurs in psychoanalysis through the analytic relationship. Here we have two ends of the continuum, one that maintains a constructionist, subjectivist position where the analytic relationship is the transmutative factor, and the other a positivist, objective reality where the curative factor in analysis is insight.

Most analysts reading this summary of their position would, I believe, consider this characterization as extreme. However, the implications of both the relational and the structuralist position lead to these extreme conceptual positions. The relational position does, however, raise many vexing questions for all Freudian positions. The authority of the analyst is a question that courses through almost every issue in psychoanalytic technique. Why assume that the analyst knows more than the patient about any given issue in the patient's life? If transference is seen as a joint construction of the patient and analyst, how is an analyst in a position to make transference interpretations and assume they have relevance to the patient's life outside of analysis? If the analyst is not in a position to make transference interpretations, then clearly the mutative factor in psychoanalysis may be solely or at least primarily the relationship between patient and analyst. Rather than continue these considerations and questions, which Steingart (1995) has taken up in great detail, I will instead try to enumerate some of the contemporary Freudian answers to the questions posed by the relational and intersubjectivity position(s).

Brenner's (1995) position on the analyst's authority is that when the analyst thinks he's right he should "stick to his guns" and continue his interpretations. When I was supervised by a structural analyst, he suggested a certain interpretation and I followed his suggestion in the following session. The interpretation led nowhere[8] and he suggested that I should have made the same interpretation again during that session. When I asked how often one would make the same interpretation, he answered as often as it takes to get through to the patient. From my perspective (today) this is not a Freudian viewpoint. If the patient's thoughts and associations are not facilitated by the analyst's intervention, Freud (1937a) (in principle) saw this as disconfirming the analyst's interpretive efforts. In this respect he had the beginnings of an operational approach to evaluate the analyst's efforts. Here Winnicott's statements about interpretive efforts are an appropriate extension of a Freudian perspective. Winnicott (1962) maintains that the analyst interprets to demonstrate not what he knows but rather the limitations of his knowledge. If something new does not appear as a result of the analyst's interpretations, then at best the interpretations are merely descriptive (or reflective) of what has already been understood in the analysis. Winnicott's view is that the interpretive effort should facilitate the analysand's efforts and lead to new places in exploring the depths of the patient's psychic realities. Bach (1985) and Steingart (1995) have stated similar views about the role of interpretation.

How does one regard the analyst's authority with respect to this view of interpretation? To consider the analyst right or wrong is perhaps asking a question from an inappropriate logical category. The question in this context is the role of interpretive efforts in facilitating the analysis, that

---

8. Of course this could have been true for many reasons and we all know that in supervision frequently the supervisee is making interpretations one week late. That is, he is applying the supervisor's suggestions from last week to this week's material.

is whether or not the interpretive effort facilitates the analytic process. At this point one could reasonably ask what does it mean to facilitate an analysis; for what purpose, or put more directly, what does the analyst consider to be the transfigurative elements in an analysis? This larger question will be asked later in this chapter but for our purposes here the analyst has the authority (as does the patient) to interpret her shared experiences with the patient and to put new meaning to these experiences. The patient and analyst have a series of shared experiences that the analyst is attempting to elucidate.[9] The final authority (in these terms) always rests with the way in which the patient is able to utilize the analyst's interventions.

So far I have deliberately not stated issues in philosophic terms, but in order to join the questions that have been asked I will venture into an area where psychoanalysts typically are one to two decades behind the philosophic and literary sources they cite. In the way that Mitchell (1988) and Hoffman (1992) have joined the issue the debate is between constructionist and realist perspectives. Is what the analyst sees real and a continuing aspect of the patient, or when the patient and analyst meet do we see a construction of two people who produce a unique series of events that have no necessary relationship to either of the two participants? The latter is the strong form of the constructionist position. For once a constructionist admits to the idea of enduring traits present in the patient (or analyst), then the pure logical form of the argument is no longer available to the constructionist. Rather at that point in time one can ask the extent to which a trait is enduring and how many traits are enduring in a given situation? If these questions are asked, then the question is a statistical question—How many and how often? The realist would argue that these questions by their very nature are the essence of realist questions.

There is another point of view that has been introduced by Ellman and Moskowitz (1980), which they called the instrumentalist point of view. Here one would say that either the realist or constructivist viewpoint should each be considered as one alternative meta-theory to be judged by the usual criteria that come into account in evaluating the efficacy of a theory. From an instrumentalist perspective one might say there is no adequate

---

9. I am writing "elucidate" here, but as I have stated it is my view that the interpretive effort is present as a means of facilitating the analytic process.

theory to account for all the phenomena. If we did research, the results would appear in the way that I just described.

The instrumentalist point of view is in accord with both the ego-psychological and the self and object Freudian position in understanding the authority of the analyst and the role of interpretation in the analytic situation. For the realist there can be only one interpretation of a given situation, since of necessity there is only reality at any given point in time. The constructionist sees even the idea of reality as a social construction and having nothing necessarily to do with an existential reality. The instrumentalist recognizes that there can be a number of views of reality but accords the theory that accounts for given phenomena the highest status. Thus an interpretive effort that facilitates the analytic process is accorded the highest status even if this interpretation seems mundane in terms of its narrative utility. The difficulty in psychoanalysis is that we have come to an empirical approach so late in the history of our discipline. It is my hope that many of us who have done research in other areas will turn our attention to the psychoanalytic situation. Although there is not space in this chapter to explore the similarities, Schafer's (1976, 1992) narrative-action language propositions have the same logical status as the constructionist position.

FURTHER COMMON GROUND AND
DIVERGENT THEORETICAL VIEWS

It would seem that there is reasonable common ground between some NYU self and object Freudians and Kohutians. Although there are points of convergence, simply including the concept of containment indicates differences between the self and object Freudians and Kohutians and intersubjectivity positions. The Freudians include the concept of aggression or destructive elements as being part of all conflicts and all transference states (and important affects to be contained). More importantly, reflecting the patient's states or adequately holding the patient is not an end of the treatment but rather, as stated, a beginning that facilitates the patient's tolerance of and ability to utilize other perspectives. Here in this conceptualization the question of a one- or two-person field is predicated on the patient's response rather than the analyst's philosophic views. Thus there are periods of time where the patient can only tolerate one person in the room and the analyst is for the patient a selfobject. If the analyst insists on a two-person field, then it will be difficult to establish analytic trust. Kleinian and structural analysts have typically insisted on being included in the analytic room as a separate source of information via interpretive efforts.

This position can tolerate the idea of two-person fields as long as the position can also realize that at times the field narrows to a one-person field. At the beginning of a treatment, as I have pointed out, there is often a tolerance by the patient for only a one-person field. If the analyst is unable to do this, then in my mind there can never be a true two-person field. By the end of treatment one hopes there is a two-person field and a useful interaction that characterizes the end of a successful analysis. The analyst's authority is subject to review at all times by the usefulness of his interventions. The development of analytic trust means that the patient may be able to reject an intervention and still accept the analyst and the analytic process. In Bach's terms the analyst has to accept the patient's subjectivity, and gradually the patient is able to integrate subjective and objective positions. If one has difficulty with the term *objective*, although there is little meaning to the term *subjective* without understanding the concept of *objective*, then one can say that as the treatment progresses the patient becomes more and more able to take and at times accept multiple perspectives. Thus if one considers psychoanalysis as a meeting of subjectivities, then as the treatment progresses the other's subjectivity becomes more important and is gradually accepted as an independent subjectivity.

If we take a comparative approach, we can say that most relational-intersubjectivity authors have written as if the analytic situation must be conceived of as a field constructed by the two participants. Most Kleinian and classical writers (see Richards and Lynch, Chapter 1, for a recent change in this position) have focused on the analysand as the person who constructs the analytic field and whose conflicts are unearthed during the course of an analysis. The self and object Freudian position is one that maintains that the analytic field changes depending on the nature of the subjectivities that are meeting and the extent to which each person can tolerate and facilitate the other. In a contemporary Freudian position the initial subjectivity that is dominant is usually the patient's, and the patient's signals should ideally determine whether a two-person field can be tolerated and utilized. Freedman's (Chapter 4) distinction concerning the ability to symbolize is a crucial one in the determination of the patient's ability to utilize a two-person field. In this vein the question is the extent to which two persons can inhabit one analytic process. I realize that I have changed the ground in terms of the traditional argument of two- versus one-person field. I have done this intentionally to provide a different focus, that is, one that attempts to rely on the patient's perceptions to determine the nature of the field.

TRANSFERENCE AND ENACTMENTS

Freud's (1905a) view that he expressed in the postscript to the Dora case was more accurate and prescient than he could have imagined. He maintained that transference was the hardest part of the treatment. Transference analysis not only was difficult for him, transference analysis was never a central aspect of his clinical work (Ellman 1991). Thus while Freud saw transference as the central vehicie of analysis, it was a vehicle that often got derailed. In my view the current focus on enactments is in part an implicit acknowledgment of the general difficulty of analyzing transference manifestations (Ellman 1998). Leaving this hypothesis aside, we can state that while all contemporary Freudians conceptualize transference as a ubiquitous occurrence, there are differences of opinion as to when transference manifestations should become the leading edge of an analytic treatment. For Brenner (1982), as a contemporary structuralist the transference is interpreted as soon as possible in the course of an analysis. Brenner's view is that the designation of a portion of the analysis as the transference neurosis is due to analysts' not interpreting transference early enough in the treatment situation. The transference should be interpreted as early and thoroughly as possible. Since Brenner sees all transference as containing libidinal and aggressive elements, the structuralist is also aware that a given transference state always contains elements of unconscious fantasy that is unlike those that are being manifested at a given point in time.

Self and object Freudians are concerned with both the transference and the therapeutic object relationship. Thus while in the case of Richard Lasky's (Chapter 10) patient all Freudians would agree with Lasky that the patient's reactions were a manifestation of transference, the central issue that divides Freudians is determining when the transference is in interpretable form. Self and object Freudians are consistently aware of the patient's state and some have maintained that a treatment consists of several transference cycles (Ellman 1991, 1997a, Freedman 1994). Often similar material will have to undergo several cycles before it is fully interpretable. Even then interpretable transference is a delicate balance where the patient's and analyst's narcissistic equilibrium is easily disrupted. One might consider this state of equipoise allowing space for the patient to create an illusory (and simultaneously real) relationship that we call transference. It is possible to conceive of the interpretable aspects of this relationship as occurring in what Winnicott called transitional space. In this space patients are able to experience transference as a created illusion and thus are more easily able to accept it as a production of their own.

> Interpretation outside the ripeness of the material is indoctrination and produces compliance. A corollary is that resistance arises out of interpretation given outside the area of the overlap of the patient's and the analyst's playing together. Interpretation when the patient has no capacity to play is simply not useful, or causes confusion. When there is mutual playing, then interpretation according to accepted psychoanalytic principles can carry the therapeutic work forward. This playing has to be spontaneous and not compliant or acquiescent. [Winnicott 1971, p. 51]

Winnicott is maintaining that the condition of mutual play is necessary for the success of an interpretive effort. This "play" occurs in transitional space and permits the patient to receive from the analyst in a manner that allows the patient the experience of creating while simultaneously keeping the experience "intensely real" for both patient and analyst. When the space can be created the conditions for interpretation have been met. Thus the self and object Freudians consider the manifestation of a consistent transference state and insight about this state crucial elements of an analysis. It is easy, however, to be induced into or induce the patient into enactments when the treatment becomes intense. By "enactments" I am not referring to momentary exchanges between patient and analyst. These momentary exchanges are often ways in which the affect is kept alive in the mutual play that Winnicott mentions. Rather, I am talking about prolonged enactments that are only beginning to be fully described in contemporary literature (Ellman 1998). Why has it taken the analytic community so long to begin to describe the interactions that occur between analyst and analysand that at times lead to enactments?

It is my view that because of the shame the classical (structural) position put into the concept of countertransference, it was rare to see an analyst talk about difficulties in the analytic situation. Hence Racker's (1968) work on countertransference became a classic in part because there were few other works that even broached the subject. In modern times Bird's (1972) seminal article on transference and Sandler's (1976) paper on role responsiveness positioned the analyst's (counter)transference or reactions as topics that could be profitably discussed. Since that time contemporary analysts such as Jacobs (1991), McLaughlin (1981, 1991), Hoffman (1983, 1992), and Renik (1993) have all put forth views about the analyst's role in enactments that at the very least allow the analytic community to talk about the analyst's reactions to the patient's transference. In my opinion it is unfortunate that a self and object Freudian perspective has not as yet been put forth.

A COMPARATIVE APPROACH

What has Winnicott added to the contemporary Freudian position? He has helped clarify the conditions necessary for interpretation and he has implicitly added to the definition of transference (Steingart 1983). In the present formulation, analytic trust leads to the creation of transitional space and the possibility of interpretable transference states. Enactments occur when interpretations are made outside of transitional space. In other words, some enactments are a result of interpretations before the patient is ready for mutual play. In Freedman's (Chapter 4) terms the requisite conditions for an interpretable transference state depend on the patient's ability for symbolization. In a similar manner Grand (Chapter 5) maintains that the capacity for self-reflection is a necessary condition to conduct an analysis. We can put together these positions by realizing that a necessary condition for self-reflection and symbolization is the occurrence of transitional space. The development of analytic trust allows for the capacity of the real and the not real to exist side by side. It also allows for the person to begin to accept aspects of the self and other without each threatening the existence of self. If the experience of self continuity is constantly threatened, then there can be no space between the self and the other; either the other will be desperately needed or dangerously close. In Winnicott's terms (which Klein adopted) when analytic trust has devel-

oped, the individual is no longer in danger of falling to bits. Gediman
(Chapter 7) I believe makes a similar distinction from a different point of
view when she invokes the concept of zone of proximal development
(ZPD). This concept borrowed from Vygotsky (1978) by Wilson and
Weinstein (1996) is a way of conceptualizing the therapeutic relationship
and transference within a single hierarchical perspective.

Up to this point the position that I have been outlining is at least
somewhat different than my reading of a Kleinian or modern Kleinian
(Schafer 1997) position. That position is similar to the contemporary
structuralists' position in the manner that the transference is interpreted.
It is my view that the Kleinians typically interpret at deeper levels than the
contemporary structuralists, but this is one analyst's viewpoint (Ellman
1996). I have based these distinctions partly on my reading of Kleinian
material and partly on a discussion of a Kleinian case presentation (Ellman 1996). Leaving depth aside, a Kleinian focus is consistently on the
here-and-now transference (Spillius 1988). Their sessions may frequently
contain a number of interpretations that are a result of a feeling or state
that they have experienced (Hill and Grand 1996). This cannot be
considered a shared analytic experience since patients are usually unaware
of their efforts to rid themselves of these thoughts and incipient affects.[10]
One question to be asked about this type of interpretive effort is the extent
to which the therapeutic object relationship guides the analyst's interventions? Or more pointedly, it is possible to consider these comparative
approaches from a vectorial perspective; one might ask when and how
often does the Kleinian analyst interpret and to what extent does the
therapeutic object relationship guide the analyst's interventions? The topic
of the therapeutic object relationship is rarely alluded to either overtly or
covertly in the Kleinian literature. On that basis one might assume that the
issue is not in the forefront of their thinking about analytic treatment.
Moreover, from a self and object Freudian position the Kleinian approach
at times disrupts the therapeutic object relationship. The analyst is put in
a position as the objective decoder of subjective states. In this respect there

---

10. To fully enter into this discussion would require an extensive treatise on projective
identification and containment. Here I can only say that I believe it is possible to find the
concept of projective identification extremely valuable while having different ideas (from
Kleinian's ideas on treatment) on how to handle the manifestations of projective identification in the treatment situation.

is a one-person field where the analysand is creating and the analyst is observing the field.

I have previously stated there is a convergence of positions between self and object Freudians and some self psychological positions; the convergence, however, dissolves as transference manifestations are consistently manifested and in turn analyzed. Since there are a number of self psychological positions I will restrict myself here to Kohut, as I put forth a quintessential self analytic position and in addition remark on what I will term an intersubjectivity-relational problem. To understand these divergent positions I will try to briefly outline my understanding of Kohut's position about the analysis of consistent transference states. Kohut advocates only interpreting the transference when the analysand perceives a break in the analyst's empathic stance. This can occur because of some action on the part of the analyst or because of part of the normal structure of the analysis (weekend breaks, summer vacations, etc.). In this mode if the analysand is in the midst of an idealizing transference, then the analyst only interprets when there is a disruption in the transference. Thus the idealizing transference itself is considered to be sufficiently transmutative to allow for the beneficial results of an analysis. This is different in three respects from all Freudian analysts: (1) All Freudians strive for the analysand to be able to receive interpretive comments from the analyst that are designed to elucidate the meaning of unconscious fantasy. It is a crucial aspect of the treatment for patients to be able to tolerate and utilize a perspective that is not part of their conscious experience. Indeed this may cause momentary disruptions in analytic trust, but if the interpretation is well timed, these disruptions will be momentary and frequently beneficial. (2) All Freudian analysts believe at some point in the treatment situation patients should be helped to understand aggressive (or destructive) aspects of their unconscious fantasy life. (3) These interpretations should at times be made when the patient is experiencing either erotic or aggressive feelings. The interpretations should not be restricted to periods when patients experience the analyst as no longer being empathically attuned to their experience.

Thus the content and the timing of the interpretive efforts of Freudians necessarily differ from Kohutians and any intersubjectivity analysts that I have encountered including Stolorow and colleagues (1987), Hoffman (1992), and Spezzano (1993). It is my view that the manner in which Kohutians interpret does not allow the patient to fully appreciate another in the therapeutic situation. The analyst by only interpreting during perceived breaks in empathy seems to indicate that patient and analyst must work to repair this situation. This is opposed to my interpretation of a Freudian position where the analyst (at least at some point in the treatment) trusts that the patient can tolerate differing perspectives between analyst and analysand. There is a seeming requirement in Kohutian analyses that the patient should quickly be put back into a mirroring or idealizing transference state. In my terminology this does not allow for the full development of analytic trust. Thus while Kohutians begin the treatment in a manner that is in accord with self and object Freudians, once patients are in a consistent transference where they can hear and utilize another, the self and object Freudians diverge from the Kohutian stance.

Up to this point I have downplayed the convergence between Freudian positions. Once the self and object Freudian senses that the patient can utilize another (or the other becomes another), then the self and object and the structural positions tend to converge. Even at these points in treatment it seems to me that self and object Freudians utilize the therapeutic object relationship in a way that is not present in structural theory. In comparison the ego-psychological position does not seem to have a place for transference interpretations in its therapeutic repertoire. The idea of cooperative work in the analysis is one that extends throughout an analysis. In at least my version of the self and object position, analytic trust is solidified when patients can take in and utilize a perspective that is distinctly different from their own conscious perspective. Thus while the ego psychological and the self and object positions converge earlier, they also diverge during periods of time that are deemed to contain interpretable manifestations of transference.

GOALS OF PSYCHOANALYSIS

I have previously stated that an analysis can be viewed as being composed of a series of transference cycles (Ellman 1991, 1996, 1997a). The cycle starts with the analysands' allowing the analyst to enter their world and the analyst being receptive to a world that penetrates various barriers including the analyst's defensive barriers. The analyst has to be willing to contain both wanted and unwanted material and return this material in a manner that is useful to the analysand. During the opening phase the analyst has to allow the patient to utilize the analytic situation in a manner that often severely tests the analyst's ability to contain and remain empathic. If the analyst can maintain this stance, it can help facilitate the analysand's ability to tolerate a two-person field. When this occurs often the analyst understands that the patient is ready and in some ways desirous of hearing interpretive attempts by the analyst. To be sure, there are some patients who desperately do not want the analyst to come near and certainly not to enter their worlds. In fact, all patients in some way or another need to fend off the analyst's attempts at interpenetration. Since I am often asked about this type of patient, I can only reiterate that it generally is precisely this type of patient where analytic trust is both hardest to develop and most crucial for the continuation of a treatment. Paradoxically often certain distant (frequently schizoid) patients can easily tolerate interpretive efforts since they are receiving these efforts in a superficial, intellectalized manner. It is exactly with this type of patient that emotional interpenetration is crucial and where the beginning phase of the treatment is both crucial and at times the longest part of the treatment. This reminds me of an anecdote about an expert in multiple personalities who maintained that once the paient's personalities had been unified, one could successfully do traditional analytic treatment with such patients. When someone asked how long this would last, he answered that the traditional treatment was usually only a matter of one or two years. The unification, however, often lasted ten to twelve years.

When the patient is ready for interpretive material a new aspect of trust is formed in the willingness to hear divergent perspectives. There are at least two different meanings of divergent perspectives: (1) listening to another's view of one's unconscious life; (2) beginning to listen to aspects of a part of the self that has been sealed off and defended against and in many ways deemed untrustworthy.

I will not at this point try to focus on the nuances of trusting another while coming into contact with aspects of the unconscious (and frequently hated) parts of the rejected self. I will only comment that Freudian ideas such as free association and evenly hovering attention are seen by self and object Freudians as analytic ideals that are achieved during the course of an analysis rather than at the beginning of a treatment. Thus many Freudians have not given up the idea of free association but see patients' ability to freely talk about what is on their mind as an achievement of analysis rather than a criteria for analyzability. In a similar manner, evenly hovering attention is something the analyst can achieve when she is able to sit back and freely listen to the patient while trusting in the analytic process. In each analysis I am positing that this is an accomplishment that is achieved gradually through a number of transference cycles and most fully in the termination phase of the analysis.

The structural and Kleinian emphasis on the patient's receptivity to the analyst is an important emphasis, but an equally important emphasis is the patients' authentically becoming active in developing their own analyzing function (developing a sense of agency through the analytic process). Here there are a number of differences within positions, so that Novick (1982), an author I respect a great deal, argues against the patient's analyzing function being an important criterion for a successful termination in analysis. From my perspective if I had to do a study on what differentiates analysis from other treatments, this would be one of the features I would stress. Thus Grand stresses the self-reflective function, while Gediman, Steingart, Bach, and Druck all in one manner or another envision the analytic process as providing an increasing sense of agency during the analysis. I have tried to stress elsewhere (Ellman 1991) that the role of the analyzing function should be seen through a wider lens than simply relegating it to verbal channels.

At a recent presentation, a Kleinian analyst told an audience that he had been mistaken in a given intervention with a patient. A discussant asked whether the analyst would discuss this mistake with the patient. The analyst answered that if one were to do this, it leads an analyst into an abyss or slippery slope, with the implication being that it is questionable whether the analyst will be able to climb back from this slippery slope. This seems to me to be a fundamental difference in perspective between this position and my understanding of self and object Freudians. Not admitting an error is in my mind either an unfortunate avoidance or more negatively it is an attempt (albeit unwittingly) to foster a certain type of idealization of the analyst. While it seems to me that certain types of personal disclosure that are becoming popular in today's analytic world are for the analyst's benefit (or indulgence), the disclosure of a mistake is one that if it is not made it is saying in effect that only the patient need be honest while the analyst has the privilege of a certain type of subtle dissembling or subterfuge. It puts a hole in the shared analytic experience and I would say it hampers the patients' ability to explore their inner world. To put this in terms that I have been using, it hampers the patients' ability to develop analytic trust. Thus while disclosure should not be avoided, it should be included only if the analyst believes it will further the analytic process.

A reader might now ask whether there aren't more differences than similarities between Freudians. I would say that since I believe the structural position is derived from the classical position in the United States, I have many criticisms of the classical position. Nevertheless, I believe that for all contemporary Freudian positions, the patient's responses to interpretations are at the core of evaluating the success of the intervention. The patient must have access to at least some of the material that led to the analyst's intervention. Both patient and analyst should have a shared experiential base or else the patient would to some extent be accepting the intervention on the basis of the analyst's authority. This from my viewpoint is anti-analytic or at the very least a factor that would stifle a shared analytic process. I think that all Freudians share in this concept. More importantly, all Freudians see conflict stemming from unconscious fantasy and uncovering these fantasies is a central goal of an analysis. All Freudians would agree that "the recognition of an unconscious, of the ego's need for defenses against intense anxieties, the assumption of the past in the transference situation with the analyst, symbolism and so on are common assumptions" (O'Shaughnessy 1997, p. 34) that they and Kleinians share. It is my view that many intersubjective, relational and interpersonal analysts do not share these assumptions. Adams-Silvan and Silvan (Chapter 3) show how important unconscious motivation is to a contemporary Freudian. Lasky (Chapter 10) demonstrates clearly that transference highlights how unconscious fantasy gains expression. Transference is the main vehicle of the analysis, although there are large differences in how one manages (facilitates) the transference in the analytic situation. For self and object Freudians, Winnicott, Kohut, and Klein can be seen as part of contemporary Freudian thought. Structural Freudians are more strongly tied to the classical literature in the United States. It seems that all Freudians can join the ego psychological Freudians in utilizing the concepts of Hartmann (1939) and Anna Freud (1936).

The treatment enters into the termination phase when mutual trust has developed (Ellman 1997b). The analyst has learned to truly listen to the patient and at times achieves evenly suspended attention. The analyst is not disrupted by the patient and the analysand is free to allow ideas to come to mind, tolerate the anxiety these ideas provoke, observe these themes, and share them with the analyst. For both analyst and analysand the other is not primarily seen as anxiety provoking, but rather can be an object to identify with, love, and occasionally destroy. Thus the analyst can comfortably be placed in transitional space and be brought back without the illusion of the analysis being lost. When both analyst and analysand can accomplish this, the analytic task is at an end. In a similar manner, if we can listen to each other's theories without becoming disrupted and tolerate the anxiety that a different theory brings with it, perhaps we can find more and more of the common ground that Wallerstein (1988) believes (or wishes) we all inhabit.

REFERENCES

Arlow, J. A. (1969). Unconscious fantasy and disturbances of conscious experience. *Psychoanalytic Quarterly* 38:1–27.
—— (1979). The genesis of interpretation. *Journal of the American Psychoanalytic Association* 27:193–207.
—— (1985). Some technical problems of countertransference. *Psychoanalytic Quarterly* 54:164–174.
—— (1990). *Methodology and reconstruction in psychoanalysis.* Paper presented at the Institute for Psychoanalytic Training and Research, New York, October.
Arlow, J., and Brenner, C. (1964). *Psychoanalytic Concepts and the Structural Theory.* New York: International Universities Press.
Bach, S. (1985). *Narcissistic States and the Therapeutic Process.* New York: Jason Aronson.
—— (1994). *The Language of Love and the Language of Perversion.* Northvale, NJ: Jason Aronson.
Balint, M. (1968). *The Basic Fault: Therapeutic Aspects of Regression.* New York: Brunner/Mazel.
Bergmann, A., and Ellman, S. J. (1985). Margaret S. Mahler: symbiosis and separation-individuation. In *Beyond Freud*, ed. J. Reppen. Hillsdale, NJ: Analytic Press.
Bion, W. R. (1967). *Second Thoughts: Selected Papers on Psychoanalysis.* New York: Jason Aronson.
Bird, B. (1972). Notes on transference: universal phenomenon and hardest part of analysis. *Journal of the American Psychoanalytic Association* 20:267–301.
Brenner, C. (1976). *Psychoanalytic Technique and Psychic Conflict.* New York: International Universities Press.
—— (1979). Working alliance, therapeutic alliance, and transference. *Journal of the American Psychoanalytic Association* 27:137–158.
—— (1982). *The Mind in Conflict.* New York: International Universities Press.

———— (1995). Some remarks on psychoanalytic technique. *Journal of Clinical Psychoanalysis* 4(4):413–428.

———— (1996). *Beyond the ego and the id.* Internet Web Site http://Plaza.Interport. Net/NYPSan/brennerhtml.

Breuer, J., and Freud, S. (1895). Studies on hysteria. *Standard Edition* 2:1–306.

Busch, F. (1995). *The Ego at the Center of Clinical Technique.* Northvale, NJ: Jason Aronson.

Carskey, M., and Ellman, S. (1985). Otto Kernberg: psychoanalysis and object relations theory; the beginnings of an integrative approach. In *Beyond Freud,* ed. J. Reppen, pp. 257–296. Hillsdale, NJ: Analytic Press.

Ellman, S. J. (1991). *Freud's Technique Papers: A Contemporary Perspective.* Northvale, NJ: Jason Aronson.

———— (1992). Psychoanalytic theory, dream formation and REM sleep. In *Interface of Psychoanalysis and Psychology,* ed. J. Barron, M. Eagle, and D. Wolitsky, pp. 357–374. Washington, DC: American Psychological Association.

———— (1996). Commentary on the British Schools of psychoanalysis. In *British Schools of Psychoanalysis,* ed. D. Hill and C. Grand, pp. 49–72. Northvale, NJ: Jason Aronson.

———— (1997a). An analyst at work. In *More Analysts at Work,* ed. J. Reppen, pp. 91–115. Northvale, NJ: Jason Aronson.

———— (1997b). Termination and long term analysis. *Psychoanalytic Psychology* 14(2):197–210.

———— (1998). Enactment, transference, and analytic trust. In *Enactment: Toward a New Approach to the Therapeutic Relationship,* ed. S. Ellman and M. Moskowitz, pp. 183–203. Northvale, NJ: Jason Aronson.

Ellman, S. J., and Moskowitz, M. B. (1980). An examination of some recent criticisms of psychoanalytic "metapsychology." *Psychoanalytic Quarterly* 49:631–662.

————, eds. (1998). *Enactment: Toward a New Approach to the Therapeutic Relationship.* Northvale, NJ: Jason Aronson.

Freedman, N. (1994). More on transformation enactments. In *The Spectrum of Psychoanalysis: Essays in Honor of Martin S. Bergmann,* ed. A. K. Richards and A. P. Richards, pp. 93–110. Madison, CT: International Universities Press.

Freud, A. (1936). *The Ego and Mechanisms of Defense.* New York: International Universities Press.

Freud, S. (1895). On the grounds for detaching a particular syndrome from neurasthenia under the description anxiety neurosis. *Standard Edition* 3:90–115.

———— (1905a). Fragment of an analysis of a case of hysteria. *Standard Edition* 7:112–122.

———— (1905b). On psychotherapy. *Standard Edition* 7:257–268.

———— (1915a). Instincts and their vicissitudes. *Standard Edition* 14:117–140.

———— (1915b). Further recommendations on the technique of psycho-analysis:

observations on transference love. In *Collected Papers*, vol. 2, pp. 377–391. New York: Basic Books, 1959.

———— (1916/1917). Introductory lectures on psycho-analysis. *Standard Edition* 15/16:243–448.

———— (1920). Beyond the pleasure principle. *Standard Edition* 18:7–64.

———— (1923a). Remarks on theory and practice of dream interpretation. In *Collected Papers*, vol. 5, pp. 136–149. New York: Basic Books, 1959.

———— (1923b). The ego and the id. *Standard Edition* 19:12–59.

———— (1926). Inhibitions, symptoms and anxieties. *Standard Edition* 20:87–172.

———— (1937a). Constructions in analysis. In *Collected Papers*, vol. 5, pp. 358–371. New York: Basic Books, 1959.

———— (1937b). Analysis terminable and interminable. *Standard Edition* 23:209–254.

Gray, P. (1973). Psychoanalytic technique and the ego's capacity for viewing intrapsychic conflict. *Journal of the American Psychoanalytic Association* 21:474–494.

———— (1982). "Developmental lag" in the evolution of technique for psychoanalysis of neurotic conflict. *Journal of the American Psychoanalytic Association* 30:621–655.

———— (1994). *The Ego and Analysis of Defense.* Northvale, NJ: Jason Aronson.

Grunes, M. (1984). The therapeutic object relationship. *Psychoanalytic Review* 71:123–143.

Hartmann, H. (1939). *Ego Psychology and the Problem of Adaptation.* New York: International Universities Press.

Hill, D., and Grand, C. (1996). *British Schools of Psychoanalysis.* Northvale, NJ: Jason Aronson.

Hoffman, I. Z. (1983). The patient as interpreter of the analyst's experience. *Contemporary Psychoanalysis* 28:1–15.

———— (1992). Some practical implications of a social constructionist view. *Psychoanalytic Dialogue* 2:287–304.

Jacobs, T. (1991). *The Use of the Self.* Madison, CT: International Universities Press.

Jacobson, E. (1964). *The Self and the Object World.* New York: International Universities Press.

Kohut, H. (1968). The psychoanalytic treatment of the narcissistic personality disorders: outline of a systematic approach. *Psychoanalytic Study of the Child* 23:86–113. New York: International Universities Press.

———— (1971). *The Analysis of the Self: A Systematic Approach to the Psychoanalytic Treatment of Narcissistic Personality Disorders.* New York: International Universities Press.

Lipton, S. D. (1977). The advantages of Freud's technique as shown in his analysis of the Rat Man. *International Journal of Psycho-Analysis* 58:255–274.

———— (1979). An addendum to "The Advantages of Freud's Technique as Shown in the Analysis of the Rat Man." *International Journal of Psycho-Analysis* 60:215–216.

Loewald, H. (1980). *Papers on Psychoanalysis.* New Haven, CT: Yale Universities Press.

McLaughlin, J. T. (1981). Transference, psychic reality and countertransference. *Psychoanalytic Quarterly* 50:639–664.

—— (1991). Clinical and theoretical aspects of enactment. *Journal of the American Psychoanalytic Association* 39(3):595–614.

Mitchell, S. (1988). *Relational Concepts in Psychoanalysis.* Cambridge, MA: Harvard University Press.

Novick, J. (1982). Termination: themes and issues. *Psychoanalytic Inquiry* 2:329–366.

O'Shaughnessy, E. (1997). What is a clinical fact. In *The Contemporary Kleinians of London*, ed. R. Schafer, pp. 30–46. Madison, CT: International Universities Press.

Racker, H. (1968). *Transference and Countertransference.* London: Hogarth.

Renik, O. (1993). Analytic interaction: conceptualizing technique in light of the analyst's irreducible subjectivity. *Psychoanalytic Quarterly* 62:553–571.

Sandler, J. (1976). Countertransference and role-responsiveness. *International Review of Psycho-Analysis* 3:43–48.

Schafer, R. (1976). *A New Language for Psychoanalysis.* New Haven, CT: Yale Universities Press.

—— (1992). *Retelling a Life: Dialogues and Narration in Psychoanalysis.* New York: Basic Books.

—— (1997). *The Contemporary Kleinians of London.* Madison, CT: International Universities Press.

Spezzano, C. (1993). *Affect in Psychoanalytic Theory and Therapy: Towards a New Synthesis.* Hillsdale, NJ: Analytic Press.

Spillius, E. B. (1988). *Melanie Klein Today: Development in Theory and Practice*, vols. 1 and 2. London: Routledge.

Stein, M. H. (1981). The unobjectionable part of the transference. *Journal of the American Psychoanalytic Association* 29:869–892.

Steingart, I. (1983). *Pathological Play in Borderline and Narcissistic Personalities.* New York: Spectrum.

—— (1995). *A Thing Apart: Love and Reality in the Therapeutic Relationship.* Northvale, NJ: Jason Aronson.

Sterba, R. (1934). The fate of the ego in analytic therapy. *International Journal of Psycho-Analysis* 15:117–126.

Stolorow, R., Brandchaft, B., and Atwood, G. (1987). *Psychoanalytic Treatment: An Intersubjective Approach.* Hillside, NJ: Analytic Press.

Stone, L. (1961). *The Psychoanalytic Situation: An Examination of Its Development and Essential Nature.* New York: International Universities Press.

—— (1967). The psychoanalytic situation and transference: postscript to an earlier communication. *Journal of the American Psychoanalytic Association* 15:3–58.

Vygotsky, L. (1978). *Mind in Society: The Development of the Higher Psychological Processes.* Cambridge, MA: Harvard University Press.

Wallerstein, R. S. (1988). One psychoanalysis or many. *International Journal of Psycho-Analysis* 69:5–21.

Wilson, A., and Weinstein, L. (1996). The transference and the zone of proximal development. *Journal of the American Psychoanalytic Association* 44:167–200.

Winnicott, D. W. (1962). Ego integration in child development. In *The Maturational Processes and the Facilitating Environment*, pp. 56–63. London: Hogarth, 1965.

—— (1965). *The Maturational Processes and the Facilitating Envionment.* London: Hogarth.

—— (1971). *Playing and Reality.* London: Tavistock.

Zetzel, E. R. (1966). The analytic situation. In *Psychoanalysis in the Americas*, ed. R. E. Litman, pp. 86–106. New York: International Universities Press.

13

Asking for Freud's Blessing

Martin S. Bergmann

As this is the last chapter, I am reminded of the story of a speaker who asked the chairman how long he should speak and was told, "You can speak as long as you wish, but we are going to lunch at 1:00 P.M." It is a quarter to one.

Sixty years ago when I was a graduate student I was impressed by a statement by Vilfredo Pareto (the Italian sociologist, 1848–1923, who was Freud's contemporary). "It is the function of the philosopher to point out logical inconsistencies in a system, but it is the function of the sociologist to discover why they persist." Mutatis mutandis, it is more important for contemporary psychoanalysts to inquire why different schools exist, rather than to search for the shortcomings in the competing systems.

Psychoanalysis was born at a crossroads between the rational humanist tradition of the eighteenth century and the interest in the unconscious, the irrational, that characterized the Romantic period of the nineteenth century. Freud investigated the irrational, but his alliance was to the humanist Western tradition.

The roots to Freud's thought go back to Greek philosophy. There is a direct line of development connecting Plato with Freud. In the "Phaedrus" (Jowett 1937), Socrates is asked whether he believes the mythological stories. He replies:

> This sort of crude philosophy will take up a great deal of time. Now I have no leisure for such inquiries; shall I tell you why? I must first know myself as the Delphian inscription says; to be curious about that which is not my concern, while I am still ignorant of my own self would be ridiculous. And therefore I bid farewell to all this; the common opinion is enough for me. For, as I was saying, I want to know not about this, but about myself: Am I a monster more complicated and swollen with passion than the serpent Typho, or a creature of a gentler simpler sort, to whom nature has given a diviner and lowlier destiny? [pp. 235–236]

It was Socrates who first noticed that artisans have a special kind of wisdom that pertained to their trade, but they do not thereby possess what he called wisdom. Socrates did not call himself a sophist, a man who knows, but a philosopher, a lover of knowledge. Today psychoanalysts are facing a similar problem: Are we artisans skilled in the removal of irrational fears and sexual malfunctioning or do we possess, because of the kind of work that we do, a special kind of wisdom? Freud, in spite of his contempt of philosophers, was a philosopher himself. He left us with the question of whether his philosophy is an indispensable part of psychoanalysis, or a private, personal outlook on the world? Waelder (1962) made a case in favor of dividing psychoanalysis from Freud's personal philosophy. Eissler (1975) drew far-reaching philosophical conclusions based on psychoanalytic premises.

The rational worldview is today under siege. Irrational movements seem to gain strength as the century comes to an end. Everywhere religious fanaticism is on the increase. We should therefore not be surprised that psychoanalysis, whose roots are in the European Enlightenment, has lost some of its appeal. Even within psychoanalytic practice we encounter patients who believe in astrology, reincarnation, and alternative medicine. These beliefs do not necessarily affect the efficacy of psychoanalytic work. For example, I have found that if such patients are encouraged to describe their previous incarnations, they turn out to represent unconscious wishes projected onto the mythical past.

In the "New Introductory Lectures" (1933) Freud insisted that psychoanalysis does not have a weltanschauung of its own.

Weltanshauung is, I am afraid, a specifically German concept, the translation of which into a foreign languages might well raise difficulties. If I try to give you a definition of it, it is bound to seem clumsy to you. In my opinion, then, a Weltanschauung is an intellectual construction which solves all the problems of our existence uniformly on the basis of one overriding hypothesis, which, accordingly, leaves no question unanswered and in which everything that interests us finds its fixed place. It will easily be understood that the possession of a Weltanschauung of this kind is among the ideal wishes of human beings. Believing in it one can feel secure in life, one can know what to strive for, and how one can deal most expediently with one's emotions and interests.

If that is the nature of a Weltanschauung, the answer as regards psycho-analysis is made easy. As a specialist science, a branch of psychology—a depth-psychology or psychology of the unconscious—it is quite unfit to construct a Weltanschauung of its own: it must accept the scientific one. . . . Psycho-analysis has a special right to speak for the scientific Weltanschauung at this point, since it cannot be reproached in having neglected what is mental in the picture of the universe. Its contribution to science lies precisely in having extended research to the mental field. [p. 158–159]

Freud never specified what he meant by the weltanschauung of science, but I found a passage in a book by Norbert Elias (1990), a German sociologist, who described what Freud must have had in mind.

There must exist more human beings like myself, that have no fear of what they will discover; apparently there are people who fear they will discover some unhappiness if they think realistically about themselves. Take Freud as an example. He wished to discover in his own way the way in which things really are, independently of what other people thought. This is the task of a scientist in the social as well as in the natural sciences. This is the ethos of a scientist. [p. 63, my translation]

There is yet another Freud. We meet him at his strongest in 1926(b).

For we do not considerate it at all desirable for psycho-analysis to be swallowed up by medicine and to find its last resting place in a text-book of psychiatry under the heading "Methods of Treatment." . . . As depth-psychology, theory of mental unconscious, it can become indispensable to all the sciences which are concerned with the evolution of human civilization and its major institution such as art, religion and social order. [p. 248]

If psychoanalysis is indispensable to the humanities and the arts, will it only affect them or will it become affected by them? Can psychoanalysis be so significant without having a weltanschauung of its own to contribute? By subordinating psychoanalysis to science Freud avoided the thorny question of whether science has a philosophy of its own and avoided dealing with the ultimate implications of his own creation.

While the quote above was written in 1926, the transition from the specialist in nervous disorders and the critic of culture began early. In "The Interpretation of Dreams" (1900) and in "The Psychopathology of Everyday Life" (1901) Freud realized that much of what he found to be typical of neuroses is of importance beyond the confines of therapy since everybody dreams and everybody forgets names and makes slips of the tongue. In 1907 Freud realized that the symptoms of individual obsessive-compulsives are identical with the commandments of Western religions, particularly those of the Catholic church and Judaism, the religions most familiar to Freud. A year later (1908) Freud found that antagonism exists between the demands of civilization and instinctual life. With that paper the specialist in nervous illnesses became a critic of civilization. In 1913 in the essay "Totem and Taboo," Freud attempted a bold interpretation as to how civilization originated and this trend of thought was continued in Freud's last book, "Moses and Monotheism" (1939). In contradiction to the claim that psychoanalysis has no philosophy of life to offer, Freud wrote a number of books, notably "Beyond the Pleasure Principle" (1920), "The Future of an Illusion" (1927), and "Civilization and Its Discontents" (1930), that must be classified as philo-sophical books. Psychoanalysts as a group did not necessarily follow Freud's lead in "Civilization and Its Discontents" and did not necessarily agree with Freud's main finding of 1920 of the eternal struggle between the libido as a life instinct and the death instinct.

Keeping these efforts in mind we can no longer claim that psychoanalysis has no weltanschauung of its own and must attempt to make explicit what it consists of.

Freud was influenced not only by Goethe, Schiller, Lessing, and Shakespeare, but also by Darwin and the antireligious and materialistic philosopher Feuerbach. Freud decided to become a physician, rather than a lawyer, under the influence of an essay on nature that was at that time attributed to Goethe. A famous slip by Freud himself, "You owe nature a death," is a parapraxis from Shakespeare's Falstaff to whom Prince Hal says, "You owe God a death." Falstaff, it will be recalled, refuses to pay before the note has become due. The slip suggests that, for Freud, nature replaced God. The reader will also recall Freud's poignant remark that happiness was not included in the plan of creation. With regard to happiness Freud reached a surprising conclusion: human happiness is attainable only when wishes of childhood become fulfilled. The fulfillment of an adult wish does not possess the capacity to make us happy unless it operates in conjunction with a childish wish. Psychoanalysis after a short period when it was allied with various progressive movements (Freud 1910b) did not aim at human happiness. The wisdom of psychoanalysis begins with the realization that psychoanalysis itself does not aim to make us happy, but only to remove the extra burden that neurosis has imposed upon man. To use an analogy, psychoanalysis does not try to eliminate all taxation, but only to eliminate a particular burdensome tax called neurosis. It aims to prepare man to be capable of tolerating the miseries of ordinary existence without adding to them.

Below the surface, but sometimes even explicitly, this book has echoed a debate with object relations theory, whose representatives are not included here. But they constitute the "significant others" to whom much of what has been said here was addressed.

In a historical context it is important to keep in mind that object relations theory has emerged from the confluence of different lines of thought. One of its roots goes back to Ferenczi and the work of his disciple Michael Balint (1968). There is a remarkable revival of Ferenczi going on (Aron and Harris 1993, Rudnytsky et. al. 1996). I participated in this revival in 1976 when I included a section on Ferenczi in a book on technique (Bergmann and Hartman 1976b), and more recently (Bergmann 1996). Ferenczi began by introducing changes in the technique of treatment and, up to 1919, Freud welcomed these changes. But when Ferenczi introduced mutual analysis, a new paradigm, less rational than that of Freud, was introduced. Freud feared that trauma as the cause of neurosis would be reintroduced at the expense of insights gained through the understanding of intrapsychic conflict. Ferenczi's two major papers (1929, 1933) were written when he was already in disagreement with Freud. Ferenczi introduced into psychoanalysis the idea that if the baby is not welcomed by love when he enters the world, he will succumb to the death instinct and will not wish to live. Ferenczi, therefore, anticipated the findings of Spitz (1945, 1946) by over a decade. In the next paper Ferenczi introduced the idea that the baby is dependent on receiving appropriate love in a dosage that he can assimilate. Otherwise, the infant becomes over-stimulated and will feel seduced, regardless of whether he was sexually abused or not, with dangerous results for his future. Ferenczi's ideas were based on Freud's death instinct theory, but, in contrast to Freud, they were clinical rather than theoretical, and contained a criticism of Freud.

The next impetus for object relations theory came from Melanie Klein (1948) and is connected with her emphasis on internal objects, both good and bad. For Melanie Klein the internalized objects have to a significant degree replaced Freud's tripartite division into ego, id, and superego. In practical terms the difference found expression in the greater emphasis on transference interpretations, which take precedence over other interpretations. As a result, the analysis is directed into the here and now of the therapist–patient relationship, often at the expense of the genetic point of view and the emphasis on reconstruction. The Kleinian analysand relives more in the transference, often at the cost of ego autonomy and the therapeutic alliance.

The third emphasis came from Fairbairn. Within three years after Freud's death Fairbairn developed a new paradigm that differed from both Klein and Freud. Fairbairn (1952) differentiated between two kinds of bad objects. Unconditionally bad objects are those that did not give love to the child. Conditionally bad objects were loving, but morally bad. To counter-act unconditional badness, the child internalizes good objects. These good objects assume superego roles and transform unconditionally bad objects into conditionally bad ones. This is also the function of religion. The believer becomes burdened by sin and is morally bad, but, at the same time, he is no longer unloved. Instead of Freud's tripartite division between ego, id, and superego Fairbairn suggested the central ego (the "I"), the libidinal ego, and finally the aggressive and persecutory ego, which Fairbairn called the internal saboteur. Because Fairbairn's metapsychology is a relatively simple one, it is easy to see that we are dealing with a third paradigm. Fairbairn is remembered less for his metapsychology than for the assertion that the libido is not pleasure seeking or discharge seeking, but object seeking.

A fourth line of development came from Winnicott, who, beginning in 1951 with his paper "Transitional Objects and Transitional Phenomenon," stressed the significance of the transitional object. In further work (1971) he created a metaphor based on the transitional object and called it the transitional space between mother and child.

> Psychotherapy takes place in the overlap of two areas of playing, that of the patient and that of the therapist. Psychotherapy has to do with two people playing together. The corollary of this is that where playing is not possible then the work done by the therapist is directed towards bringing the patient from a state of not being able to play into a state of being able to play. [p. 38]

Forcefully Winnicott described the interplay between love and hate:

> After "subject relates to object" comes "subject destroys object" (as it becomes external); and then may come "*object survives* destruction by the subject." But there may or may not be survival. A new feature thus arrives in the theory of object-relating. The subject says to the object: "I destroyed you," and the object is there to receive the communication. From now on the subject says: "Hullo object!" "I destroyed you." "I love you." "You have value for me because of your survival of my destruction of you." [p. 90]

The ideas expressed in this paragraph are derived from Freud's dual instinct theory, but Winnicott found a new way of looking at what goes on between the therapist and the difficult analysand. Winnicott became the most admired among object relations theorists.

A fifth line of development leads back to the Hartmann group and particularly to the work of Spitz (1965) and Mahler's whole work. "It can never be sufficiently stressed that object relations take place in a constant interaction between two very unequal partners, the mother and the child. Each provokes the response in the other; that this interpersonal relationship creates a field of constantly shifting forces" (Spitz 1965, p. 204). Such observations mark the transition from ego psychology to object relations theory. Freud himself was not an object relations theorist because he envisioned the baby as born in a state of primary narcissism. The Hartmann school transformed the term *primary narcissism* to mean the undifferentiated matrix out of which different developments will ensue. One of the most important developments was from the need-satisfying state to the reaching of object constancy. When the latter stage is reached the child becomes capable of loving. The Hartmann group was not openly critical of Freud, but as I have shown elsewhere (Bergmann 1998a) they too modified Freud's paradigm in many significant ways.

Object relations theorists, like Freudians, are not a monolithic group, but they all share one important idea: they believe that Freud, because he was a self-analyzer, created psychoanalysis on the model of one-person psychology, with the analyst's role restricted to observer and interpreter. Object relations theorists see psychoanalysis as a two-person psychology. We have all been influenced by the two-person paradigm, but not to the same degree. To illustrate the difference I select a 1996 paper by Thomas Ogden. Because of space limitations I will not do justice to that paper and concentrate only on the interpretation of one dream. Dr. Ogden's patient dreamt:

> "An old man was sitting in his study reading. It was like your office, but it wasn't actually your office. It was dark and had a dank, seedy feeling to it. People were peering through the window at him. I was one of them. It was terribly important to be perfectly still so as not to be caught. I was afraid I would pee. He seemed like a depressed, dirty old man. I thought he was only pretending to read or forcing himself to read. I also had the feeling that he was trying to turn himself on sexually by reading, but it wasn't working." [p. 1130]

Dr. Ogden's comments:

> It was at this point that the very disturbing thought occurred to me that Ms. A. must have been watching me watch her. . . . Everything seemed to have suddenly and unexpectedly been reversed: what had been private had become public; what had felt like simple curiosity had become prurient interest. [p. 1130]

Ms. A. and I in the (asymmetrically) shared experience of this transference-countertransference drama, had each in our way insisted that we are not the outsider to the parental intercourse, but were "really" adults participating in it. . . . The old man (simultaneously representing me, the patient's internal world, and the analytic relationship) was depressed and lonely, going through the motions of reading or perhaps attempting to escape his depression by means of solitary, empty sexual excitement. [p. 1131]

While the Freudian analyst would inevitably ask for free associations for any dream, Dr. Ogden uses his own countertransference reaction as a substitute for the free associations of the patient. As a Freudian psychoanalyst I am accustomed to forming a hypothesis after I hear a dream. I then listen to the free associations in order to confirm or disconfirm my hypothesis. In the absence of free associations I can only offer my hypothesis: the dream contains a memory of the patient as a child observing her father looking at pornographic literature and masturbating. Should my hypothesis turn out to be correct through the free associations of the patient, I would add that, at that moment, the patient realized that the mother is not a satisfactory sexual partner to the father and this realization in turn stimulated her own oedipal excitement (the need to pee), but at the same time debased the image of the father, hence the deadness.

The work of supervision with candidates and beginning therapists usually consists of helping the beginner to bridge the gap between case and paradigm. Today we no longer enjoy the luxury of certainty that our paradigm is, objectively speaking, the best. We have learned that irrational subjective factors, including our own personal analyses, often determine the choice of the paradigm. If the analysis was a successful one we retain the paradigm of our analyst. If it failed, we will seek another. It is even possible that if Dr. Ogden had tried the Freudian paradigm, or I his, neither one of us would profit. For analysts differ in the kind of paradigm in which they can be most productive.

THE EVOLUTION OF MY THERAPEUTIC POINT OF VIEW

When I became a psychoanalyst in New York after World War II the Hartmann period was in full swing. In 1958 a symposium, "Psychoanalysis,

Scientific Method and Philosophy," was organized under the chairmanship of Sidney Hook (1959). In that symposium the opening statement was made by Hartmann himself with his well-known paper "Psychoanalysis as a Scientific Theory" (1959). To the dismay of a younger generation of psychoanalysts, Hartmann could not hold his own against the criticism of the philosopher of science Ernst Nagel. In 1962 Waelder, in a review of the symposium, repaired some of the damage, but a loss of faith had taken place.

Waelder's attempt to rescue the scientific status of psychoanalysis was to create a hierarchical order of the data. On the first level are the data of observations that every psychoanalyst collects; they form the level of observation. The interconnections of these data form the level of clinical interpretation. When these data are generalized, the level of clinical generalization is reached. These levels lead to theoretical formulations and result in a clinical theory. Further abstraction leads to the level of metapsychology. Finally, since Freud had a tendency toward philosophizing, there are also Freud's philosophical ideas.

The advantage of Waelder's hierarchy was that one can stop at any level without feeling that he is no longer a psychoanalyst. Its disadvantage became clearer to me much later: the structure does not reflect the history of psychoanalysis. Freud himself did not gradually go up the ladder; all the phases were there from the beginning. Neither psychoanalysis nor, for that matter, any other science proceeded in this orderly fashion. It was Kuhn's (1962) *Structure of Scientific Revolutions* that showed me Waelder's error. But for many years I and my students found his formulation the answer to the Hook symposium.

A new journal, the *Journal of Psychoanalysis and Contemporary Thought*, was founded under the leadership of Benjamin Rubinstein with the explicit aim of making psychoanalysis subject to a more rigorous scientific scrutiny. In 1976 George Klein published his book *Psychoanalytic Theory: An Exploration of Essentials*, which contained such challenging chapters as "Is Psychoanalysis Relevant?" and "The Ego in Psychoanalysis: The Concept in Search of Identity." That book signaled a revolution among Rapaport's students against Freud's metapsychology. Special publications under the heading of "psychological issues" became the literary expression of this group. For David Rapaport psychoanalytic metapsychology was the glory of psychoanalysis and Chapter 7 in *The Interpretation of Dreams* (Freud 1900) was the text that all of us felt obliged to master. Many of Rapaport's students were psychologists who were admitted into psychoanalytic training after they promised to use psychoanalysis as a research tool and refrain from practicing psychoanalysis. It is conceivable that their rebellion against psychoanalytic metapsychology was an indirect expression of their revolt against the restriction to practice.

The second book that had a powerful effect on the psychoanalysts of my generation was Thomas Kuhn's *The Structure of Scientific Revolutions*, first published in 1962 and enlarged in 1970. It was Kuhn who introduced the concept of paradigm, which I have used so often. To Kuhn a scientific paradigm is a time-limited concept, but while it dominates the thinking of a given scientific community it serves as the model for the problems raised and the solutions found that interest this particular group. Kuhn also noticed that in rare circumstances two paradigms can coexist peacefully. Here are some of Kuhn's ideas that influenced our thinking on psycho-analysis:

- Observation and experience can and must drastically restrict the range of admissible scientific belief, else there would be no science. But they cannot alone determine a particular body of such belief. An apparently arbitrary element, compounded of personal and historical accident, is always a formative ingredient of the beliefs espoused by a given scientific community at a given time. [p. 4]
- Normal science, for example, often suppresses fundamental novel-ties because they are necessarily subversive of its basic commit-ments. . . . The very nature of normal research ensures that novelty should not be suppressed for very long. [p. 5]
- The extraordinary episodes in which that shift of professional commitments occurs are the ones known in this essay as scientific revolutions. They are the tradition-shattering complements to the tradition-bound of normal science. [p. 6]
- Scientific fact and theory are not categorically separable, except perhaps within a single tradition of normal-scientific practice. [p. 7]
- Competition between segments of the scientific community is the only historical process that ever actually results in the rejection of one previously accepted theory or in the adoption of another. [p. 8]

Kuhn's examples were taken entirely from the natural sciences, but they are translatable into the problems we were struggling with. When

Breuer and Freud in 1895 published their findings in *Studies on Hysteria* they did not so much modify an already existing paradigm; they created a paradigm where none existed before. The sexual and incestuous ideas that formed the basis of hysteria evoked indignation and revulsion; Breuer and Freud did not have to dethrone a previously existing paradigm.

> Thus the recognition of the illness as hysteria makes little difference to the patient; but to the doctor quite the reverse. It is noticeable that his attitude toward hysterical patients is quite other than towards sufferers from organic diseases. He does not have the same sympathy for the former as for the latter. [Freud 1910a, p. 11]

When Freud gave up both the seduction theory as the cause of hysteria and the hypnotic technique, he exchanged one paradigm for another. The analysts who broke ranks with Freud can be seen as offering a different paradigm. When a paradigm appears as too radically different, a break is usually unavoidable. The different schools of psychoanalysis can be seen as working under different paradigms. Kuhn's concept of a paradigm carries with it tolerant connotations. It introduced into psychoanalysis a greater degree of relativity than was characteristic of Freud.

Freud, as many of the great scientists of the nineteenth century, experienced nature as a "lady" with many secrets. The scientist attempts to wrestle these secrets from a reluctant "nature." When the scientist succeeds, "history" grants him immortality. This was a romantic view of science. Using the tools that Freud himself gave us we can see this view as a magnificent sublimation of the yearnings that belong to the Oedipus complex, nature being the mother that the oedipal son possesses when he deciphers her secret, and history is the father who reluctantly blesses this conquest. It is conceivable that Freud himself contributed to the loss of power of that metaphor.

Following Kuhn we can see the early disciples who defected from Freud's teaching as offering other paradigms than the one he developed. To see psychoanalytic schools as offering different paradigms comes closer to Freud's ideal that psychoanalysis shares with science a weltanschauung; whereas the belief that Freud actually held, which equated different paradigms with resistance of those who were insufficiently analyzed and thereby reserving for himself the one and only truth, is much closer to a religious point of view, a view that Freud abhorred. Under Kohut's influence I learned to see the history of psychoanalysis not as a war between the forces of light and the forces of darkness, but as the construction of different paradigms, each one having its own strong points as well as its weaknesses. This relativism increased my capacity to understand the history of psychoanalysis. Lawrence Friedman (1997), in his plenary address to the American Psychoanalytic Association, uncovered some of the personal reasons that led Freud to create his paradigm:

> So vivid is the image of Freud as Discoverer that we sometimes forget that a proud man here is a proud man there. As a self-proclaimed physician, Freud had pride in his practice and in his person. He hated to have his bluff called. He disliked having patients show him he was wrong when he told them they would go into a trance. He did not want his authority to be dependent on his patient's response. [p. 23]

Once the cathartic method was exchanged for free associations, Freud became less dependent on his patients. Whatever the patient brought up in his free associations was useful for making interpretations.

> Freud found that he lost leverage when he engaged patients too wholeheartedly. They would play out their neurosis on the instrument of his therapeutic desire. He had to retain autonomy not just to make discoveries but to keep himself free of the patient's manipulation, and the patient free of his. [p. 29]

What Freud understood as the resistances of the analysand, Friedman sees as Freud's inclination to see through everything and the creation of an adversarial attitude which became the hallmark of Freud's technique.

Freud (1917) wished to be remembered as the third in the chain that included Copernicus and Darwin. Copernicus deprived us of the illusion that our earth is in the center of the universe, and Darwin forced us to accept that we were not divinely created, but slowly evolved out of the animal kingdom. Freud inflicted upon us a third humiliation, that we are not masters of our own house and are dependent on unconscious forces over which we have no control. For the scientific status of psychoanalysis, it was essential that it be classified as a discovery and indeed much, but by no means all, of what constitutes psychoanalysis can make claim to the status of discovery.

Discovery in the natural sciences demands that if one person had not made this discovery, another person at another time would have reached the same conclusion. It is historically documented that had Darwin not discovered his evolutionary theory, Wallace would have done so. Scientists must race against each other to make their discoveries. In principle the atomic bomb could have been discovered under Hitler or Stalin with consequences too terrible to contemplate. It is not so with psychoanalysis. Although Freud made very basic discoveries, psychoanalysis as an amalgam of investigation and treatment can be better understood as Freud's creation. Had Freud not lived, other techniques of mental therapy would have been discovered, but psychoanalysis with its complex structure could never had been "discovered" by anyone else. Being a creation, and not strictly speaking a discovery, psychoanalysis is vulnerable to other competing attempts to improve upon the original model.

The question of what is and what is not psychoanalysis has been a subject of a long debate. In the encyclopedia articles of 1923 Freud offered a complex definition consisting of three parts. He saw psychoanalysis as

1. a procedure for investigating mental processes;
2. a method of treatment;
3. a collection of information leading to a new scientific discipline.

I discussed the implication of this definition elsewhere (Bergmann and Hartmann 1976a). It was the second point of this definition, psychoanalysis as a method of treatment for neurosis, that occupied center stage and became the disputed ground for different schools. To me, it seems that a shift to the third part of the definition, the collection of information leading to a new scientific discipline, should receive more attention. If we follow this line of thought, we can say that any method of treatment that is based on the data collected by the analytic method deserves to be called psychoanalysis. The ideal method of treatment chosen should be based on our psychoanalytic understanding of our patients' personality structure and how most profitably to approach them. We must lose the fear that obsessed Freud that the gold of psychoanalysis will be diluted by some copper of psychotherapy.

Since psychoanalysis is both a technique of investigation and a theory of treatment, it consists of two different paradigms. Classical psychoanalysis assumed that the two coincided, that explanation and cure go hand in hand. If this were so, then making the unconscious conscious as rapidly as possible would be the shortest road to cure. The history of psychoanalytic technique, as I portrayed it in 1976, demonstrated that the two do not coincide. Adherents of different paradigms claim that theirs is capable of producing a better and shorter cure, but what constitutes cure is by itself so complex that no paradigm has emerged as victorious.

In my plenary address to the American Psychoanalytic Association (Bergmann 1993) I suggested that the dichotomy between loyalists and heretics is no longer adequate to describe what happened in the history of psychoanalysis. We need a tripartite division, which I labeled as extenders, modifiers, and heretics. The new category I introduced was that of the modifier. Unlike the dissenters that left or were expelled from psychoanalysis, the modifier accepts some or most of Freud's basic tenets. However, he wishes to modify an important aspect of theory or technique. Modifiers, I noted, create schisms and evoke controversies, but they have an enormous advantage in that they keep psychoanalysis alive. Had psychoanalysis been divided only between extenders and heretics, stagnation would have set in long ago. Although I was not aware of it at that time, in retrospect my classification is only a variation on the theme introduced by Kuhn.

I must admit that my subdivision is far from perfect. It is not always easy to draw the line between modifier and heretic (Richards 1994). Wilhelm Reich's book *Character Analysis* (1933) is the work of a modifier, but his Orgone therapy (1942) is the work of a heretic writing outside the confines of psychoanalysis. Similarly, Kohut's (1971) book on narcissism was the work of a modifier, but his *Restoration of the Self* (1977) is, for many, more than a modification of psychoanalysis.

In the history of psychoanalysis Ferenczi was the first modifier (Bergmann 1996). He disagreed with Freud, but did not wish to start his own movement. What fate held in store for him, had death not intervened, will remain unknown. The first organized psychoanalytic modification was achieved by Melanie Klein when Anna Freud's effort to expel her and her followers failed. In her memorandum Anna Freud said:

"Though the idea of an open forum for psychoanalytic teaching may seem tempting at first glance, I personally doubt that it could be carried out effectively and whether the results would not fall far short of the intentions. . . . If such teaching procedure had been adopted from the beginning of psychoanalytic development, psychoanalysis of the present day would include the theoretical and technical teachings of, for instance, Stekel, Adler, Jung, Rank, etc. . . . Psychoanalytic societies, . . . after all were founded for the propagation and development of the more or less unified and consistent theory and method. Such disintegration of psychoanalytic societies and psychoanalytic teaching may on the other hand be inevitable. In this case further progress and development will again, as in the earliest times of analysis, have to be expected from the efforts of single individuals and not from the activities of societies and institutes. [King and Steiner 1991, pp. 633]

Fortunately for the history of psychoanalysis in Great Britain, Anna Freud's fears did not materialize. At this point we should look more closely at what is generally called the classical technique. Opponents of this technique often speak of it as if it were still in full bloom. In my view no analyst today, not even Paul Gray or Arlow, can lay claim to the title classical psychoanalyst. The classical period came to an end after World War II and Fenichel's classic of 1945 is the great monument to this era. Since then we have learned too much from too many sources to call ourselves classical psychoanalysts. In a forthcoming monograph (Bergmann 1998a), I show that Hartmann and his followers were no less modifiers of the classical technique than Melanie Klein or Kohut. The debate among psychoanalysts as to who is the legitimate heir to Freud is a political or a theological argument and not a scientific debate. All schools of psychoanalysis have retained some of Freud's teaching and criticized and discarded others.

In addition to the well-known modifiers who originated new schools of psychoanalysis, within every clinical group modifications have taken place. Bibring's (1953) paper on depression introduced a major modification when he saw depression essentially as an illness of helplessness. Berliner (1958) achieved a similar change when he conceptualized the masochism of the child as a response to the sadism of the parent. He transformed masochism into an object relations theory. His was an early attempt to see masochism as emerging from the pathological relationship between caregiver and child.

In different periods different thinkers hold leading positions. In the 1960s and 1970s Hartmann was the most revered American psychoanalyst. His name hardly appears in the current literature. At the conference that generated this book, the analysts most frequently mentioned, besides

Freud, were Winnicott and Loewald. Otto Fenichel and Ernst Kris, whose contributions were very significant to me, were hardly mentioned.

Basic issues in psychoanalysis seldom come to a conclusion. Most of the issues that agitate our discussions are not within our power to resolve. Can the psychoanalytic interview answer the question whether the infant is born in a narcissistic state devoid of object relations as Freud assumed? Is the infant born with maximum sadism, as Melanie Klein assumed? Is the infant born in the undifferentiated state that Hartmann's ego psychology postulated? Can the psychoanalytic interview answer the question whether there is a primary femininity in women? So much of what is basic to the understanding of human beings takes place so early in life, a period in which memories and wishes are of necessity confused. Much that is relevant is not recalled but acted out in transference, and the actions of patients are subject to different interpretations.

What is surprising as psychoanalysis reaches it hundredth anniversary is not that changes in technique and theory have taken place, but how much that Freud discovered is still valid today. Freud's ideas on the importance of the unconscious in deciding the basic determinants of our lives, such as the choice of profession, the choice of our mate, our philosophy of life, and the structure of our neuroses, have been confirmed over and over again. Other basic ideas of Freud have also withstood the test of time—the value of free association as a source of discovery has been confirmed; that every analysis involves resistance has also remained true; that transference reactions are inevitable in every analysis and must be analyzed if an analysis is to deepen remains a basic tenet; human sexuality does not begin with puberty and is preceded by an active period of a powerful infant sexuality that succumbs to repression during the latency period, only to be revived during adolescence. Adolescence is charged with finding new nonincestuous love relationships for the older incestuous ones. When adolescence fails to accomplish this task, mental illness in one form or another takes place.

Freud's great discovery was the crucial role that the Oedipus complex plays as the nucleus of the neuroses. How Freud made this discovery we can read in the letter to Fliess of October 15, 1897 (Masson 1985). In his own self-analysis Freud discovered only mild derivatives of the Oedipus complex, love for the mother and hostility toward the father. What enabled him to divine the Oedipus complex, with all the horror that this discovery evoked, was the fact that he was familiar with *Oedipus Rex* and *Hamlet.* These two works of literature presided over the discovery. Because literature was present at the discovery of the Oedipus complex, a close relationship between psychoanalysis and the arts was present from the very beginning. In its aim to remain rational, psychoanalysis was a child of the Enlightenment, but because of its interest in the morbid and the irrational, it was also the child of Romanticism.

Within the classical model, the Oedipus complex, with its many variations both positive and negative, was conceptualized as the nucleus of the neuroses. Only reluctantly did Freud venture into the earlier preoedipal phases of development. After Freud we have learned how rich and how conflictual the preoedipal period can be and we learned to appreciate the importance of ego deficits in addition to intrapsychic conflict. Although we appreciate earlier phases that antedate the formation of the Oedipus complex, the Oedipus is still the shibboleth by which the Freudian analyst can be recognized. If all goes well, if the mother is good enough and no illnesses or external catastrophes contaminate the picture, the newborn infant can successfully navigate Mahler's symbiosis and separation individuation phases and arrive at the oedipal stage without impairment. But no good parent can save the child from the hazards of the Oedipus complex and no one surmounts the Oedipus complex without paying a price. While the Oedipus complex creates neuroses and problems of development, the fate of those who remain arrested on a preoedipal level is more tragic.

Only the narcissist, like Shakespeare's Richard III, or the pervert deny the oedipal taboo, at their own peril. A note of pessimism accompanies the Freudian analyst as he looks upon the price civilization extracts. It is this tragic core that limits our popularity. To a Freudian analyst, the Oedipus complex is the inevitable and universal source of guilt. It is the psychological basis for the Christian belief in original sin. Even after the incest taboo has been established, oedipal guilt persists in the unconscious. Overcoming our oedipal wishes is the major contributor to making us civilized human beings. There are other reasons for the Freudian tragic view, including the extraordinarily strong wish that many people have in relinquishing the wish to be both sexes. Kubie (1974) gave to this wish the status of a drive that is opposed to libido and highly self-destructive. Other analysts see the wish to be both sexes as a pathological response to the humiliation inflicted upon the child by the exclusion from the primal scene. To these responses must be added early traumatic experiences in infancy that often are responsible for the fact that aggression and envy have become so powerful that we cannot offer such patients meaningful help.

Jung seems to have been the first to grasp this tragic moment. His wish to gain popularity for psychoanalysis contributed to his break with Freud. The Freud–Jung correspondence (McGuire 1974) is so very interesting because the intrapsychic battle within Jung himself unravels. We see how Jung's need to transform psychoanalysis into a new religion gradually gains ascendancy. Winnicott (1964) has pointed out that Jung's basic personality structure was psychotic. His encounters with Freud, and particularly their habit of discussing their dreams, threatened Jung's stability and forced him to create his own paradigm. In 1977 Kohut took up the problem once more when he tried to differentiate "Guilty man" from "Tragic man." If it is true, as many psychoanalysts today believe, that the two analyses of Mr. Z. (Kohut 1979) represent his analysis and his self-analysis, then, their great differences notwithstanding, both Jung and Kohut followed Freud's example, analyzing themselves and through their own self-analysis reaching a different paradigm.

There is another idea that always had a special appeal to me. Both Freud (1912) and Reik (1948) emphasized that genuine insight is accompanied by a sense of surprise for both analyst and analysand. To make new discoveries, the Freudian analyst must maintain his own self-analysis alive. Orthodoxy of any kind forces us to live on the capital accumulated by previous generations, and this is the enemy of creativity. It is what we discover that makes our work interesting.

Paradoxically, in spite of the emphasis on surprise, if we were to rely only on our "third ear," the communication of our analysands would very soon overwhelm our understanding of them. Psychoanalytic training enables the candidate, before he even meets his patient, to employ an internalized paradigm that helps him to put order into the free associations, memories, dreams, and transference reactions that he obtained from the analysand. As we learn more about our patients, we build up an inner map. This inner map helps prevent us from going astray. It is based in part on our own analysis and our own self knowledge. It is also based on our clinical experience with previous patients. Because this map is derived from sources other than what the patient has contributed, it is in danger of distortion; strictly speaking, once we reach a certain depth, every patient is unique and the encounter is a new one. The map is therefore continually in need of revision.

Every psychoanalytic paradigm corresponds in some ways to the actual psychic reality of the analysand. At the same time, no paradigm can capture the total psychic reality of the analysand. What paradigm best mirrors psychic reality is the subject of debate between competing psychoanalytic schools. However, since psychoanalysis not only seeks to discover the psychic reality of our patients but also to bring a change into the preexisting equilibrium, it is at least conceivable that a more limited paradigm, devoid of complexity, is more effective in bringing about change.

In spite of his heroic self-analysis, Freud was subject to self-deception, no less than other mortals. Much of what he regarded as the fruit of his scientific labors turned out to be the inheritance of the cultural prejudices of the Victorian era in which he grew up, and these prejudices colored his views, particularly those on femininity and feminine sexuality. The errors he made in this area were particularly costly. The profession today is primarily that of women and every woman psychoanalyst studying this history has to forgive Freud the errors he made in the way he understood women.

Two other limitations of Freud must be mentioned. Although he wrote a brilliant analysis of a case of paranoia in 1911, the study was based on a published book and not on an encounter with a living psychotic individual. Freud was not comfortable with psychotic patients and he buttressed the discomfort by the belief that psychotics are incapable of forming a transference (1914a). In spite of the effort of Paul Federn (1952), one of Freud's earliest adherents, and many others, psychotics remained outside of the therapeutic, if not the theoretical, orbit of psychoanalysis. Even in 1954 when Leo Stone, under the rubric of the "widening scope" of psychoanalysis, urged that borderline cases be included in the scope of psychoanalysis, Anna Freud (1954) opposed this effort. Freudian psychoanalysis paid a heavy price for narrowing its scope to the neuroses (see Green 1975).

In the classical model, perversion, like psychosis, was an object of psychoanalytic interest, but was largely considered unsuitable for psychoanalysis. The foundations for the classical paradigm on perversion go back to Freud (1905). The paradigm was summarized in Fenichel (1945):

Perversions and morbid impulses are pleasurable, or at least are performed in the hope of achieving pleasure, whereas compulsive acts are painful and performed in the hope of getting rid of pain. . . . Guilt feelings may oppose his (the pervert's) impulses; nevertheless at the moment of his excitement he feels the impulse as ego syntonic, as something he wants to do in the hope of achieving positive pleasure. [p. 324]

Persons who react to sexual frustration with a regression to infantile sexuality are perverts; persons who react with other defenses or who employ other defenses after the regression are neurotic. [p. 325]

Perversion was seen as a fixation point of the libido on pregenital stages of the libido. Because the pervert's wishes are ego syntonic and because they bring pleasure, Fenichel and the Freudian psychoanalytic tradition maintained that perversions were largely inaccessible to psychoanalysis.

The classical paradigm prevailed until after World War II. This was followed by a period that I call paradigm confusion, when many different ideas competed with each other without any one emerging as victorious (Socarides 1962).

In the 1960s and 1970s a new paradigm on perversion emerged through the work of Joyce McDougall (1964, 1978), Janine Chasseguet-Smirgel (1970, 1985), and Masud Khan (1979). These authors created a new paradigm for the understanding and treatment of perversions. The reformulation was based on a number of new ideas, namely, that in perversion the sexual drive has been captured by the death instinct, and that the pervert is less interested in pregenital sexuality than in the destruction of the gender differences, as well as generational differences and often life itself. The pervert does not idealize the person he loves, but idealizes some aspect of the sexual act itself.

The pervert circumvents the shock of the primal scene (McDougall 1972) by denying that intercourse demands two people of different genders. He creates an illusion of another, nongenital sexuality, which he considers as superior. Perversions are sexual defenses against depression or psychosis.

When representatives of different schools of psychoanalysis meet to discuss a case, such as two symposia in *Psychoanalytic Inquiry* (Miller and Post 1990, Pulver et al. 1987), or a prolonged discussion in 1994 of psychoanalytic facts in the *International Journal of Psycho-Analysis* (Ahumada 1994, Caper 1994, Filho 1994, Gardner 1994, Gribinski 1994, Ornstein and

Ornstein 1994, O'Shaughnessy 1994, Quinodoz 1994, Riesenberg-Malcolm 1994, Sandler and Sandler 1994, Schafer 1994, Spence 1994), it is evident that every school organizes the chaotic material that the analysand presents to the analyst according to its own paradigm. What we offer is not a permanent truth, but rather different kinds of organizations, each one with its own advantages and each one with its own limitations.

One of the statements that I have always quoted with particular pleasure was Fenichel's, that the subject matter of psychoanalysis is the irrational but its method is rational. It is not easy for us to give up this belief and yet it seems to me that we have to accept that our basic convictions, and particularly the school to which we belong, contain a large measure of irrationality, and it is this irrationality that is responsible for the vehemence in which psychoanalytic controversies often take place.

Over twenty years ago I debated dream theory with Hanna Segal. In my opening remarks I wondered, that being of approximately the same age and coming from the same region in Europe, what would have happened if I had gone to England and she to the United States? Would I be speaking as a Kleinian and she responding as a psychoanalytic ego psychologist? Hanna Segal would have none of my politeness. She told the audience that as she came to England she was given Anna Freud's (1937) *The Ego and the Mechanisms of Defense* and Melanie Klein's (1932) *Psychoanalysis of Children*. There and then she became a Kleinian and would have become one regardless of circumstance. We have to agree that there was a basic affinity between Klein and Segal, but to claim that this affinity was based on rational considerations would, in my opinion, be a mistake. We have to accept not only the fact that every analyst meets the analysand with his own countertransference, but that the irrational plays a major role in our adherence to one school or another. Since analyses take place within the framework of particular schools, the irrational roots that bind us to a particular school are not likely to be questioned.

At this point we encounter a contradiction worth noticing. To be able to put the communications of our analysand into a useful frame of reference we must internalize the dominant paradigm of the school in which we receive our training. Similarly, when we teach or write we can do so more easily from a well-defined point of view. However, when we are puzzled by something in our patients, we are better therapists if we have internalized different points of view in the course of our training. Even when one is not a Kleinian one can find that at certain crossroads, the interpretation of projective identification is indicated. Similarly, one need not be a Kleinian to observe that at a particular point our analysand is struggling to overcome the influence of a powerful internalized bad object. By the same token, one need not be a Kohutian to note the absence of the needed self-object in the life of our analysands. Paradoxically, although we need an internalized cohesive structure to interpret, our capacity to be good listeners and good therapists is enriched if we have in our preconscious ideas that belong to a number of paradigms other than our own.

AMBIVALENCE TOWARD FREUD

One of the difficult truths unearthed by Freud is the significant role that ambivalence plays in all human relationships. After the first wave of falling in love the couple has to face their differences and this introduces a note of ambivalence into their relationship. Parents and children cannot hope for a conflict-free love relationship across the generations. The same holds true for our relationship to the founder of psychoanalysis. Toward him our ambivalence stems from two sources: the inevitable ambivalence that every son and daughter face toward their parents, and the realistic ambivalence that much of what Freud discovered was erroneous, or partially mistaken, and requires revision. Freud thought that he forced reluctant nature to yield to him one of her cherished secrets and, to the extent that he discovered the enormous role that the unconscious plays in our lives, he was right. But today we must accept that Freud's was only one paradigm, and does not constitute a sufficiently strong gestalt to resist encroachment of other paradigms.

There is yet another Freud who, at least twice in his life, had the courage to change fundamentally the paradigms that governed his thinking. I am referring to Freud, who at the turn of century abandoned the seduction theory as the cause of neurosis and, once again, in 1920 and 1923, added the dual-instinct theory and the structural point of view to the topographic one. The right to reformulate basic concepts when better ones can be formulated is part of our historical professional identity. In so doing Freud threw caution to the wind and made controversy within psychoanalysis inevitable. Analysts had to be divided as to their attitudes toward the death instinct. It is not irrelevant to point out that the Kleinians accepted the death instinct, while the ego psychologists, including Fenichel (1974), opposed it. Another division that logically resulted from the structural theory was whether our main task is the amelioration of the harshness of the superego as Franz Alexander (1925) and Strachey (1934) maintained or whether, following the tenets of ego psychology, our main effort should be to free the ego from the encumbrances of the mechanisms of defense. These issues were debated in the Marienbad Symposium (1937), which took place in 1936.

The Freud who continued to reexamine his work and did not fear to change paradigms has become my professional ego ideal. It is the Freud who, like Oedipus, wished to know the truth wherever the truth will lead. It is the Freud who had the courage to analyze himself, and particularly the courage to discover within himself during World War I that he had unconscious wishes that his sons should be killed at the front.

Understanding the history of psychoanalysis will compel us to face the fact that the changes in the basic paradigms are continually taking place, but the rate of change has accelerated in recent times. Psychoanalysis seems to reflect our culture as a whole, where changes are taking place more rapidly than in earlier times.

As I watched the proliferation of different schools within psychoanalysis, it became increasingly clear to me that we need a better history of psychoanalysis if we are to understand our differences. I am working on a book (1998b) to be entitled *Wrestling with Freud*. I have taken my title from a myth reported in Genesis 32:24–26.

> And Jacob was left alone; and there wrestled a man with him until the breaking of the day, And when he saw that he prevailed not against him he touched the hollow of his thigh; and the hollow of Jacob's thigh was out of joint, as he wrestled with him. And he said, let me go, for the day breaketh. And he said I will not let thee go, except thou bless me.

I recall as a child puzzling over this myth. How can wrestling, with which I was thoroughly familiar, end on a blessing rather than a victory? And yet the myth is quintessentially biblical. The struggle between the hero and God belongs to the realm of myth, but the asking for a blessing from the adversary is a postmythological idea. No Homeric hero would have understood it. Nor will the metaphor have meaning to an Orthodox Jew or an orthodox analyst.

Freud's father was named Jacob, but Freud himself made no use of the biblical myth, despite what he told us in his autobiography (1925): "My deep engrossment in the Bible story (almost as soon as I had learned the art of reading) had, as I recognized much later, an enduring effect on the direction of my interest" (p. 8).

In what sense am I asking for Freud's blessing? I cannot obtain the approval of the historical Freud, for I know that he wished his correspondence with Fliess to be burned. He had considerable contempt for what he called the "so-called posterity," and he did not want us to know of his personal struggle when the main ideas that constitute psychoanalysis first emerged. Freud wished to bequeath us an idealized version of psychoanalysis.

We have no right to blame him. Freud felt that he had already revealed more than he cared to when he published his own dreams in 1900. The reason he gave for publishing his own dreams was that dreams of neurotics were suspect. At this point Freud was not candid, for he had already reached the conclusion in his own self-analysis that he was not entirely normal. I assume that a powerful impulse for self-disclosure accompanied Freud's self-analysis. Later on, the wish for privacy won ascendancy and Freud regretted his self-disclosure. As a result of his self-analysis Freud realized that the line of demarcation between neurosis and health is a fluctuating one and that the medical effort to dichotomize health and illness has only a limited applicability to the ubiquitous intrapsychic conflict that is the price we pay for culture; the price extracted determines our adjustment or maladjustment to the culture in which we live.

Instead of the myth of the struggle between Jacob and God (not just with an angel as the attenuated version of this myth has it), Freud preferred the statement by Goethe:

Was du ererbet von deinen Vatern hast,
Erwirb es, um es zu besitzen

What thou hast inherited from thy fathers, acquire it to make it thine. [*Faust*, part I, scene I]

The quote appears on the very last page of the posthumously published (1940) *Outline of Psycho-Analysis*. These are almost the last lines we have from Freud's pen. We generally assume that what we inherit we need not acquire. However, Goethe believed, and Freud admired this belief, that the two are not opposed to each other, but what we inherit we must work to acquire in order to make it our own. Without such a work of internalization we are doomed to remain blind followers.

For me personally, and I believe for all of us Freudian analysts today, Jacob's asking for the blessing after the struggle is relevant. For unlike the early circle of Freud's disciples we cannot and should not continue to defend every view that Freud ever held. We know how frequently he was mistaken. But, for us, the question is what predominates? The awe before the magnitude of his discoveries, the gratitude for Freud's opening the way to us for the understanding of the unconscious, or our disappointments in what he failed to understand or misunderstood? If the former prevails inwardly, we continue his work and thus are entitled to ask for his blessing.

I wish to conclude with the statement of why I am a Freudian. After my father, Freud was the person who influenced me most deeply. I identified myself with him and his work. Freud (1933) himself denied that psychoanalysis was a weltanschauung. He believed that psychoanalysis only participates in the weltanschauung of science. Here, too, he was mistaken. For many psychoanalysts, including myself, psychoanalysis itself became a way of looking at the world. Freud was my ego ideal. I have read and reread him, taught him and argued with him since my adolescence. I have read his biographies, and remembered many of his sayings and even his jokes. To be a Freudian means to know Freud, to make him a living reality within us and to remain convinced that he has bequeathed to us a line of inquiry that goes on and on, rather than as some who claim that it is a cul de sac. We all have parricidal wishes; like Shakespeare's Prince Hal, we, at times, try to put on our heads the crown Freud left behind him. Alternatively, we find some other leader to whom we offer this crown. But when we surmount our aggression, our parricidal wishes, and accept our own limitations, we return to Freud as having given us the basic ideas that keep our sprit of inquiry alive. It is my feeling of gratitude toward Freud that made me ask for his blessing in this chapter.

REFERENCES

Ahumada, J. L. (1994). What is a clinical fact? Clinical psychoanalysis as inductive method. *International Journal of Psycho-Analysis* 75:949–962.

Alexander, F. (1925). A metaphysical description of the process of cure. In *The Scope of Psychoanalysis, 1921–1961: Selected Papers of Franz Alexander*, pp. 205–224. New York: Basic Books, 1963.

Aron, L., and A. Harris, eds. (1993). *The Legacy of Sandor Ferenczi*. London: Analytic Press.

Balint, M. (1968). *The Basic Fault: Therapeutic Aspects of Regression*. London: Tavistock.

Bergmann, M. (1993). Reflections on the history of psychoanalysis. *Journal of the American Psychoanalytic Association* 41:929–955.

––––––– (1996). The tragic encounter between Freud and Ferenczi and its impact on the history of psychoanalysis. In *Ferenczi's Turn in Psychoanalysis*, ed. P. Rudnytsky, A. Bokay, and P. Giampieri-Deutsch, pp. 145–159. New York: New York University Press.

––––––– (1998a). *The Hartmann Era and Its Contribution to Psychoanalytic Technique*. Forthcoming.

––––––– (1998b). *Wrestling with Freud*. Forthcoming.

Bergmann, M. S., and F. Hartman, eds. (1976a). What is psychoanalysis? An examination of the assumptions and the language of psychoanalysis. In *The Evolution of Psychoanalytic Technique*, pp. 2–16. New York: Basic Books.

––––––– (1976b). The controversy around Ferenczi's active technique. In *The Evolution of Psychoanalytic Technique*, pp. 110–145. New York: Basic Books.

Berliner, B. (1958). The role of object relations in moral masochism. *Psychoanalytic Quarterly* 37:38–76.

Bibring, E. (1953). The mechanisms of depression. In *Affective Disorders*, ed. P. Greenacre, pp. 13–48. New York: International Universities Press.

Breuer, J., and Freud, S. (1895). *Studies on Hysteria. Standard Edition* 2.

Caper, R. (1994). What is a clinical fact? *International Journal of Psycho-Analysis* 75:903–913.

Chasseguet-Smirgel, J. (1970). *Female Sexuality: New Psychoanalytic Views*. Ann Arbor: University of Michigan Press.

––––––– (1985). *Creativity and Perversion*. New York: Norton.

Eissler, K. (1975). The fall of man. *Psychoanalytic Study of the Child* 30:589–646. New Haven, CT: Yale University Press.

Elias, N. (1990). *Über sich selbst (About Myself)*, ed. A. J. Heerma, W. van Voss, and A. van Stolk. Frankfurt: Suhrkamp.

Fairbairn, R. (1952). *An Object-Relations Theory of the Personality*. New York: Basic Books.

Federn, P. (1952). *Ego Psychology and the Psychoses*, ed. E. Weiss. New York: Basic Books.

Fenichel, O. (1945). *The Psychoanalytic Theory of Neurosis*. New York: Norton.

––––––– (1974). A review of Freud's *Analysis, Terminable and Interminable. International Review of Psychoanalysis* 1:109–116.

Ferenczi, S. (1929). The unwelcomed child and his death instinct. In *Final Contributions to the Problems and Methods of Psychoanalysis*, ed. M. Balint, pp. 102–107. New York: Basic Books, 1955.

—— (1933). Confusion of tongues between adult and child: the language of tenderness and passion. In *Final Contributions to the Problems and Methods of Psychoanalysis*, ed. M. Balint, pp. 156–167. New York: Basic Books, 1955.

Filho, G. V. (1994). Conceptualisation of the clinical psychoanalytical fact. *International Journal of Psycho-Analysis* 75:1041–1049.

Freud, A. (1937). *The Ego and the Mechanisms of Defence*. London: Hogarth.

—— (1954). The widening scope of indications for psychoanalysis: Discussion. *Journal of the American Psychoanalytic Association* 2:607–620.

Freud, S. (1900). The interpretation of dreams. *Standard Edition* 4 and 5.

—— (1901). The psychopathology of everyday life. *Standard Edition* 6:1–279.

—— (1905). Three essays on the theory of sexuality. *Standard Edition* 7:125–243.

—— (1907). Obsessive actions and religious practices. *Standard Edition* 9:115–127.

—— (1908). Civilized sexual morality and modern nervous illness. *Standard Edition* 9:177–204.

—— (1910a). Five lectures on psycho-analysis. *Standard Edition* 11:3–55.

—— (1910b). Leonardo da Vinci and a memory of his childhood. *Standard Edition* 11:59–137.

—— (1911). Psycho-analytic notes on an autobiographical account of a case of paranoia (dementia paranoides). *Standard Edition* 12:3–84.

—— (1912). Recommendations to physicians practising psycho-analysis. *Standard Edition* 12:109–120.

—— (1913). Totem and taboo. *Standard Edition* 13:1–163.

—— (1914). On narcissism: an introduction. *Standard Edition* 14:73–107.

—— (1917). A difficulty in the path of psychoanalysis. *Standard Edition* 17:135–144.

—— (1920). Beyond the pleasure principle. *Standard Edition* 18:3–64.

—— (1923). Two encyclopaedia articles. *Standard Edition* 18:235–259.

—— (1925). An autobiographical study. *Standard Edition* 20:7–74.

—— (1926a). Inhibition, symptom and anxiety. *Standard Edition* 20:87–174.

—— (1926b). The question of lay analysis. *Standard Edition* 20:179–258.

—— (1927). The future of an illusion. *Standard Edition* 21:5–56.

—— (1930). Civilization and its discontents. *Standard Edition* 21:64–125.

—— (1933). New introductory lectures on psycho-analysis. *Standard Edition* 22:179–258.

—— (1939). Moses and monotheism. *Standard Edition* 7–137.

—— (1940). An outline of psycho-analysis. *Standard Edition* 23:144–207.

Friedman, L. (1997). Ferrum, igneous and medicina: return to the crucible. *Journal of the American Psychoanalytic Association* 45(1):21–40.

Gardner, M. R. (1994). Is that a fact? Empiricism revisited, or a psychoanalyst at sea. *International Journal of Psycho-Analysis* 75:927–937.

Green, A. (1975). The analyst, symbolization and absence in the analytic setting. *International Journal of Psycho-Analysis* 56:1–22.

Gribinski, M. (1994). The stranger in the house. *International Journal of Psycho-Analysis* 75:1011–1021.

Hartmann, H. (1959). Psychoanalysis as a scientific theory. In *Essays on Ego Psychology*, pp. 318–350. New York: International Universities Press.

Hook, S. (1959). *Psychoanalysis Scientific Method and Philosophy*. New York: New York University Press.

Jowett, B., trans. (1937). *The Dialogues of Plato, Vol. 1*. New York: Random House.

Khan, M. (1979). *Alienation and Perversions*. New York: International Universities Press.

King, P., and Steiner, R., eds. (1991). *The Freud-Klein Controversies, 1941–1945*. London: Tavistock/Routledge.

Klein, G. S. (1976). *Psychoanalytic Theory: An Exploration of Essentials*. New York: International Universities Press.

Klein, M. (1932). *Psychoanalysis of Children*. London: Hogarth.

——— (1948). *Contributions to Psycho-Analysis, 1921–1945*. London: Hogarth.

Kohut, H. (1971). *The Analysis of the Self*. New York: International Universities Press.

——— (1977). *The Restoration of the Self*. New York: International Universities Press.

——— (1979). The two analyses of Mr. Z. *International Journal of Psycho-Analysis* 60:3–27.

Kubie, L. S. (1974). The drive to become both sexes. *Psychoanalytic Quarterly* 43:349–426.

Kuhn, T. (1962). *The Structure of Scientific Revolutions*. Chicago: University of Chicago Press.

Marienbad Symposium. (1937). The theory of the therapeutic results of psychoanalysis. (Papers by E. Glover, O. Fenichel, J. Strachey, E. Bergler, N. Nunberg, and E. Bibring.) *International Journal of Psycho-Analysis* 38:125–188.

Masson, J., trans./ed. (1985). *The Complete Letters of Sigmund Freud to Wilhelm Fliess, 1887–1904*. Cambridge: Harvard University Press.

McDougall, J. (1964). Homosexuality in women. In *Female Sexuality: New Psychoanalytic Perspectives*, ed. J. Chasseguet-Smirgel, pp. 171–212. Ann Arbor: University of Michigan Press.

——— (1972). Primal scene and sexual perversion. *International Journal of Psycho-Analysis* 53:371–384.

——— (1978). *Plea for a Measure of Abnormality*. New York: International Universities Press.

McGuire, W., ed. (1974). *The Freud/Jung Letters: The Correspondence Between Sigmund Freud and C.G. Jung*, trans. R. Manheim and R. F. C. Hull. Bollingen Series 94. Princeton: Princeton University Press.

Miller, J., and Post, S. (1990). How theory shapes technique: perspectives on a self-psychological clinical presentation. *Psychoanalytic Inquiry* 10(4):459–624.

Nunberg, H., and Federn, E., eds. (1974). *Minutes of the Vienna Psychoanalytic Society, 1906–1918*, vol. 3. New York: International Universities Press.

Ogden, T. (1996). The perverse subject of analysis. *Journal of the American Psychoanalytic Association* 44(4):1121–1146.

Ornstein, P. H., and Ornstein, A. (1994). On the conceptualisation of clinical facts in psychoanalysis. *International Journal of Psycho-Analysis* 75:977–994.

O'Shaughnessy, E. (1994). What is a clinical fact? *International Journal of Psycho-Analysis* 75:939–947.

Pulver, S., Escoll, P., and Fischer, N., issue eds. (1987). How theory shapes technique: perspectives on a clinical study. *Psychoanalytic Inquiry* 7(2):141–299.

Quinodoz, J. M. (1994). Clinical facts or psychoanalytic clinical facts? *International Journal of Psycho-Analysis* 75:963–976.

Reich, W. (1933). *Character-Analysis: Principles and Technique for Psychoanalysts in Practice and Training*. New York: Orgone Institute Press, 1945.

——— (1942). *The Function of the Orgasm*. New York: Orgone Institute Press.

Reik, T. (1948). *Listening with the Third Ear*. New York: Farrar, Straus.

Richards, A. D. (1994). Extenders, modifiers, heretics. In *The Spectrum of Psychoanalysis: Essays in Honor of Martin S. Bergmann*, pp. 145–160. New York: International Universities Press.

Riesenberg-Malcolm, R. (1994). Conceptualisation of clinical facts in the analytic process. *International Journal of Psycho-Analysis* 75:1031–1040.

Rudnytsky, P. L., Bokay, A., and Giampieri-Deutsch, P., eds. (1996). *Ferenczi's Turn in Psychoanalysis*. New York: New York University Press.

Sandler, J., and Sandler, A. (1994). Comments on the conceptualisation of clinical facts in psychoanalysis. *International Journal of Psycho-Analysis* 75:995–1010.

Schafer, R. (1994). The conceptualisation of clinical facts. *International Journal of Psycho-Analysis* 75:1023–1030.

Socarides, C. (1962). Theoretical and clinical aspects of overt female homosexuality. *International Journal of Psycho-Analysis* 10:579–592.

Spence, D. P. (1994). The special nature of psychoanalytic facts. *International Journal of Psycho-Analysis* 75:915–925.

Spitz, R. A. (1945). Hospitalism. *Psychoanalytic Study of the Child* 1:53–74. New York: International Universities Press.

——— (1946). Hospitalism: a follow-up report. *Psychoanalytic Study of the Child* 2:113–117. New York: International Universities Press.

——— (1965). *The First Year of Life: A Psychoanalytic Study of Normal and Deviant Development of Object Relations*, in collaboration with W. Godfrey Cobliner. New York: International Universities Press.

Stone, L. (1954). The widening scope of indications for psychoanalysis. *Journal of the American Psychoanalytic Association* 2:567–607.

Strachey, J. (1934). The nature of the therapeutic action of psycho-analysis. In *Psychoanalytic Clinical Interpretation*, ed. L. Paul, pp. 331–360. New York: Free Press, 1963.

Waelder, R. (1962). Psychoanalysis, scientific method, and philosophy. *Journal of the American Psychoanalytic Association* 10:617–637.

Winnicott, D. W. (1951). Transitional objects and transitional phenomena. In *Collected Papers: Through Paediatrics to Psycho-Analysis*. London: Tavistock, 1958.

——— (1971). *Playing and Reality*. London: Tavistock.

——— (1964). Review of C. G. Jung, *Memories, Dreams and Reflections*. *International Journal of Psycho-Analysis* 45:450–455.

Index